False, Fleeting, Perjur'd Clarence

George Duke of Clarence
1449-1478

False, Fleeting, Perjur'd Clarence

George, Duke of Clarence 1449–78

M. A. Hicks

ALAN SUTTON
1980

Alan Sutton Publishing Limited
17a Brunswick Road
Gloucester GL1 1HG

First published 1980

British Library Cataloguing in Publication Data

Hicks, Michael A
False, fleeting, perjur'd Clarence.
1. Clarence, George Plantagenet, *Duke of*
2. Great Britain - History - House of York, 1461-1485
I. Title
942.04'4'0924 DA247.C/

ISBN 0-904387-44-5

Typesetting and origination by
Alan Sutton Publishing Limited.
Photoset Plantin 10/12.
Printed in Great Britain
by Redwood Burn Limited
Trowbridge & Esher.

Table of Contents

Illustrations

Plates page

Acknowledgements

Acknowledgements and thanks for permission to reproduce photographs are due to the Ashmolean Museum, Oxford for plate 3; to the Bodleian Library, Oxford for plates 5 and 11; to Lord Brocket for plate 1; to Lord Middleton and Nottingham University Library for plate 8; to the National Portrait Gallery, London for plates 6 and 14; to the Master and Wardens of the Skinners Company, London for plate 4; to the Society of Antiquaries of London for plates 2 and 7; and to Brian Waters for plate 15.

Preface

This book, the culmination of a decade of study, offers me the welcome opportunity to acknowledge my obligations to those who assisted me. I was still an undergraduate when Charles Ross first excited my interest in fifteenth-century England. Then and ever since he has supported and guided me, as teacher, as examiner, as referee, and as fellow student. His influence amounts to much more than my relatively few references to his *Edward IV*, which was so largely anticipated in discussion. To Mr. T.B. Pugh I owe my scholarly method, some valuable ideas and this fruitful topic of research. Dr. Roger Highfield started me off on my thesis, before handing me over to John Armstrong, whose blend of profound learning, kindly criticism and illuminating insight was just what I required. All four instilled in me the approach pioneered by the late K.B. McFarlane. My research would have been impossible without the willing assistance of the staff at the Public Record Office, British Library, Bodleian Library and many other repositories, whose efforts were much appreciated. I am grateful to the Institute of Historical Research for electing me to a Research Fellowship for the academic year 1973-4. Dr. Gerald Harriss examined the thesis and Miss Margaret Condon read the draft of this book: both gave good advice, which I hope I have used to full advantage. Dr. Pierre Chaplais, Dr. Alan Thacker and Dr. Carole Rawcliffe certainly contributed more in private discussion than they can have realised. To Peter Hammond of the Richard III Society I am indebted for an introduction to my publisher. I have been sustained by the consistent and selfless encouragement of my parents and my wife Cynthia, especially the latter, who has had to read, re-read and indeed live with Clarence more than anyone else. Ultimately, however, I am solely responsible for any remaining defects.

Michael Hicks

Winchester,
March 1980

TABLE I: EDWARD III's DESCENDANTS AND TITLE TO THE CROWN 1461-78

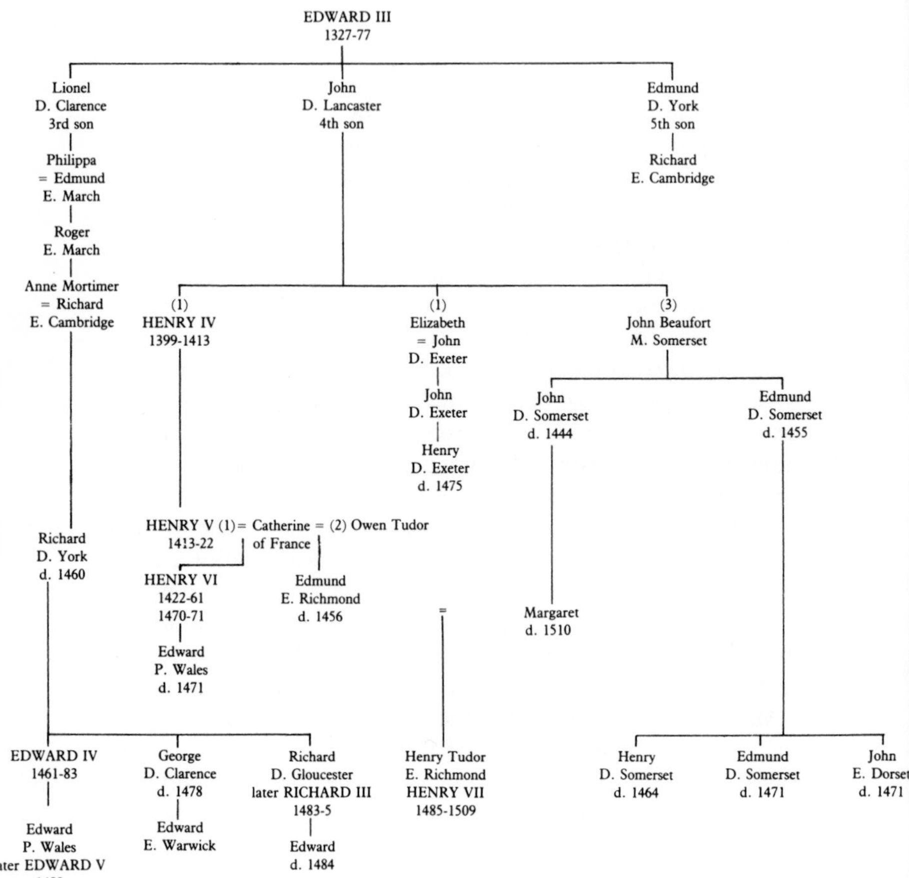

Chapter I

Birth, Youth and Early Career 1449-69

1. Cadet of the House of York

George Plantagenet, the future Duke of Clarence, was born into one of the greatest families of fifteenth-century England. He was justifiably proud of his lineage, for he was a prince of the blood royal three times over. His father was Richard, third Duke of York, only son of Richard, Earl of Cambridge and his first wife, Anne Mortimer. Cambridge was the younger son of Edmund of Langley, first Duke of York, the fifth son of King Edward III. Duke Edmund's elder son was Edward, second Duke of York, who was killed in 1415 at the battle of Agincourt. He was predeceased by his younger brother Cambridge, who had been executed earlier in the same year for complicity in the Southampton plot. In this way Cambridge, George's grandfather, forfeited not only all that he possessed, which was not much, but also his title to the dukedom of York. To this diminished inheritance he left two children, Richard and Isabel.

Anne Mortimer, George's grandmother, was the only sister and heir of Edmund Mortimer, Earl of March and Ulster, who died in 1425. The earldom of March had been created in 1327 for Roger Mortimer of Wigmore. The earldom of Ulster, the patrimony of the de Burgh family, had descended to Elizabeth de Burgh, wife of Lionel, Duke of Clarence, the third son of Edward III. It was their daughter Philippa who married Edmund Mortimer, Earl of March (d.1381). Richard was thus heir to both these earldoms. His title was not affected by his father's forfeiture. It is hardly surprising that successive kings of England regarded him as rightful Duke of York.

Duke Richard's long minority was spent in the household of Ralph Neville, Earl of Westmorland. His countess was Joan Beaufort, daughter of John of Gaunt, Duke of Lancaster, granddaughter of Edward III, sister of Cardinal Beaufort and great-aunt of Henry VI. She was her husband's second wife: by his first he had nine children, by her another thirteen. Most of these made good marriages: Richard, William, George and Edward were to sit in parliament as Earl of Salisbury, Lord Fauconberg, Lord Latimer and Lord Abergavenny; several of their sisters's husbands did likewise. Their brother Robert sat first as Bishop of Salisbury, later as Bishop of Durham. The young Duke of York married the youngest child Cecily Neville and was thus connected by marriage to almost the whole of the English nobility.

The duke's own family was less extensive but equally important. His sister Isabel had married twice. Through her first husband, Thomas Grey of Heton (Northum.), the duke was related to William Grey, later Bishop of Ely. Through her second marriage to Henry Bourchier, Count of Eu and later Earl of Essex, the duke was connected to the latter's brothers Thomas, Archbishop of Canterbury, William, Lord FitzWarin and John, Lord Berners and their half-brother the Duke of Buckingham. When he himself had children the Duke of York found distinguished spouses for them: at his death his daughters Anne and Elizabeth were Duchesses of Exeter and Suffolk.[1]

Richard, Duke of York was not merely well-connected. He was the wealthiest English magnate from the end of his minority in 1432 until his death in 1460. At its peak his net income above unavoidable expenses may have approached £5,800 a year. This was rivalled by only two other contemporary magnates, Humphrey Stafford, Duke of Buckingham (d.1460) and Richard Beauchamp, Earl of Warwick (d.1439), whose net incomes may have attained £5,020 and £4,400 respectively.[2] A mere handful of other magnates received half this amount a year. The income of Duke Richard was not confined to the issues of his estates: he also enjoyed the king's wages as lieutenant in France and Ireland.

Duke Richard's expenditure was as impressive as his income. It is hard to believe that his household cost him less than the £2,200 spent by the Duke of Buckingham in 1444.[3] This figure did not include expenditure on clothing or jewellery: one jewelled collar,

TABLE II: GEORGE PLANTAGENET'S NEARER RELATIVES IN THE 1450s

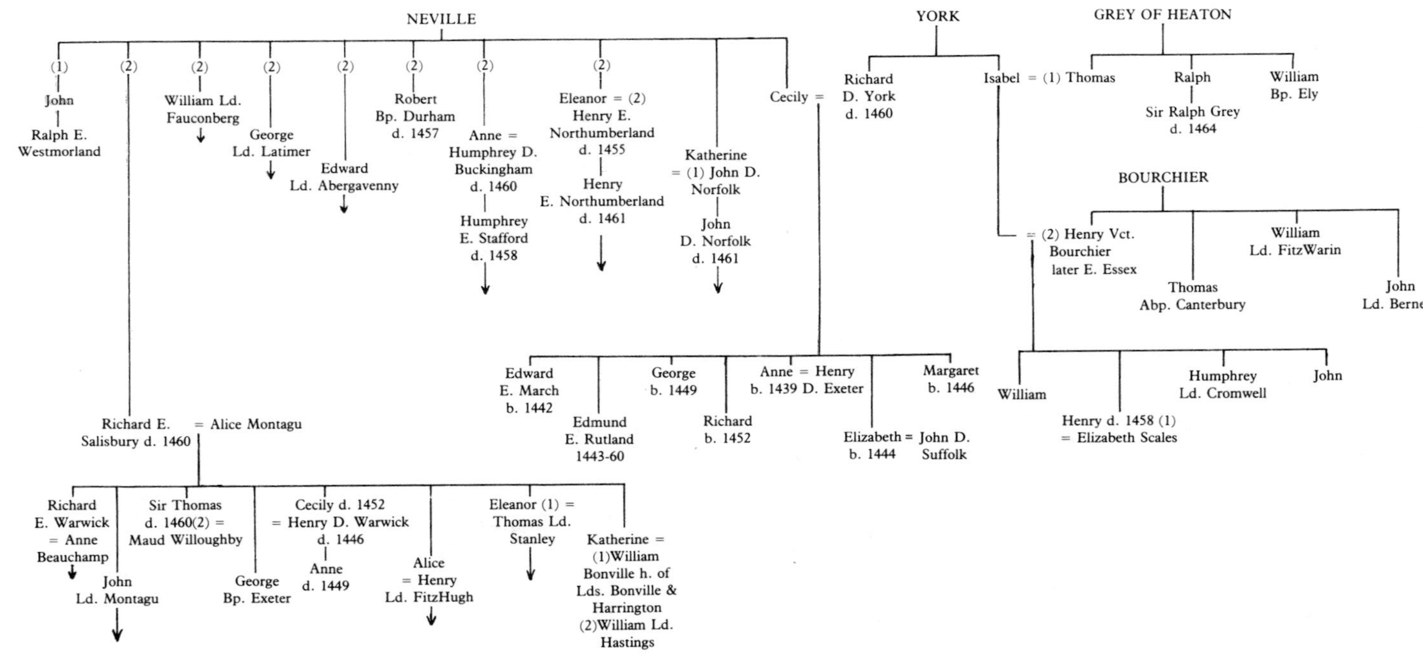

doubtless exceptional, cost 4,000 marks (£2,666 13*s*. 4*d*.). The fees of the ducal retainers totalled over £900. He paid the highest marriage portion known in medieval England: this was the 6,500 marks (£4,333 13*s* 4*d*.) agreed in 1445 for the betrothal of Anne, his daughter, to Henry Holland, later Duke of Exeter.[4] As the latter was Henry VI's heir general, he might one day have become king and Anne queen. Duke Richard was equally ambitious for his eldest son Edward, for whom he sought a daughter of the King of France,[5] although Henry VI himself had to be content with the daughter of the Duke of Anjou. In his later years, after 1450, receipts from his estates, especially those in Wales, probably fell[6] and he left large debts, but it is unlikely that this was reflected in his style of living: it certainly did not force him to curb his ambitions.

It was into this atmosphere of great wealth, lavish expenditure, important connections and exalted ambitions that the duke's children were born. Seven reached adolescence. There were four sons, Edward (b.1442), Edmund (b.1443), George (b.1449) and Richard (b.1452) and three daughters, Anne (b.1439), Elizabeth (b.1444) and Margaret (b.1446). Anne, betrothed in 1445, may have left the parental household at once. The others may be divided into two groups. One consisted of the two elder sons, near the same age and six years older than their next brother. They appear to have had a separate establishment in the fourteen-fifties and may have had little to do with their younger brothers. The latter and the daughters probably remained in their mother's care, as they were in 1459, especially as Richard was a sickly child.[7] Perhaps it was in these years that Margaret developed the affection for George, three years her junior, which she displayed later in life.

George was the fifth son of the duke but at his birth only two others survived. He was born at Dublin on 21 October 1449, when his father was lieutenant of Ireland. His christening was distinguished by the presence as godfathers of the heads of the rival Anglo-Irish houses of Butler and FitzGerald, respectively Earls of Ormond and Desmond, as Duke Richard employed the opportunity to bring them together. It took place in the church of St. Saviour.[8] Nothing more is known of George's life until 1459, when his father's political activities forced him to attention. It is unlikely that he attracted much of Duke Richard's interest, as George was still not in his teens when his father died. He was the third surviving son. He could not expect to inherit anything from his father, who might however buy an heiress for his wife. Alternatively a career in the church was open to him. Probably neither had been seriously considered. In 1459-61 his prospects altered radically.

Duke Richard had played a major part in the affairs of France and Ireland and wished to do the same in England, where both his wealth and birth gave weight to his views. But he was denied his natural position by the group of magnates who controlled the government and managed it at home and abroad with equal lack of success. They were headed by Edmund Beaufort, Duke of Somerset, who developed from the rival into the enemy of Duke Richard. The fourteen-fifties were punctuated by a series of attempts by the latter to obtain control of the government, either by peaceful or violent means. One such incident resulted in a skirmish in 1455 at St. Albans at which Somerset was killed. Both then and in 1453 the Duke of York temporarily seized power as Protector. Renewed tension led to further clashes in 1459 at the battles of Blore Heath and Ludford. The latter was an almost bloodless skirmish in the vicinity of Duke Richard's marcher castle of Ludlow (Salop.): his force dispersed and he himself fled to Ireland.[9]

Within Ludlow castle during the battle were the Duchess of York and her two younger sons. The town and castle were sacked and they were taken prisoner.[10] At the parliament at Coventry that followed, the duke, his two elder sons, the Earls of March and Rutland, the duchess's brothers the Earl of Salisbury and Lord Fauconberg, Salisbury's son the Earl of Warwick, and others were attainted as traitors. They thus forfeited all their estates. The Duchess of York submitted to Henry VI's mercy. He pardoned her, assigned 1,000 marks (£666 13*s.* 4*d.*) per annum from her husband's estates for the support of herself and her children, and confided them to the custody of her sister Anne, Duchess of Buckingham.[11]

In June 1460 the Earls of Warwick, Salisbury and March and Lord Fauconberg returned. On 10 July 1460 they fought a battle at Northampton against the king's forces, where the Duke of Buckingham, husband of the Duchess of York's custodian, was killed. Henry VI himself was captured. A parliament was summoned. The Duke of York delayed his return from Ireland until shortly before it was due to meet. Landing at Chester, he proceeded to Ludlow, being met in state by his duchess on the way, and went to London.[12]

At the parliament he seated himself on the royal throne and laid claim to the crown of England. He was no longer content merely to control the government of Henry VI. He was aware that he was heir of Lionel, Duke of Clarence (d.1369), the elder brother of John of Gaunt, Duke of Lancaster (d.1399), from whom the claim of the Lancastrian kings derived.[13] His title was marred by two descents through the female line but he persisted in it. It required acceptance that the crown of England was governed by the laws of real estate and the overthrow of a dynasty already sixty years old. The parliamentary peerage, even those who were his supporters, were extremely reluctant to accept his title, but eventually they arranged a compromise.

King Henry would remain king for life but the claim of his son was set aside in favour of the Duke of York. York was considerably older than Henry VI, so it was unlikely that this would benefit him personally. As heir to the crown he was provided with lands. For the remainder of his life he described himself in letters as 'true and legitimate heir of the kingdoms of England and France and of the lordship and land of Ireland'.[14] This radically altered the expectations of his son George, who was no longer merely a younger son of a great magnate, but potentially son and brother of kings. His future was assured.

The settlement was shortlived. Queen Margaret and many magnates refused to accept it and resisted by force. The Duke of York set out to impose it on them, but was killed at the battle of Wakefield. Also slain was his son Edmund, Earl of Rutland. The queen's army marched southwards and on 17 February 1461 defeated the Earl of Warwick at the second battle of St. Albans. At this time the Duchess of York was at London, perhaps at Baynard's Castle, together with her younger children. The importance of George and Richard was much increased by the death of her husband and second son, so, for safekeeping, she sent them overseas to Utrecht to the protection of the Duke of Burgundy. They were treated with respect by Duke Philip.[15]

A fortnight after their departure, on 4 March 1461, their brother Edward proclaimed himself king as Edward IV. On 29 March, at Towton in Yorkshire, he decisively defeated the Lancastrians. Henceforth he enjoyed general recognition as king.

Edward's supporters were pleased to hear of Philip's favourable reception of his brothers, as they hoped for a treaty with Burgundy, and even speculated that 'one of these brothers will marry the daughter of Charles',[16] that is Mary of Burgundy, sole daughter of Philip's heir Charles the Bold, Count of Charolais. While Philip did not share this desire, he nevertheless hoped for amity with England and saw the presence of the new king's brothers as an opportunity to display his friendship. He sent for them. They were at Sluys on 17 April and on the morrow they proceeded to Bruges, accompanied by the papal legate as a mark of respect. Duke Philip lodged them in the town of Bruges, surrounded them with his officers and did all he could to honour them. He even visited them at their lodgings on their arrival. He fêted them and they attended a banquet in their honour given by the town of Bruges. Afterwards Philip despatched them with an escort of his palace guards and courtiers to Calais,[17] whence they sailed to England.

The court of Burgundy was the most magnificent in Europe and its splendour had been paraded before these two small boys in their honour. One cannot tell what impression it made on them, although their conduct must have been unexceptional, since it did not draw the attention of the narrators, who were more interested in the actions of Duke Philip. Several of the writers state their ages. Usually they underestimate them: Waurin, for example, thought they were eight and nine.[18] Perhaps they were small for their age. The difference in age of George and Richard is also understated, which may reflect on their physical development.

2. The King's Heir 1461-6

On their return to England the brothers were received with great deference at Canterbury and proceeded to London where they probably met their brother, now King Edward IV, on or about 12 June 1461.[19] They were his nearest male relatives and George was his heir. Edward appointed George steward of England for the coronation, but as 'he was but yonge and tender of age, my lord Wenloke was assigned to hime to receive the bills' of those claiming honorary offices at the coronation.

The ceremonial of the coronation began with the progress of Edward IV into London on 26 June. He was met at the Tower by his brothers among others and they were among the twenty-eight knights of the Bath he dubbed that evening. The heralds were paid for their assistance and received an additional twenty marks

(£13 13*s.* 4*d.*) 'for the yefte and largesse of oure derest beloued bretheren at the same place made knightes'.[20] Next morning, clad in blue gowns with white silk trimmings, they rode ahead of the king in procession to Westminster. It was on the following morning, Sunday 28 June, that Edward was crowned at Westminster Abbey. A splendid banquet followed. On Monday and Tuesday Edward wore his crown.[21] In attendance were the lords spiritual and temporal and his brothers, although it is unlikely that they played an active part.

On the Monday, after the crown-wearing in Westminster Abbey, George accompanied his brother to the palace of the Bishop of London, where a banquet was held in his own honour. £10 was given to the heralds 'for the yefte and largesse of oure Feest holden in oure paleys at London . . . for the makyng of oure derest beloued Brother the Duc of Clarence', and they were given a further twenty marks (£13 13*s.* 4*d.*) for the creation of his ducal estate.[22] The choice of title was significant, for it emphasised that the claim of the house of York was hereditary, stemming from Lionel, Duke of Clarence, second son of Edward III. It had been taken from Lionel's wife's honour of Clare, later a possession of the Earls of March, of Richard, Duke of York, and ultimately of Edward IV. George's creation demonstrated that he was Edward's heir; their youngest brother Richard had several months to wait before he was created Duke of Gloucester. A few months later Clarence was elected a knight of the Garter.[23]

By his creation as a knight and duke any lingering doubt about George's future was allayed. He was to remain a layman, to be a great magnate, and as his brother's heir might even one day become king. In the meantime he was no more than a boy, not yet twelve years of age, and a minor in his brother's custody.

At his accession Edward was faced by the problem of what to do with his two young brothers and his unmarried sister Margaret. They were of political importance but were not yet of much use to him. He did not leave them in the care of their mother, the Dowager-Duchess Cecily. There is a shortage of direct evidence about their careers at this date. George and Richard enjoyed annuities of £40 attached to their titles, the third-penny of the counties whose name they bore. That of Richard was indeed derived from Gloucestershire but George's annuity, since his title was not taken from any shire, was payable at the receipt of the exchequer.[24]

George, Duke of Clarence as constable of Queenborough. From a set of *c.*1595; possibly based on a lost original.

Princess Margaret also enjoyed a pension from the same source. Sometimes Edward authorised additional payments. Such disbursements can be traced through the records of the exchequer.

When the payment was made in cash a record was sometimes made of the agent into whose hands it was paid. In Easter term 1462 Clarence received £20 by the hand of John Peke. On 16 February 1464 £60 was paid to the same agent and on 9 May £25 was received by John Kendall.[25] More often the sum was assigned to another source, usually a sheriff or escheator, and sometimes he failed to pay the money. In such cases Clarence's remedy lay in action of debt at the exchequer of pleas. On 5 December 1463 he received a tally for £10 payable by John Green, escheator of Kent and Middlesex, which was served on 1 January following: despite having sufficient money, Green declined to pay. On 1 February a bill was presented on Clarence's behalf reciting the circumstances and seeking payment of the sum and damages of 10 marks (£6 13*s* 4*d*.) The barons of the exchequer ruled that the duke should recover the sum plus damages of £1. Acting for the duke was John Kendall. In two other cases in the same term, against the sheriffs of Hampshire and Gloucestershire, Clarence also recovered the money due. In the former instance Kendall was again his attorney.[26]

A similar pattern emerges for Princess Margaret. Payments made on her behalf in Easter term 1462 and on 9 May 1463 were received by Peke. Later, until July 1467, they were normally by hand of John Kendall, who also acted as her attorney in actions of debt.[27]

Neither Peke nor Kendall were ordinary attornies. Peke, who had been a servant of the Duke of York and was to be a lifelong follower of Clarence, was a yeoman of the crown and thus a member of the king's entourage. He was probably deputising for Kendall, who was cofferer of the king's household,[28] the official responsible for paying the king's everyday expenses. Kendall's involvement in the affairs of Clarence, of Margaret, and probably of Gloucester too, indicates that their needs were also being met by the royal household.

This impression is confirmed by the account for 1461-2 of the keeper of the great wardrobe, Robert Cousin. On the orders of the king he worked on the repair and re-equipment of a tower at Greenwich for the use of the king's brothers and sister and supplied them with clothing. Clarence received a pair of stockings, thirteen russet gowns, a velvet jacket and doublet, two other velvet gowns, a long and short gown with satin trimmings, two gowns of kendal and another of damask that Cousin had made for him. There is no such list for Gloucester but certain garments, in particular two green cloth gowns, were supplied for the 'aforesaid lords of Clarence and Gloucester'. He also paid a tailor to make a gown for the Lady Margaret and mended a kirtle for her.[29]

Cousin's expenses were miscellaneous in character. They included the cost of conveying clothes and other items for the brothers from London to Greenwich and on another occasion for the carriage of stuff belonging to the king and his brothers by pack horse from London to Leicester. Another time they were separated from the household and Edward ordered the exchequer to contribute towards the cost of Clarence's journey.[30] This evidence that they were not always with the king also shows that they depended on his household not only for money but for transport. Cousin's account suggests that they were normally at Greenwich rather than in the king's company.

Perhaps this was why Edward made the decisions that resulted in a lost privy seal writ of 30 September 1462 to Robert Cousin. Cousin ceased to cater for their needs on an ad hoc basis, as the need arose, but instead supplied each, not only Clarence, with all things necessary for their stores as well as their immediate wants. The existence of a store implies immobility, a stable establishment. This gains support from the character of the goods supplied: a pillow, bolsters, a standing coffer, two small chests, three hundred carpet hooks, three hundred tenterhooks, six pounds of laton wire, one hundred shoe nails, two hundred lattice nails, and seven hundred and fifty assorted nails. Clearly Clarence was equipped with furniture and the means to repair his abode. This was true of Gloucester and, to a lesser extent, of Margaret. Clarence was supplied with horse harness, including ten bits for coursers and others for two hackneys, so they were less dependent on the king for transport. The sheer bulk of the goods supplied points to the same conclusion. An indication that they continued to reside in the same place is that the receipts given for the goods were drawn up on the same date, 30 September 1462. Probably they still lived at Greenwich.

In addition to their nurse, doubtless still in their service, John Skelton esquire and others waited on the dukes.[31] Already in 1461-2

Clarence (but apparently not Gloucester) had henxmen or pages of honour, probably two in number, for whom Cousin provided two jackets. By September 1462 there were four for whom Cousin provided: it was presumably they who slept on mattresses and bolsters, while Clarence used a featherbed and pillow of down. In view of the small size of his establishment, they were probably intended as companions of his own age. In the king's household henxmen were boys of noble birth, who had their own servants and were continually supervised by the master of henxmen. It was his task to instruct them in languages, divinity and other school subjects, in etiquette, courtesy in word and deed, and table manners, and to ride, joust and wear armour, dance, sing, and play the pipe and harp.[32] These were accomplishments that the king's brother also needed to acquire and which at eleven he would not already know. Perhaps one should envisage him and these other youths being taught by their unknown master. Unfortunately one cannot tell how thorough or successful the teaching was. In later life Clarence was more than usually pious and possessed considerable charm. Robert Cousin supplied him with a shooting glove, a quiver and four dozen bowstrings, so he must have learnt archery. He was given a saddle with an old fashioned harness, a gilded saddle, and bits for horses, so he must have learnt to ride. Cousin had already supplied him with a sword and sword belt, when in December 1463 King Edward gave him three embroidered caparisons, two jousting harnesses and two cuirasses which had belonged to Henry Beaufort, Duke of Somerset,[33] an enthusiastic jouster. Later, in battle, the duke performed with credit but, so far as we know, he never engaged in any public tournament.

Clarence was provided with all that he could possibly need. Everything was of the utmost magnificence. To supply him the great wardrobe had purchased the luxury fabrics of many countries: cloth of gold from Venice and Genoa, baldachin woven with gold thread from Lucca, silk from Damascus, hats from Cologne, cloaks from Ireland, linen for sheets from Holland, Brussels, Champagne and Flanders, cloth from Frisia. There were furs of marten, ermine, sable and minever, lambskins, and hats made from beaver. The woollen cloth included motley, kendall, kersey, worsted and Frisian, besides blanket and fustian for blankets. There was velvet, silk, satin, sarsenet, tartarin, bockram, baldachin, leather and even canvas. Often these were trimmed with gold thread, silk or satin.

The quantities were enormous: to make gold thread 2lb. 7oz. of Venetian gold was supplied; 7½ stone of feathers were provided for featherbeds, 571 marten furs for various purposes. If one were not aware that later Clarence received more, one would suppose it sufficient for a lifetime.

Even a stationary household requires some organisation. Grooms were needed to tend the horses, cooks to prepare meals and others to serve them, chaplains to pray and clerks to write letters and accounts. There was particular need for a secretariat. Clarence was lieutenant of Ireland; the lands granted him by the king had to be administered; as patron of ecclesiastical livings he had to make presentations. As lieutenant protections were issued and appointments were made by the duke's letters patent. One such, dated at Westminster on 1 April 1463, by which Clarence appointed the Earl of Desmond as his deputy in Ireland, apes royal formulae almost exactly. It begins:

> 'George Duke of Clarence and lord of Richmond lieutenant of our most dread lord King's land of Ireland to all whom these letters reach greeting'.

After the dating clause, without any indication that Clarence was a minor, his seal was affixed.[34] Similar letters were certainly issued for other purposes, such as presentations to livings, although the full text of such letters does not survive.[35] The seal was in the custody of the chancellor who, by at least Michaelmas 1462, was Master John Tapton, Dean of St. Asaph.[36]

The approval of Tapton, but not necessarily of Clarence, was needed for the issue of letters under the ducal seal. Later Edward was to establish councils to manage the affairs of his sons Edward and Richard, yet these councils were not always mentioned in the letters they issued. The absence of references to a council in Clarence's letters, therefore, does not mean that one did not exist. Almost certainly both he and Gloucester possessed them: they were needed to manage their estates, finances and other business. Some of the early grants of land to Clarence specifically included the income, even though he was not of age, so some machinery must have been created to relay the money to him; the grant of Boston (Lincs.) to the duke was announced to the local tenants after the annual audit of accounts in 1462; and in 1463, in Clarence's name, one William Burgh was retained as constable of the ducal castle of Prudhoe

(Northum.) by 'the surveyor of his livelihood'.[37] This is all that is known of the duke's administration. What is clear, however, is that Clarence's administration was itself subject to the king's overriding authority.

It is probable that all grants of Edward IV were made in response to petitions from the recipient, sometimes oral but usually in writing. Normally such petitions consisted of a draft of the king's grant, setting out in full what was wanted, preceded by a brief request clause; if the king was amenable, his letter patent would copy the draft verbatim. Grants to Clarence originated from similar petitions, which survive among the chancery warrants. This is true even of his earliest grants. From where did the initiative come? Presumably not from the duke himself, a mere boy too young to manage his own affairs. Besides the petitions contained much detailed information, on the rent and term of leases for example, which must have been based on searches among the records of the chancery and exchequer. When all this was assembled in a petition, it was not necessarily approved in full: Edward often struck out entries before signing the bill. This demonstrates that the petition was not prepared under his supervision. Unless one postulates that some petitions were rejected and do not survive, one must suppose that Edward indicated in general terms what he was willing to give, that the research for and draft of the petition were the work of Clarence's writing office, and that the king then vetted the result. Whether the need for the grant was first indicated to the king is to proceed further than the evidence permits. It is worth noting that some grants followed windfalls, such as the gift of estates that immediately followed the death of the Earl of Kent in 1463. Did Clarence's servants rush to assert his claim to anything that was going or did Edward automatically allot some of the spoils to his brother? Clarence's clerks were not outstandingly efficient: they duplicated some grants, for example.

When he first occurs, Tapton was acting not only as Clarence's chancellor but also in a financial capacity.[38] Probably at this early date he was the dominant figure in the duke's household, which became bigger as Clarence grew older. By March 1465 the great wardrobe was providing not only for his henxmen but also for his heralds and footmen; by March 1466 his entourage could be regarded as a multitude; and in 1468 it was anticipated that his riding household would consist of 188 persons. By then the chancellor had been joined as dignitary by the chamberlain, steward, treasurer and controller of the household and by the secretary.[39] This illustrates the increasing formality and organisation of the household as the duke turned from boy into great magnate.

Although relatively little is known of Clarence's everyday life, there are several moments when he steps into the limelight. For example, there is a report of the burial at Bisham Abbey of Richard Neville, Earl of Salisbury and his son Thomas Neville on 15 February 1463. Salisbury was Clarence's uncle and had died with Richard, Duke of York at Wakefield. Among those at the funeral were the late earl's brother Lord Latimer, his surviving sons Richard, Earl of Warwick, John, Lord Montagu, and George, Bishop of Exeter, his daughters Lady Stanley and Margaret, later Countess of Oxford, and the king's sister Elizabeth, Duchess of Suffolk and her husband. But none of these was treated as reverently as the guest of honour, the Duke of Clarence. He was escorted by two barons to the offering, where he gave 6*s*. 8*d*. more than anyone else. Baldachin cloth was offered to the corpses in reverse order of rank: Clarence was last to present it, taking precedence over his brother-in-law the Duke of Suffolk.[40]

Such deference was calculated to fill him with his own importance. He was the elder of the king's two brothers and his heir. On 12 September 1462 Edward gave an annuity to Lord Stanley, in recognition of services done and to be done to the king and to his brothers Clarence and Gloucester, his loyalty to any children of the king to take precedence.[41] Likewise when Lord Grey of Codnor was retained by Lord Hastings in 1464, he reserved his loyalty to the Duke of Clarence: it is unlikely that Grey was referring to a prior contract with the duke but to the latter's claim on his allegiance as heir to the throne. Such reservations were commonplace when the heir was the king's son. A further indication of the relative importance with which the dukes were regarded is provided by an account of their visit to Canterbury on 27 August 1463: John Stone wrote of 'the lord George Duke of Clarence with his brother'.[42]

Clarence responded to such adulation with arrogance. In front of him, both in the procession to high mass in Canterbury cathedral and at other places, he had a sword carried point uppermost. Both dukes had accompanied Thomas Bourchier, Archbishop of Canterbury.[43] It was probably at this time that the archbishop had the custody of the two brothers, for which — much later — he was rewarded.

The archbishop's custody was shortlived. The different importance and age of the two dukes resulted in them being treated differently. Richard was in the household of the Earl of Warwick before Michaelmas 1465, when the earl was granted the custody and marriage of Lord Lovell in recompense for Richard's expenses.[44] Already in 1464-5 the Earl and Countess of Warwick, Lord Hastings, Lord FitzHugh and the Duke of Gloucester had together made offerings at the high altar of St. Mary's collegiate church, Warwick and the minstrels of earl and duke were together at Stratford later in the same year. A book containing a treatise of the duties of a page, which appears to be in Gloucester's handwriting, may date from this time. He does not again appear in view until the early summer of 1469. For the whole of the intervening period he was probably in Warwick's care.

Clarence, meanwhile, was increasingly important. He may have been under the general supervision of Lord Stafford of Southwick, with whom he was several times associated, but he was not in his custody. On 22 April 1463 he attended a chapter of the order of the Garter for the first time: also present, his brother knights, were the king, two earls and eight barons. Clarence was not yet fourteen years old. On 26 May 1465 he again acted as steward of England, this time at the coronation of the queen and in person. He celebrated Easter 1466 at Salisbury as guest of the bishop, Richard Beauchamp. At Winchester on 18 July 1466 he acted as a commissioner of oyer and terminer at a treason trial:[45] he had often been appointed to commissions before but, so far as we can tell, he had never previously officiated. By then he was no longer a minor, having done homage for his lands on 10 July 1466. He was nearly seventeen years of age.

The formalities involved in declaring him of age had been set in motion, before 30 January 1466, when the master of the rolls issued the necessary certificate.[46] It may be presumed, as Clarence was so young, that it was Edward who initiated the process, and it was certainly he who authorised his coming of age, just as he had earlier admitted his brother as a minor to the Garter chapter. Edward's decisions were based on first hand acquaintance. He believed, apparently consistently, that Clarence could be relied upon and that his political usefulness outweighed his inexperience. Had he thought otherwise, Clarence would have remained a minor, perhaps for the four years remaining until his twenty-first birthday. Edward's confidence enabled Clarence to court patronage and become a channel for others to the king's ear. His own service became attractive. Events suggest that he was precocious and his conduct adult: soon after he had control of his affairs, he set off for his lordship of Tutbury and was at once immersed in administrative reform and litigation.[47] He was already a political force.

3. Clarence in Politics 1464-9

It was at a great council at Reading, which first met on 14 September 1464, that King Edward announced his marriage to Elizabeth Grey. The Burgundian chronicler Jehan de Waurin describes a scene in which the king voluntarily declared his intention of marrying her, listened to objections and then overruled them.[48] As the marriage had already taken place and as Waurin is frequently wrong about English affairs, it is safer to rely on Gregory's chronicle. This indicates that Edward's statement was made against his will, because negotiations had reached the point where he had to make a firm decision whether to marry Bona of Savoy.[49] Such an account agrees with the diplomatic situation at the time. It also appears that no announcement was intended as it was only on Michaelmas day, a fortnight after the opening of the council, that Elizabeth was received as queen. Whatever Edward's plans for her, he evidently did not intend to present her to the council as queen.

All the sources agree that the immediate and general reaction of the council was hostile. The marriage was clandestine, itself a cause for censure. The queen was not a virgin, had been married before and had children, which were other sources of objection. It was also thought dishonourable, as Polydore Vergil and Dominic Mancini put it, because it was motivated by 'blynde affection, and not by reule of reason'. It served no purpose of state and squandered one of England's few diplomatic cards — the king's freedom to marry. Mancini and Vergil decried her humble origins and 'meane caulying', and even Waurin, who knew of her continental connections, thought her unsuitable for such a prince.[50]

This assessment has generally been accepted by modern historians with the exception of Professor Lander. While concentrating mainly on blots on other escutcheons, Lander also argued that such objections to Elizabeth were not justified. Admittedly her father Richard Wydeville was not noble, but he was head of a long-

TABLE III: THE WYDEVILLE KINDRED IN 1464

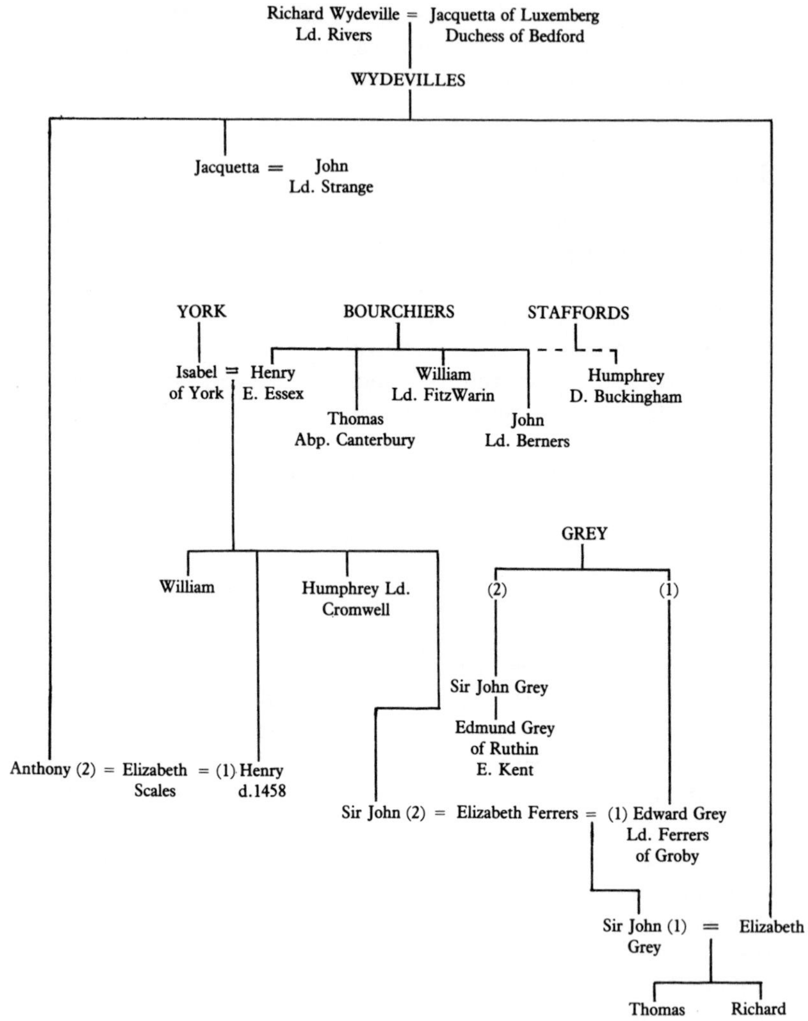

established county family of importance. Moreover her mother Jacquetta, Duchess of Bedford was not only widow of a royal prince, the son of Henry IV, brother of Henry V and Regent of France, but also daughter of a Count of St. Pol, a scion of the house of Luxemberg. Other members of this family, to whom Jacquetta was related, had been Holy Roman Emperors, Kings of Bohemia and of Hungary. On the basis of his wife's dower and his own service Wydeville had become a royal councillor, had been created Lord Rivers and a knight of the Garter, and by 1464 the family was established among the lesser nobility. Three of his children had married well. Jacquetta had married John, Lord Strange of Knockin. Elizabeth had married Sir John Grey (d. 1461), eldest son and heir of Edward, Lord Ferrers of Groby (d. 1457), a cadet of the Greys of Ruthin. Edward's widow Elizabeth Ferrers had taken as her second husband Sir John Bourchier, a younger son of the Earl of Essex. Another of the earl's sons, the late Henry Bourchier, was first husband of Elizabeth Scales:[51] she had remarried to Anthony Wydeville, in her right Lord Scales. Although Elizabeth Grey's relations with her mother-in-law were not cordial, such connections were valuable. Through them kinship could be claimed with the five Bourchier peers, the Stafford family and even the house of York. There were few aristocratic families to which they were not in some way related. These kinsmen rapidly perceived that the advancement of the Wydevilles could benefit them. Three of the nobles who married Elizabeth's sisters were already related to them. After the initial shock, the marriage was accepted.

Such an argument is quite convincing, but it is purely hypothetical and fails on several grounds. First of all, Jacquetta's lineage was not enough. One recalls Commines's later comment that Jacquetta's son was no fit match for the heiress of the duchy of Burgundy, 'for he was a mere earl and she the greatest heiress of her time'.[52] How much less suitable was her daughter for King Edward, greatest heir of his time. Indeed Waurin, who was acutely conscious of her continental connections, said as much and his comment is conclusive. Secondly, a careful examination of the Wydevilles's background reveals that they were not heirs of the longstanding gentry family but merely cadets, almost landless and dependent on royal wages and Jacquetta's dower. Without her dower, indeed, they could not have supported the estate of baron, yet without it they could expect to be in the relatively near future, when she died.

Edward IV. Portrait, *c*.1530.

Queen Eizabeth Wydeville. Copy, 16th century.

Admittedly Lord Rivers's eldest son Anthony was assured of a baronial income from his wife's estates, provided that she did not predecease him leaving no children, as ultimately she was to do. The Wydeville marriages were not particularly impressive either, for they were contracted with decidedly minor noble families. As for their more eminent connections, these only mattered if they acknowledged the Wydevilles and acted on their kinship. Lady Ferrers, however, took pains to prevent Elizabeth from recovering three manors of her jointure and Elizabeth's son, her own grandson, from inheriting the family estates; in this she was encouraged by her second husband, who enlisted the aid of his Bourchier father the Earl of Essex, his uncles the Archbishop of Canterbury and Lord Berners, and his brothers William and Thomas.[53] The Bourchiers, of course, were another family indirectly related to the Wydevilles. Another nobleman who should have regarded them as cousins, but in fact denounced them as upstarts, was Edward IV as Earl of March! Finally, the Wydevilles themselves were aware of their relatively obscure origins and tried to camouflage them: why else did they so persistently stress their continental connections on ceremonial state occasions?[54] Why did Richard Wydeville quarter his arms with those of Beauchamp of Hatch and take the title of Lord Rivers, rather than Wydeville? The answer appears to be that he wished to stress relationship, not yet traced, with the earlier noble houses of Beauchamp and of Redvers, formerly Earls of Devon and lords of the Isle of Wight and Ongar (Essex). When he was granted his title he also secured Rivers's fee in Northamptonshire. Later, in 1465, he, his wife and son paid a high price for the lordship of Wight. Like that later parvenu Lord Burghley, the Wydevilles did their best to manufacture a noble lineage.

The great council of 1464 had cause to regard Elizabeth as unfit to be queen and even for snobbery towards the Wydevilles themselves. On the other hand, the second part of the argument remains valid: the great council and the nobility, particularly those closely connected to the Wydevilles, had no choice but to accept and make the best of the new situation.

Clarence may have shared his elder brother's contempt for the upstart Wydevilles or may have regarded them as cousins. Mancini states that he made his hostility known 'by his bitter and public denunciations of Elizabeth's obscure family'.[55] Mancini was writing to explain the situation nineteen years later without experience of its development. He was influenced by hindsight, including the later disputes of queen and duke which led to the latter's death. For events in 1464 his testimony is unreliable. There is no other evidence of hostility at this date. Quite the contrary, in fact.

Clarence was certainly in Edward's favour on 30 August 1464. On that date he was granted the county of Chester during pleasure.[56] As this was the traditional patrimony of the Prince of Wales, the grant was tantamount to recognition of him as Edward's heir. It never took effect, doubtless because of the announcement of Edward's marriage. Any overt hostility would have earned Edward's wrath and Clarence would have ceased to benefit from his patronage. But it was precisely during this period, between August 1464 and July 1465, that the main endowment of the duke occurred. Furthermore, Edward gave Clarence four tuns of red wine and £100 towards his celebrations at Christmas. The duke escorted Elizabeth into Reading Abbey for her formal presentation as queen and later presided over her coronation.[57] At the very least he bowed to the *fait accompli*. He may even have welcomed it.

The marriage marked a turning point in English politics. It had been a faction that made Edward king. It had consisted of several magnates, in particular Richard Neville, Earl of Warwick and Salisbury, and the retinue of Edward himself as head of the house of York. Edward's leading retainers were Humphrey Stafford of Southwick, William Herbert of Raglan, Walter Devereux, William Hastings, John Dynham and Walter Blount. From this faction Edward had drawn his first councillors and principal officials.

Most important was the Earl of Warwick, the wealthiest contemporary magnate and head of the house of Neville. He was captain of Calais, warden of the Cinque Ports, great chamberlain of England, lieutenant of England north of the River Trent, and warden of the West March towards Scotland. With his brother John, from 1464 Earl of Northumberland, he destroyed Lancastrian resistance in the north; another brother George, Bishop of Exeter, was chancellor of England; an uncle, Lord Fauconberg, was steward of the king's household; four sisters were wives respectively of the Earl of Arundel, two barons and the heir of another two baronies, while his aunts were married into almost every other noble family. Edward IV was his first cousin. Kinship reinforced Warwick's natural pre-eminence and like earlier Nevilles he was to use marriage to strengthen his grasp on political power. He was the dominant influence on government and enjoyed a personal ascendancy over the young king, whom he could induce to act against his better judgement; away from Warwick's presence, however, Edward was always capable of independent action.[58]

At Edward's accession Warwick was able to work in concert with the York retainers. Three of them — Herbert, Devereux and Blount — were former retainers, who had held important office under him in Wales and Calais.[59] Another was Lord Hastings, who held the potentially vital office of chamberlain of the king's household, which carried with it control over access to the king and unrivalled opportunities for personal intimacy. To secure his goodwill, Warwick arranged for Hastings to marry his sister Katherine, a youthful widow: in addition to her valuable jointure of £400 a year, Warwick persuaded Edward to settle on them extensive lands over and above those which Hastings was granted on his own behalf.[60] Each of the six York retainers was ultimately ennobled, although Blount had to wait until 1465 and Dynham until 1467. Each enjoyed Edward's patronage and was assigned responsibilities. Stafford and Dynham were active in the West Country, Herbert and Devereux (now Lord Ferrers of Chartley) in Wales, Hastings at court and Blount as treasurer of England. None rivalled Warwick.

Gradually the faction altered. The Earl of Kent died and was replaced as household steward by a non-Neville. By 1464 the struggle of York and Lancaster was resolved, and even some Lancastrians accepted Edward as king and accommodated themselves to changed circumstances. One who had already done so was Lord Rivers, a councillor by at least 1463. The basis of government broadened from a faction to embrace much of the nobility. The Yorkist councillors and the new men, who owed everything to Edward, were responsive to his will and were willing agents of his policy. Warwick, however, was not content merely to execute policy but expected to formulate it. His military resources were no longer necessary, but he failed to adapt to a diminished role. He was the main protagonist of a pro-French foreign policy, for which Edward had little sympathy. The accord for which he worked, based on a matrimonial treaty with France, was wrecked by the king's marriage. He himself had been made to appear ridiculous. Early reports, which suggested that he was about to rebel, indicate how violent was his immediate reaction. Nevertheless he reconciled himself to the situation and even escorted the new queen into

Reading Abbey for her formal recognition.[61]

Lord Rivers was already a royal councillor but his daughter's marriage greatly enhanced the family's importance. They had legitimate claims on King Edward's generosity. Rivers was created an earl and appointed treasurer of England, an office which not only carried extremely valuable emoluments but might enable him to enrich himself.[62] The queen was supplied, not without difficulty, with an adequate dower, carved mainly from the duchy of Lancaster. Her household and estates became the means to reward other members of her family. Jaques Haute, for example, was carver in her household and Martin Haute became receiver of her Northamptonshire estates.[63] Actually the Wydevilles received relatively little endowment because by 1464 Edward had largely dissipated the enormous fund of patronage in his hands in 1461. Yet royal patronage was only one possible source of advancement.

In medieval England the marriage of a daughter was a business matter. The father of the bride paid a marriage portion on which depended in part the rank of the bridegroom and the size of the jointure settled on them. The 200 marks (£133 13*s.* 4*d.*), which was all that Lord Rivers paid for Elizabeth's marriage, had bought only the heir of a minor barony and an inadequate jointure. In 1464 he still had five unmarried daughters, but now he was an earl, the king was his son-in-law, and a match with his family was attractive for other than financial reasons. The king's personal intervention or the promise of royal favour could decisively influence such transactions.

It was in this way that Edward advanced his wife's relatives. It was due to his initiative that the Duke of Buckingham, the heirs of the Earls of Arundel, Kent, Essex and Lord Herbert, the heiress of the Duke of Exeter, and the Dowager-Duchess of Norfolk married Katherine, Margaret, Eleanor, Anne and Mary Wydeville, Thomas Grey and John Wydeville respectively. He had given the custody of the estates of Humphrey Stafford, late Duke of Buckingham (d. 1460), to his widow and half-brother at a fixed rent, which he waived on 28 April 1464 in return for the marriage and wardship of the young duke, properly at the disposal of the late duke's executors.[64] The duke was married to Katherine Wydeville soon after Edward's wedding. It was also at Edward's instance that the marriage of Anne Holland was bought from the Duchess of Exeter. In three other cases Edward settled substantial lands on the magnates's heirs and their Wydeville brides and/or paid the marriage portion. Probably he did likewise in the other case. Altogether, it is quite clear that these marriages were of the king's making and, since the inducements offered were well above the market values, that his intervention was decisive.

It was on this basis that support for the Wydevilles grew. It comprised their relatives, their servants and now their new in-laws. These included the king's sister Anne, Duchess of Exeter, Lord Herbert, and the Earls of Essex, Arundel and Kent. Essex was uncle of the king and head of the Bourchier family, now tied to the Wydevilles by several strands. John Bourchier, Lord Berners became chamberlain to the queen, his son Humphrey one of her carvers, and his wife Margery was to be the constant attendant of the Princess Elizabeth. Anne Wydeville, wife to William Bourchier, remained in attendance on the queen.[65] The Bourchiers were a closely knit family: Lords Berners and Cromwell were constantly associated, Lord FitzWarin collaborated with his brother the Earl of Essex,[66] and the latter with their brother Thomas, Archbishop of Canterbury. As the archbishop, earl, Berners and FitzWarin were half-brothers of the late Duke of Buckingham, it comes as no surprise that the Countess of Essex received a gift from the Duchess of Buckingham at Writtle (Essex) in July 1463.[67] The archbishop and duchess shared the custody of her late husband's estates, and he and Essex acted in August 1467 as trustees of their niece Joan Stafford, Lady Beaumont. So too did her surviving brothers John and Henry Stafford and her new stepfather Walter Blount, now Lord Mountjoy.[68] He was the second husband of the Duchess of Buckingham. The Staffords were themselves bound to the Wydevilles by the marriage of the Duke of Buckingham and Katherine Wydeville. Sir Henry Stafford's wife Margaret Beaufort, Dowager-Countess of Richmond had a son Henry Tudor in the household of Lord Herbert, where she visited him on several occasions.[69] Herbert was not merely father-in-law of Mary Wydeville but brother-in-law of Walter Devereux, Lord Ferrers of Chartley.

The tying of these bonds occurred in the years 1466-7 and had a major effect on domestic politics. It was not that Lord Rivers 'could induce Edward IV to do exactly what suited the Wydevills',[70] except in the matter of marriages, but that Edward took a liberal view of his obligations to the Wydevilles. He tried hard to establish every member of the family and supported their efforts to help themselves. His advisers wisely ingratiated themselves with the

Wydevilles, who in turn drew some of them into their service. There was little change in Edward's advisers or those with access to him, but most of them became connections of the Wydevilles. The Bourchiers, for example, included at least three councillors in the archbishop, Berners and Essex, who was a former treasurer; Edmund Grey of Ruthin, the new Earl of Kent, and Lord Mountjoy were both councillors and former treasurers,[71] and belonged to the group of York retainers, just as Herbert and Ferrers did. Rivers as treasurer now held a key position.

The council was not the only forum of debate. As important, if not more so, were those who had access to the king's chamber and could influence him privately. The provisos of exemption from the 1465 act of resumption survive. On the provisos the clerk of parliament stated who had delivered them after the king had signed them. They belong to February and March 1465, when the politically important might all be expected in parliament. As they related to a matter that touched everybody, all those able to obtain access to the king might be expected to have done so. Twenty-two named individuals did, including twenty councillors. They included all the chief officers of state and household, namely the chancellor and treasurer of England, the keeper of the privy seal, the steward, chamberlain, treasurer and controller of the royal household, and the chief butler of England. There were several bishops; the Earl of Warwick, his two brothers, and his client Lord Wenlock; Rivers, Scales, Archbishop Bourchier, Essex, Berners and Cromwell, Herbert and Ferrers, and Mountjoy, all of them Wydevilles or Wydeville kin.[72] Not all were of equal importance and it is likely that later, when the Wydevilles were better established, they themselves would have been more prominent.

Clarence also participated in the delivery of provisos. A few months later, on 26 May 1465, he was to preside over the coronation of the new queen:

> 'The Duq of Clarance Stywarde of Englond ryding in the hall on horsebak his coursour rychely trapped hede & body to the grounde with Crapsiur rychely embroiderd & garnyst with spangyls of golde'.

He led the procession into Westminster Abbey, held the basin for the queen for her ablutions after the ceremony, led the procession to the banquet and there supervised the coronation feast. Before the ceremony King Edward created thirty-eight knights of the Bath: he also made two new earls and a baron, probably after the service.[73] The king's new kin were present in large numbers. To the Wydevilles a large connection was desirable, but it certainly strained Edward's capacity to give. The number of kinsmen eager to serve Edward was not matched by the avenues open to them.

Clarence and Queen Elizabeth were fortunate to receive priority in the king's provisions. Later Edward was unwilling to alienate crown, duchy of Lancaster or duchy of York property. As there were no new forfeitures during 1464-9 and several attainders were reversed, no more land came into his hands. Edward could not lavishly endow the new kin that he had acquired and the new peers that he had created: they had to compete for his largesse. He had to satisfy demands made on him by specific cash rewards; by enlarging his household, members of which enjoyed annuities; and by the exploitation of his rights of wardship and marriage. The latter may have had profound implications.

If Edward was to avoid the enmity of the previous grantee, he had to compensate him for the loss of property resumed by the crown. In 1465 when Lord Rivers was appointed treasurer, the ruffled feelings of Lord Mountjoy were smoothed by elevation to the rank of baron and the gift of 1,000 marks (£666 13*s*. 4*d*.) in cash.[74] When the Earl of Worcester was sent to Ireland as deputy, he sold his other offices: the office of chief justice of North Wales was bought by King Edward for £200 and given to Lord Herbert; the constableship of Porchester castle was surrendered to Lord Scales; the stewardship of the household, which he vacated, was given to the Earl of Essex and the constableship of England to Lord Rivers.[75]

In this dearth of patronage it was attractive to employ Edward's powers over land to enlarge the fund available. In 1467 several manors were resumed from the Archbishop of York and given to Lord Stafford of Southwick.[76] It was later believed that the trial of Sir Thomas Cook was staged to obtain his possessions by the Duchess of Bedford and Earl Rivers; on other occasions the Wydevilles gave solid grounds for such accusations. There were even greater advantages in manipulating attainders: on Henry Courtenay's attainder in 1469, the chronicler Warkworth reports that 'menne seyde the Lord Stafford of Southwyke was cause of the seyde Herry Courtenayes death';[77] he was certainly the main beneficiary. One day the constellation of offices held by the Earl of Warwick might be resumed.

The implications of such actions were serious: even more so was Edward's distribution of royal wards. The marriages of the queen's brother and sisters had been arranged largely through Edward's intervention, only the Duke of Buckingham being a royal ward, but in the late fourteen-sixties Lords Herbert and Rivers enjoyed a virtual monopoly of marriages in the king's gift. In Easter term 1469 Earl Rivers bought the wardship and marriage of John, Lord Zouche for £1,000.[78] George Neville, son of the Earl of Northumberland and potentially the greatest contemporary heir, was to be considered as bridegroom for Edward's daughter Elizabeth. As treasurer, Earl Rivers had in his gift the wardship, marriage and custody of the estates of politically less important heirs; among beneficiaries were his son Lord Scales and Lord Herbert. The Herbert gains were yet more extensive. On 20 January 1467 Lord Herbert's heir married Mary Wydeville. The day before his daughter Margaret Herbert married Thomas Talbot, Viscount Lisle, whose wardship and marriage he held. On 23 June 1467 for 800 marks (£533 13*s.* 4*d.*) Edward sold him the wardship and marriage of John, Lord Grey of Powys, who married Anne Herbert. Henry Tudor, rightful Earl of Richmond, was brought up in the Herbert household and was intended for Maud Herbert. Also in the household by 1468 was Henry Percy, heir to the barony of Poynings and eldest son of the attainted third Percy Earl of Northumberland;[79] perhaps he too was intended to marry a Herbert, as he later did. The success of Herbert's marriage policy bears witness to his influence with the king, to which the Croyland chronicler testifies,[80] and which was reflected in his rapid advancement from Welsh squire to great magnate with an income of £2,400.

The methods that the Herberts and Wydevilles used to build up their power were abrasive and illustrate their ambition and lack of scruple. None of their projects, however, were as potentially explosive as Herbert's marriage policy. Apparently he planned the reversal of past attainders to supply his daughters's bridegrooms with magnate estates and cared nothing for possible repercussions.

Henry Percy was heir to the Poynings barony through his mother. Should he marry a Herbert, it is difficult to believe that the Herbert-Wydeville connection would not have joined with his own powerful relatives, such as the Earl of Kent, to secure his restoration to the family earldom, as was to occur during 1469-70. This entailed the dispossession of the current occupants of the Percy estates, that is the Earl of Warwick in Cumberland and Yorkshire, his brother of Northumberland in Northumberland, and the Duke of Clarence in Yorkshire, Lincolnshire and elsewhere. The potential victims were well-aware of the danger. In 1469 a Yorkshire rebellion led by Robin of Holderness called for Percy's restoration. Clarence was unwilling to surrender the estates and John Neville was to regard compensation offered later as inadequate.[81] Herbert was already Warwick's personal enemy, the result or cause of a feud over the lordship of Newport,[82] and apparently had no qualms over dispossessing him.

Henry Tudor was heir of his mother Margaret Beaufort, daughter and sole heiress of John, Duke of Somerset (d.1444). He was also by right Earl of Richmond, as Herbert recognised,[83] as son and heir of Edmund Tudor (d.1456), whose earldom and honour had lapsed in 1461. Had he married Maud Herbert, he too could have relied on the Wydeville-Herbert connection for support, as well as the family of his stepfather Henry Stafford; later they united in his favour. The occupant of the honour, the Duke of Clarence, again had no intention of relinquishing it.

Compensation was not necessarily attached to such restorations and in the situation of the late fourteen-sixties, when the king had little to give, it was unlikely to be adequate. An obvious parallel was the situation in the twelfth century, when political conditions had created more heirs than lands. Nor were these the only dangers of Herbert's marriage policy. His son had been created Lord Dunster, to the displeasure of the Earl of Warwick,[84] apparently because of his own tenuous claim. Viscount Lisle's link with Herbert was fraught with peril: as coheir of Elizabeth Berkeley, Countess of Warwick, he inherited a claim to the Berkeley barony in Gloucestershire, to which Herbert was a powerful neighbour, which claim Lisle pursued by force; he had claims to the estates of the earldom of Shrewsbury that his grandfather had settled on his father; and his grandmother Margaret, Countess of Shrewsbury, daughter of Richard Beauchamp, Earl of Warwick by Elizabeth Berkeley, conveyed to him a claim to the Warwick earldom and to the enfeoffed lands of the late earl.[85] If Lisle revived these disputes, he was likely to receive Herbert's support and it was possible that Herbert could secure King Edward's intervention on his behalf.

Warwick was confronted by a threat to his earldom and, more immediately, to his predominance in the north. While these represented the most crippling and direct threat to his personal power, they were not the only ones. His brother Northumberland was bound to lose heavily if the Percies were restored; his other brother the archbishop had already lost lands to Stafford of Southwick — an ominous warning aimed at Warwick himself. It is unlikely that it escaped Warwick's notice, when arranging his sister's marriage to the impecunious Earl of Oxford, that Oxford was coheir of Lady Scales, childless wife of Anthony Wydeville; in 1466 Anthony persuaded her to convey her inheritance to his trustees, thereby ensuring that on her death he would retain them to the loss of the rightful heirs, Oxford included.[86] The Wydevilles also annoyed another brother-in-law, Lord Hastings, who seems never to have made common cause with them. Hastings was a relative of Lady Ferrers of Groby and through her of the Wydevilles. In 1464 the queen, then plain Elizabeth Grey, had sought his help, apparently to obtain an audience with the king to plead her case against Lady Ferrers. Hastings complied on the exacting condition that Elizabeth's heir would marry his as yet unborn daughter and that he would share any proceeds.[87] When Elizabeth's efforts were crowned with unforseen success and she became queen, the arrangement lapsed: Hastings could expect nothing else. Elizabeth, however, may have nursed animosity towards him; her brother Scales never seems to have trusted him;[88] and one of the Wydeville marriages, between Sir John Wydeville and the Dowager-Duchess of Norfolk, prevented Hastings from making good royal grants of the duchess's jointure.[89] A magnate as reliant on dynastic support as Warwick could not ignore such affronts; probably, indeed, they were brought to his attention by kinsmen, who expected him to put things right. Unfortunately he no longer had the power.

The Neville estates and power had been built up by exploiting kinship to the crown and moments of political ascendancy, notably the coups of 1455 and 1461. The queen's marriage, followed at once by the rupture of his nephew's engagement to the Exeter heiress, was a severe blow to Warwick, but like everyone else he accepted the new situation and tried to make the most of it. In the late fourteen-sixties, however, Wydeville influence at court was growing and that of Warwick was waning. They advanced partly at the expense of Lord Hastings, one of his intermediaries with the king. It was probably the loss of another ally that caused him to object to the replacement as treasurer of Lord Mountjoy by Lord Rivers,[90] even though Mountjoy himself harboured no rancour. Finally, in 1467,

Warwick's brother Archbishop Neville was dismissed as chancellor,[91] a blow that was compounded by the appointment as keeper of the privy seal of Thomas Rotherham, apparently a Wydeville protegé. Nothing demonstrates Warwick's weakness more than his withdrawal from court and denunciation of his enemies, actions reminiscent of the Duke of York's similar conduct in the fourteen-fifties and just as unsuccessful.

Warwick had to contest the Wydevilles's growing power at court both because of Herbert's designs on his estates held by royal grant and because control of his hereditary estates depended on his capacity to exclude rival claimants from a fair hearing by the king.[92] Similar influence would be needed by his heirs. Warwick had no son, only two daughters who were heiresses of his Montagu, Beauchamp and Despenser possessions; his nephew George Neville was heir to the Neville inheritance itself. Warwick's daughters needed to marry husbands sufficiently powerful to keep their inheritance. All three were great heirs, who in normal circumstances could expect little difficulty in attracting worthy spouses. But Edward's intervention in the marriage market for his Wydeville sisters-in-law had removed the most eligible bachelors and George Neville's betrothed, Anne Holland, was married instead to the queen's son. Earlier Warwick had obtained the restoration of John de Vere to the earldom of Oxford and had married him to his sister Margaret. He could not provide for his daughters. He was certainly aiming high: his ward Francis, Viscount Lovell was married not to his daughter but to his niece Alice, daughter of Lord FitzHugh. This lends credence to Waurin's otherwise unsupported statement that Warwick wanted to marry both his daughters to brothers of Edward IV. Edward forbade it and thwarted the necessary dispensation.

These were probably the supplementary grievances to which the Croyland chronicler refers. Like continental writers, such as Thomas Basin, he thought that Warwick's breach with the Wydevilles was due to differences on foreign policy.[93] Even after Edward's marriage Warwick pressed for an alliance with France, in which he was influenced by his personal liking for Louis XI and animosity for Charles the Bold. His negotiations continued until mid-1467. Apparently he still believed that he could win over opinion in England, including the king, and made promises accordingly.[94] Edward, however, favoured the Burgundians, who had helped him become king, with whom England had strong commercial ties, and because of the threat of France. An embassy appointed on 26 March 1466 was to treat, among other things, for the marriage of 'our dearest brother George, Duke of Clarence and Mary daughter of our aforesaid kinsman the Count of Charolais'. The Burgundians wished only to treat for a marriage between Charles the Bold and Margaret of York.[95] This marriage, which took place in 1468, was accepted by Margaret at a great council at Kingston in October 1467. The treaty was already complete in June 1467. Edward linked it with an offensive war against France. The Wydevilles, as relatives of the Count of St. Pol, favoured Burgundy and, as they owed all to Edward, were willing agents of his policies. They initiated and dominated the tournament of Lord Scales and the Bastard of Burgundy in June 1467, which coincided with Edward's dismissal as chancellor of Archbishop Neville.[96] On his return Warwick was furious, withdrawing to his estates, and Edward said unforgivable things. By mediation of Archbishop Neville and Earl Rivers, a reconciliation was patched up at the Coventry great council of January 1468 between Warwick and Stafford of Southwick, Herbert and Audley.[97] It was not sincere. Henceforth Warwick could not influence Edward or achieve his ends by peaceful means.

The Duke of Clarence was present at the tournament, the dismissal of Archbishop Neville, and the preliminaries of Margaret's marriage,[98] but did not support the foreign policy of the king and the Wydevilles. The projected marriage to Mary of Burgundy was short-lived and may not have been seriously intended. More attractive was Warwick's francophile foreign policy. During April and May 1467 he and Louis XI reached an understanding which involved the partition of Burgundy. Clarence would have Holland, Zeeland and Brabant, Louis the rest. The project enjoyed Clarence's support. When Edward rebuffed the French embassy, it was welcomed by the duke and earl.[99] Had the understanding been implemented, Louis would have found another husband for Margaret of York. But Edward was not interested.

Clarence's domestic relations with those about the king were not good. He had been appointed lieutenant of Ireland and indented for it with the king on 30 April 1467, but he was not allowed to go there. Instead the Earl of Worcester was sent as deputy and it was he, not Clarence, who enjoyed the emoluments of office.[100] Their relations were not improved by Clarence's dispute with Worcester and the latter's sister Philippa, Lady Roos over the lordship of Wragby (Lincs.), a quarrel that Clarence lost.[101] In 1468 Clarence was again at odds with opinion at court, certainly including Worcester and Hastings, over a Derbyshire feud.[102] Clarence shared with Warwick the threat to his estates posed by Lord Herbert's sponsorship of Henry Tudor and Henry Percy and, in the prevailing circumstances, could not count on compensation. Edward declared that he intended 'to lyve uppon my nowne [except] . . . in grete and urgent causes', a statement that suggested that no more lands would be made available for compensation. Although Clarence was exempted from the 1467 act of resumption, his proviso limited his landed income to 5,600 marks (£3,733 6*s*. 8*d*.) and reversions of 1,000 marks (£666 13*s*. 4*d*.). He had almost reached this level, which in no way matched his ambitions, for in 1468 he planned spending even more on his household alone.[103] He was unable to expand his estates with Edward's help.

Clarence found that his influence was less than the deference accorded to him had suggested. Edward thwarted his hopes of territorial advancement at home and abroad. Perhaps he could marry an heiress. The obvious candidates were Warwick's daughters but Edward forbade the match. There were no other eligible English candidates. The duke was a pawn in Edward's diplomacy. This did not result in his marriage in 1466 and it might not in the future. It was not necessarily in Edward's interests to arrange further marriage treaties and, if he did, it would be because they were attractive to him. Clarence was unwilling to wait as long or as patiently as his sister Margaret. Therefore he joined Warwick in opposition.

4. Clarence and Warwick 1464-9

Although separated in age by over twenty years, Clarence and Warwick were first cousins. In the years when he was Edward's principal supporter Warwick must have met the duke frequently. Both attended the funeral of the Earl of Salisbury in 1463 and together they escorted the new queen into Reading Abbey a year later.

The chronicler Waurin states that the plan to marry Warwick's daughters and Edward's brothers was first mooted at Cambridge in

1464. This appears too early, for Clarence did not come of age until July 1466, Gloucester for another three years. Yet Waurin's story may have some basis in fact. He depicts Edward's reaction as rage and prohibition of the marriage. Warwick and Clarence persisted with it.[104] Master Lacy was despatched to Rome to secure the necessary dispensation for consanguinity. During the summer of 1467 Archbishop Neville tried to influence negotiations with the aid of the papal legate, with whom he enjoyed friendly relations.[105] The refusal of a dispensation by Pope Paul II may have been connected with Edward's success in 1467 in obtaining a cardinalate for Archbishop Bourchier, not Archbishop Neville. Negotiations on behalf of the princes continued, this time through Edward's own proctor James Goldwell, which resulted in a dispensation on 14 March 1469.[106]

The marriage policy complemented Warwick's foreign policy. After the birth of Edward's daughter Elizabeth, it was unlikely that Clarence and his wife would ever become King and Queen of England. Louis XI's proposal to carve a principality out of Burgundy for Clarence was attractive to Warwick. The duke also found it alluring, as it offered the prospect of immediate advancement. After Edward had thwarted the proposed partition of Burgundy, Clarence like Warwick may have remained committed to a pro-French foreign policy.

In 1467 Clarence was still only seventeen, immature and inexperienced. As a commissioner of oyer and terminer, he amused himself at the expense of a fellow justice who had fallen asleep.[107] But he was ambitious, knew what he wanted, and was determined to obtain it. He wished to marry Isabel Neville. He wanted real power at court and a larger share of royal patronage: alliance with his rivals's enemy was one means to these ends. The 1468 ordinance of his household illustrates his grandiose notion of his own importance but it is unlikely, at first, that he contemplated usurpation. Warwick certainly did not overlook the possibility. From the start he must have foreseen the need to eliminate his enemies by force and impose some physical restraint on Edward: the association of the king's brother might silence any opposition. As the greatest magnate apart from himself, Clarence was a worthy husband for his daughter.

Such aims contradict the rumours that Warwick was implicated in the Lancastrian plots in 1468, which, according to pseudo-Worcester, was believed by Edward himself. They appear in several continental sources. There were widespread but ineffective Lancastrian conspiracies, involving Jasper Tudor in Wales, Master Ralph Mackerell in East Anglia and, from the indictments, Sir Thomas Hungerford and Henry Courtenay in the south-west and others in London.[108] The course of Margaret of Anjou's policies towards England from 1467 cast doubt on any rapprochement before 1470.

The dispensation was granted at Rome on 14 March 1469. Its arrival made Clarence's marriage possible. The site selected was Calais castle, where Warwick was captain. In February the earl had been commissioned to investigate land tenure in the Pale of Calais, sufficient justification for his presence there. Edward, who had also intended to visit Calais, changed his mind[109] and instead went on a pilgrimage in East Anglia.

On 7 June 1469 Clarence arrived at Canterbury, where he was received with all honour by the Prior and convent of Christ Church. He remained for two days at the prior's lodging with a household of impressive size. Afterwards he went to Sandwich, where he found the Earl of Warwick and Bishop of London. They were soon joined by Archbishop Neville and the Prior of Christ Church. The former blessed Warwick's ship, the Trinity, on 12 June. The borough of Sandwich was generous in gifts: beneficiaries included the Earl and Countess of Warwick, Lord Wenlock, Sir Walter Wrottesley and Sir John Guildford. Clarence was given six capons and six gallons of wine.[110] The Duchess of York was at Sandwich for four days to see Clarence. The Countess of Warwick went to Calais independently and the others dispersed. Warwick accompanied Clarence to the duke's castle of Queenborough (Kent), but on 28 June he was in London, whence he wrote to Coventry informing the city of the intended wedding.[111] Three days later a licence was obtained from Cardinal Bourchier for the marriage to be celebrated at Calais,[112] but on 4 July the Earls of Warwick and Oxford and Archbishop Neville were still at Canterbury. They crossed the Channel on 6 July and on 11 July Archbishop Neville married Clarence and Isabel Neville in the presence of Warwick

> 'and v other knyghtes of the garter, and many other lordes and ladies and wurshipfull knightes, well accompanied with wise and discreete esquires, in right greate numbyr to the laude preysinge of God, and to the honoure and wurship of the world' . . .[113]

The following day Warwick, Clarence and the archbishop issued a manifesto under their seals, in which they stated their intention of remedying evil government. It recited the evils that had led to the deposition of three earlier kings:

> 'First, where the seid Kynges estraingid the gret lordis of thayre blood from thaire secrete Councelle, And not avised by them; And takyng abowte them other not of thaire blood, and enclynyng only to theire counselle, rule and advise, the wheche persones take not respect ne consideracion to the wele of the seid princes, ne to the comonwele of this lond, but only to theire singuler lucour and enrichyng of themself and theire bloode, as welle in theire greet possessions as in goodis; by the wheche the seid princes were so enpoverysshed that they hadde not sufficient of lyvelode ne of goodis, wherby they myght kepe and mayntene theire honorable estate and ordinarie charges withynne this realme' . . .

From such evil counsel stemmed taxation, illegal prests, the alienation of royal demesne and civil disorder. Such evils were again present, due to the king's evil councillors. The manifesto proposed their dismissal and punishment, the resumption of grants made to them, and the assignment of sufficient lands to support ordinary charges without need for taxation or forced loans.

Such charges are commonplaces of political propaganda. They are the eternal cry of those out of power against those who are in, motivated less by the desire to right wrongs than to transfer the fruits of power to themselves. Yet this is no reason to dismiss them, for such manifestoes were surely designed to justify the actions of the authors, to attract support, to still potential resistance. To achieve such aims propaganda had to appeal to contemporary grievances. As the manifesto said, the king's favourites had insinuated themselves into the king's innermost counsels, supplanting the Nevilles and doubtless others. Much of Edward's recent alienations, which included parts of the crown estate and duchy of Lancaster, had passed to them; large sums had been spent buying them offices and marriages. By 1469 Herbert and Rivers were among the richest of the peerage. It was at least partly as a result that Edward failed to live on his own resources, as he had promised in 1467, and had spent the war-tax then granted on ordinary expenses: Rivers and his wife, important exchequer annuitants, had gained by securing payment of longstanding arrears. Wydevilles and Herberts were concerned primarily with self-advancement, rather than the good of the commonwealth, in pursuit of which they had perverted justice.[114] This was effective propaganda, which won some popular support.

Warwick was concerned primarily to destroy his enemies, the 'evil councillors', whom the manifesto named as Earl Rivers, the Duchess of Bedford and their sons, William Herbert, now Earl of Pembroke, Humphrey Stafford of Southwick, now Earl of Devon, Lord Audley and Sir John Fogge. Audley, Stafford and Herbert were already among Warwick's enemies in 1468. Those outside Edward's patronage would not resist the punishment of those who controlled it. The list reassured any others who might have feared reprisals.

The manifesto announced that Warwick, Clarence and the archbishop would be at Canterbury on 16 July 1469 and summoned thither all true subjects arrayed for war. The need to appeal to a Kentish audience may account for Fogge's presence on the list. Earl Rivers himself had a house at the Mote, Maidstone and other lands in north Kent; his relatives, the Fogges and Hautes, were prominent Kentish gentry. Warwick, Clarence and some of the Calais garrison landed at Sandwich. They were reinforced by contingents from Sandwich, Lydd and New Romney, for Warwick was warden of the Cinque Ports. They included his lieutenant, Sir John Guildford. Another force joined them at Canterbury and they proceeded via London to Northampton.

Even before Clarence's wedding Warwick had arranged for rebellions by his supporters in the Midlands and the north to supplement his own rising in Kent. Nominally led by Robin of Redesdale, the northern rebellion entailed the mobilisation of Warwick's northern retainers. Among those who later required pardons were Lord FitzHugh, Warwick's brother-in-law and his deputy as warden of the West March; Sir Richard Salkeld, Warwick's deputy as constable of Carlisle, and the Carlisle garrison; and, most important of all, many Richmondshire gentry from near Warwick's lordship of Middleham.[116] Robin of Redesdale's forces proceeded southwards, defeating Edward's tardily assembled army at Edgecote, near Banbury in Oxfordshire. Among those killed were sons of Lords FitzHugh and Greystoke; Henry Neville, son of the idiot Lord Latimer, and his brother-in-law Oliver Dudley; and John Conyers, son of Warwick's steward of Middleham.[117]

Before the wedding Warwick had written to Coventry, and doubtless elsewhere, to order the muster of men to resist the northern rebels. In fact, of course, he intended them to participate in the insurrection. Like Warwick himself the Midlanders missed the battle of Edgecote, but it is probable that they did rise, since they were held principally responsible for the death of Earl Rivers. Midlanders were predominant among the thirty-four men whom the Duchess of Bedford later accused of her husband's murder.[118] Among them were John Langstrother, Prior of St. John, who had been associated as preceptor of Balsall with the Earl of Warwick during the fourteen-fifties; Sir Edward Grey of Asteley (Warw.), brother-in-law and enemy of the queen, one of Warwick's councillors; Sir Geoffrey Gate, his marshall at Calais;[119] his retainers and tenants John Hugford of Edmundscote (Warw.), William Berkeley of Weoley (Worcs.), Thomas Stafford of Middleton (Berks.), Thomas Wake of Blisworth (Northants.), John Hay of More End (Northants.), and James Hyet of Lydney (Gloucs.); and nine artisans of Coventry, who had apparently responded to his letter of summons.

The rising was thus based on three elements of Warwick's power: his dominance of the north, founded on his estates and his military authority as warden; his importance in Kent as captain of Calais and warden of the Cinque Ports; and his Beauchamp and Despenser estates in the West Midlands. As far as one can tell, nobody came from his Welsh marcher lordships or his estates in southern England. None of those killed or accused have been identified as Clarence's men, although he, like the Earl of Oxford,[120] probably mobilised his retinue. Clarence himself was not accused of killing Earl Rivers. The rebellions had been planned by Warwick and the results were achieved with his resources alone. It was probably Clarence who instigated the attack on Lord Scales's house at Middleton (Norf.), for it was organised by John Jenney, steward of the honour of Richmond in Norfolk.[121]

King Edward himself was slow to realise how extensive and how dangerous the rebellions were. When he did, he sent Earl Rivers to safety — an indication of his military value — and summoned the new Earls of Pembroke and Devon to his aid. Had they co-operated, their support might have been enough. Edward did not issue commissions of array, the recognised way of mobilising support, perhaps because those loyal to him could not be relied on to protect his favourites. We know that Clarence's marriage, in spite of Edward's prohibition, was widely expected and was well-attended by the political élite, including five knights of the Garter; even Cardinal Bourchier co-operated. Perhaps historians have under-estimated the appeal of Warwick's coup. Others than he may have suffered by the cornering of the marriage market and royal patronage: the Earl of Kent, for example, objected to Pembroke's advancement in North Wales, without lasting effect; Humphrey Bourchier, Lord Cromwell, husband of one of the Cromwell coheirs, had grounds for offence and even alarm in Lord Scales's designs on the inheritance of the other coheir, his sister-in-law Maud, Lady Willoughby; the Duke of Norfolk, who was trying to wrest Caister castle from the Pastons, was confronted by the Pastons's prospective in-laws, Lord Scales and Sir John Wydeville; and Lord Hastings, as we have seen, had similar grievances. Other lords of the king's blood, perhaps even the Bourchiers, may not have been averse to breaking the favourites's grip on power. Without supporting Warwick in rebellion, such magnates, if mobilised by the king, might themselves have required some curbing of his favourites.

After the battle of Edgecote Earl Rivers, the Earl of Pembroke, Sir Richard Herbert and Sir John Wydeville were executed at Northampton on the orders of Warwick and Clarence; Thomas Herbert was also executed; and the Earl of Devon was killed at Bridgewater. Edward himself was almost alone when he was arrested by Archbishop Neville, who handed him over to Warwick and Clarence. At Coventry on 2 August, he was at Warwick from 8 to 12 August,[122] and at Middleham (Yorks.) by 25 August.

With the deaths of the leading 'evil councillors', the aims of the manifesto were largely achieved: only the resumption of grants to them and the assignment of revenues to support the ordinary expenses of government remained to be done. Warwick, however, wanted more than was set out in the manifesto: he undoubtedly expected a decisive say in foreign policy and access to royal patronage. Edward would hardly have submitted indefinitely and might even contemplate revenge. It was therefore necessary to control his actions. He was a prisoner. His obedience was assured by a scarcely veiled threat of deposition. The manifesto had compared the conduct of his councillors to those of three deposed kings: it was an obvious inference that, if he did not attend to reform himself, he would be deposed. Essential to the threat was a credible alternative. Rumours that Edward was a bastard were current at home and abroad. A continental source attributed them to Warwick.[123] This might enable the claims of Edward and his daughters to be set aside in favour of the Duke of Clarence. Such an approach would create problems, since magnates who accepted the destruction of the king's favourites might not prefer Warwick in their place and would certainly oppose any attempt to change the king. Of course deposition was only a threat, which Warwick is unlikely to have wished to carry out.

In the meantime the rebels tried to govern with the king in restraint on the pattern of the fourteen-fifties. Thomas Wake accused the Duchess of Bedford of sorcery and the case was considered by a council at Warwick before 'diuers of the lordes'. The council summoned a parliament for 22 September 1469.[124]

After these initial consultations, Warwick withdrew with the king to Middleham, and tried to control affairs from there. He communicated with the council at London by signet letters and oral messages. Archbishop Neville went north, apparently to consult him, before 10 September.[125] He was therefore absent from a council meeting on 12 September, which was attended by Cardinal Bourchier, four other bishops including the chancellor and keeper of the privy seal, three lesser clerics, and Lords Mountjoy, Dynham, Dacre and Ferrers. An earlier letter to the council assumed the presence of both archbishops, the chancellor and Clarence.[126] Others who probably attended were Langstrother, the new treasurer, and the Earl of Essex. The most vital matters before them concerned public order.

The most serious disturbances were in Norfolk, where the Duke of Norfolk was still contesting Sir John Paston's occupation of Caister castle.[127] Even when the Wydevilles had drawn his attention to it, Edward had taken no effective action. By 21 August the duke was blockading the castle. The council intervened, offering arbitration, 'appoyntementys and rewll made by the lordys of the Kyngys concell whych be to my seyd lord of Norffolk nere kyne', namely that the matter should be arbitrated by the council, by Cardinal Bourchier, Clarence, Archbishop Neville or Essex. The intervention, which was at Clarence's instigation, was confided to Walter Writtle, whom he had recommended: Writtle received full authority in his credence from all the lords. The terms were considered so honourable that Norfolk would be ill-advised to refuse them, but he declared that they were no better than those offered before. He demanded the surrender of the castle and rejected

Archbishop Neville as arbiter. Instead, he declared that 'he wul not spare to do as he is purposyd for no duke in Ynglond', a clear reference to Clarence who had twice written to him, and resumed the siege. The besiegers thus earned the 'obloquy of all men', and Norfolk's retainers, some of whom had never been enthusiastic, became alarmed and regretted that they had ever begun the siege. They made excuses to Writtle, trying to escape censure for crimes already committed and recommending arbitration by the council. Writtle pointed out that this proposal had already been rejected. He warned them that the council was unlikely to be well-disposed to their excuses unless amends were made, for example, by persuading Norfolk to end the siege or make a truce. Truces followed, from 18 to 22 to 25 September, but then, short of supplies and munitions, the castle capitulated on 27 September. Yet, by the mediation of Clarence, Cardinal Bourchier and other lords, Norfolk granted a safe-conduct to the garrison, so further bloodshed was avoided. This had been the constant aim of the government.

There was also plenty of disorder elsewhere, in Wales and the north. The parliament was cancelled, the true reason probably being that it was not expedient to hold it while disorders persisted 'in diuers parties of this our[e] land' . . . If the shire elections could not be controlled but might be occasions for disorder, parliament might not provide the show of strength that Warwick needed. Some form of assembly was held at York, probably a great council. The lords of the council were absent in the north from 15 September and a delegation of barons of the Cinque Ports were there from 22-29 September.[128]

At the parliament it was probably intended to reduce the Wydevilles, Herberts and other opponents to permanent insignificance by resuming their lands. Perhaps Warwick and Clarence were to receive permanent control of the government. However, a Lancastrian rebellion led by Humphrey Neville of Brancepeth (Durh.) proved beyond Warwick's capacity to quell and he was forced to release the king.[129] No permanent measures had been taken, apart from the various executions, and the political initiative was surrendered to the king.

Chapter II

Reconstruction and Readeption 1469-71

1. Edward IV's Recovery of the Initiative October 1469 - February 1470

Edward IV had been released, but he still had little freedom of action. The Croyland chronicle plausibly states that Edward wanted revenge for the offences committed against his royal dignity.[1] He was in no position to exact vengeance, for Warwick's victory had deprived him of his most fervent supporters. One of them, Humphrey Stafford, Earl of Devon, had died without leaving male issue, so his earldom died with him. Another, the Earl of Pembroke, left a minor as his heir. His Herbert retinue, so important in Wales, had been so badly mauled at Edgecote that it was of no immediate use to the king. The third of them, Earl Rivers, had depended on influence at court and the dowerlands of his wife. His son Anthony succeeded as Earl Rivers, but could not inherit his mother's estates. Those manors which he did hold as Lord Scales were small, scattered and conferred little political power; his court connections were at a discount late in 1469. The Herbert-Wydeville marriage alliance survived, but was not militarily significant. None of the husbands of the queen's sisters yet had control of their inheritances. Edward had too little committed support for a military offensive against his late captors.

However, he could rely on the loyalty of the peerage as a whole to prevent any repetition of the coup d'etat. On his entry into London after his release, Edward was escorted by a powerful group of magnates, among whom Sir John Paston observed two dukes, three earls and three barons.[2] They were a representative company, not confined to the king's servants. The Bourchier-Stafford group, represented by the Earl of Essex, Lord Mountjoy, Sir John and Sir Henry Stafford, was most important. It is not known to have had any reason for hostility towards Warwick and Clarence: indeed Essex and Mountjoy, like Hastings and Dacre of the South, had co-operated with Warwick and Clarence's shortlived government. Other escorts were related to them: John Neville, Earl of Northumberland was Warwick's brother, Lord Hastings was his brother-in-law, others had been in his service. They probably counselled moderation rather than resort to force. They were a powerful group, who might be expected to influence Edward's course of action.

They might also be expected to influence the policies of Warwick and Clarence, the strength of whose faction had been clearly demonstrated at Edgecote and after. They enjoyed the active support of two other earls, Shrewsbury and Oxford, of the Archbishop of York, and of Lords FitzHugh, Stanley and Scrope, and at least the sympathy of others. Clarence was the king's brother. As the most powerful faction they required consideration. The deaths of Rivers, Pembroke and Devon had removed some of the complaints in their manifesto. Other grievances could be satisfied if Clarence, Warwick and their supporters received a share of royal patronage and a part in royal government commensurate with their actual power. Otherwise there might be further bloodshed. This was in nobody's interest, least of all that of Warwick and Clarence, whose victory at Edgecote had borne few fruits. In view of their strength, they may have expected a favourable compromise, perhaps even predominance in the royal council.

Immediately after his release Edward acted in a hostile manner towards the Earl of Oxford and Archbishop Neville. Commissions of array issued on 29 October were clearly directed against Warwick and Clarence, who were not named in them. The king's household servants spoke against them.[3] Edward himself soon saw the need for terms. According to the Croyland chronicler, there passed between the king and the dissident magnates 'messages and embassies',[4] which were followed by a great council. Quite a lot is known about it: it met in the parliament chamber, had sessions on 6 and 9 November, and did not break up until after Christmas. Some guesses may be hazarded about its composition: certainly there were three dukes, four earls, six barons and six bishops[5] apart from Warwick's faction. It was an exceptionally full and representative

TABLE IV: EDWARD IV'S BID FOR SUPPORT 1469-70

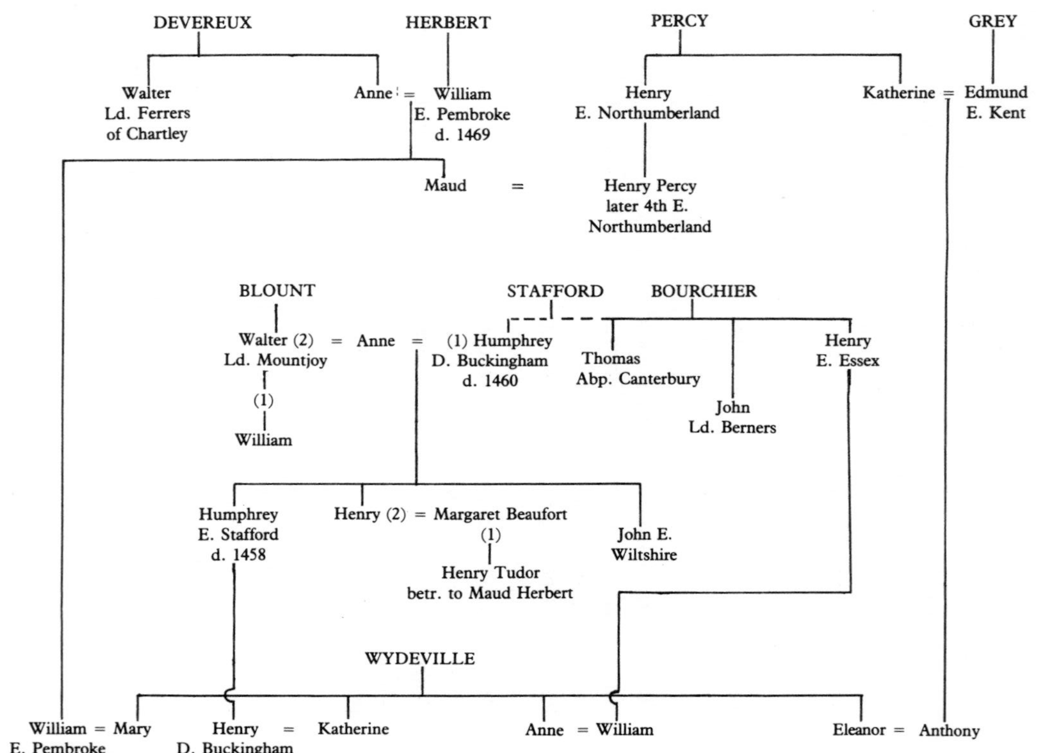

meeting of the magnates of the realm.

Polydore Vergil thought that it was the moderate line taken by the council that resulted in an agreement:

> 'Both thauthorytie and also intreatie of the nobylytie so movyd the mynde of the king and earle, that, uppon mutuall promyse of assurance made, the earle himself and the duke of Clarence came to London, gardyd with a sclender crew of soldyers in respect of so great danger, and had at Westmynster long talke with the king concerning composytion'.[6]

This agrees with the account in the Croyland chronicle, which states that they came on an appointed day: this must have been before 18 November, when Edward accepted the fealty of the Prior of St. John.[7] This was one of the confederates's few gains. As a result of their pressure, Edward granted a general pardon for all offences committed before Christmas, a later day than he wished,[8] but he made no other concessions.

Apart from lending money and acting as mediator, the council presided over the resettlement of the crown and the redistribution of the custodies, offices and escheated lands that had been held by the three dead earls. Their deaths had reduced the pressure on Edward's patronage and gave him greater freedom for political manoeuvre. As we shall see, his policy was not one of temporisation.

From the moment of his release Edward seems to have decided to assign a political role to his youngest brother Richard, Duke of Gloucester, who was now seventeen years old. Lacking in political experience, he had been brought up in Warwick's own household, so he should not have been offensive to anyone. In any case Edward had a duty to provide for him. Gloucester was appointed constable of England in place of Earl Rivers, was granted the honours of Clitheroe and Halton in Lancashire and Cheshire, and on 14 November was conveyed the lordship of Sudeley (Gloucs.). By warrant dated 19 October Edward ordered the exchequer to pay £100 to Gloucester at once; another warrant on 6 November ordered the further payment of five hundred marks (£333 6*s.* 8*d.*) 'towardes thexpenses of his houshold and other charges by him to bee borne by oure ordinaunce and commaundement'. A third warrant ordered payment of £100 for household stuff that he required 'er he departe hens'.[9] This referred to his impending departure for Wales, where disturbances following Pembroke's death had necessitated the despatch of Lord Ferrers in September. Edward deprived Warwick and Hastings of all the offices which they had obtained during his captivity, notably as chief justices of North and South Wales. Instead Gloucester was appointed chief justice of South Wales on 16 October and chief justice of North Wales on 6 November. By 16 November Gloucester was also steward of all the duchy of Lancaster lordships in South Wales formerly held by Pembroke and (during Edward's pleasure) chief steward, approver and surveyor of the principality of Wales and the earldom of March. On 29 October he was appointed commissioner of array in the three border counties and obtained further powers subsequently.[10] Edward had delegated to him overriding, indeed viceregal, authority throughout Wales. Gloucester presumably set off soon after the middle of November.

As Gloucester was inexperienced, he was probably guided by Lord Ferrers of Chartley. He was a lifelong supporter of the house of York in Wales, a royal councillor, and an associate and brother-in-law of the late Earl of Pembroke. The second Earl of Pembroke was a minor, but on 15 November the dowager-countess was granted custody both of him and his estates.[11] The countess was Anne Devereux, sister of Lord Ferrers: at this time she was apparently living at his residence at Weobley and he probably enjoyed the oversight of the Herbert estates and retainers. On 2 November he himself was granted the offices of steward, receiver and constable of the three marcher lordships of Hay, Huntington and Brecon during the minority of the young Duke of Buckingham.[12] The Herbert connection, still vital to Edward, remained intact. Even Gloucester's appointments were temporary in character: he held the posts of chief justice only for the duration of Pembroke's minority, the other offices at pleasure. Thus his promotion was merely a temporary substitute for Herbert power, not an infringement, and would end when the second Earl of Pembroke came of age.

Herbert power in Wales was hardly more important than the custody of two of the late earl's wards, Henry Percy and Henry Tudor. The latter threatened to upset Edward's plans. Since 1462 Henry Tudor had been a Herbert ward and was intended as husband for Maud Herbert. His mother Margaret Beaufort, Dowager-Countess of Richmond, was wife of Sir Henry Stafford, second son of the first Duke of Buckingham. Edward wanted to enlist the political support of the Staffords. Margaret remained closely interested in her son, whom she visited at Raglan and to whom she sent frequent messages. On Pembroke's death she wanted custody of her son. There was thus a conflict of interest between the Herberts and Staffords, into which Edward was drawn: he was in danger of alienating powerful supporters, whether he upheld the Herbert title or not. Margaret was looking for legal loopholes. Her receiver-general, Reginald Bray, paid for

> 'serches in the escheker & with Thomas Bayan clerk of the parlement & the wrytyng of ij copyes of a acte & a provysion for my lord of Richemounde mater'.

He also organised a search in chancery, paying 'for the copy of my lord Pembroke patentz for the warde and mariage of my lord of Richemounde'. He travelled to Weobley, other agents did the same, and one Davy was deputed to wait on Henry Tudor. Bray paid the expenses of a conference at the Bell Inn in Fleet Street on 31 October, attended by

> 'my lord and my lady . . . with theyre feliship & lernyd counsell to haue a comynicacion with the lord Ferys & my lady of Pembroke Counsell for the Wardship of my lord of Richemounde'.

The legal counsel were presumably Master Starkey and Richard Eton, to whom Bray paid 6*s*. 8*d*.; Starkey was recorder of London. Apparently their efforts were crowned with success, as Bray later paid for the 'writyng of lettres patentz and acte for my lordes of Richemound mater of the kynges graunte'.[13] Instead Edward made concessions to the Herberts over their other ward.

The wardship of Henry Tudor had threatened to thwart all Edward's efforts to win the support of the powerful Bourchier-Stafford connection, which was no less coherent than in 1464. In right of his wife, Sir Henry Stafford had sufficient resources to support the way of life of an earl. So had his brother John, in right of his wife Constance, heiress of Henry Green: Edward created him Earl of Wiltshire.[14] He did not endow him, so he must have been among the poorer earls. On 27 October he was appointed steward of the duchy of Cornwall.[15] John was on good terms with his brother Henry, whom he had visited at Woking (Surr.) on 16 August: they had played cards together and hunted in Windsor park. Henry frequently corresponded with his mother, the Dowager-Duchess of Buckingham, to whom he gave a grey ambling horse in September or October. During Edward's captivity at Warwick, Henry had relied for information on his stepfather Lord Mountjoy. Mountjoy and his two stepsons were among Edward's escort into London in October: clear evidence that they saw eye to eye in politics.

Mountjoy was a former treasurer of England and a trusted servant of the king. His heir William Blount was appointed master forester of Kingswood (Gloucs.), Petherton and Fulwood (Soms.) on 19 October and of Exmoor (Devon) and Racche (Soms.) on 26 November.[16] He was presumably meant to co-operate with his stepbrother Wiltshire and their cousin, the Devonshire magnate Lord FitzWarin. On the advice of the council Blount was also appointed sheriff of the sensitive counties of Nottingham and Derby, where Warwick and Clarence were particularly powerful. A more tactful choice could hardly have been found: his father Mountjoy, a former client of Warwick, was currently steward of Clarence's honour of Tutbury (Staffs.); William himself was administering Clarence's estate at Wirksworth (Staffs.) as Warwick's understeward.[17]

The ties between Staffords and Bourchiers remained strong. So did those between the Bourchiers and the crown, which Edward strove to reinforce. Cardinal Bourchier now lent £700 in return for, among other things, the custody of the lands and person of Richard Neville, Lord Latimer.[18] Richard was his great-nephew, grandson of his brother John, Lord Berners, still chamberlain of the queen. On 13 November Sir Thomas Bourchier was appointed constable of Leeds castle, Kent. The head of the family, the Earl of Essex, was steward of Edward's household: their kinsman Bishop Grey was the new treasurer of England.[19] Altogether they were given every incentive to become Edward's partisans.

The second of Pembroke's wards had been Henry Percy, eldest son of the attainted third Earl of Northumberland. Probably Pembroke had intended to secure his restoration as earl. Warwick and Clarence had taken the threat seriously and had incarcerated him in the Tower. It was there that on 27 October he took an oath of fealty to Edward in the presence of Cardinal Bourchier, two bishops, two dukes and five barons. He was released on sureties of £8,000, to be cancelled if he appeared before the king again on 26 May 1470. The Earls of Arundel and Kent, Bishop Grey and Lord Ferrers stood surety for him. Two of these, Grey and Kent, were close relatives; Ferrers represented the Herberts. His support was probably in return for Percy's promise to marry Maud Herbert, which he had done by Michaelmas 1472.[20] Edward had enlisted maximum magnate participation in Percy's release, which was desirable in view of the repercussions. If Percy kept the terms of his bail, he was almost certain to be restored to the family earldom. The bonds were cancelled, probably prematurely, as Percy was authorised to enter his father's inheritance on 25 March 1470.[21] Yet it is clear that his restoration was considered imminent: the acts of the November council presume it.

The reversal of the attainder of the third Earl of Northumberland entailed the dispossession of those occupying his estates. The three principal sufferers would be Clarence, Warwick and John Neville, Earl of Northumberland. Edward did not compensate the first two, but he was more concerned about Northumberland. He had been consistently loyal, earning his earldom in battle against the Lancastrians, and had stood aloof from the summer rebellion of his brothers. He had even been among those who escorted Edward into London on his escape. He was too valuable an ally for Edward to offend.

Edward did his best to compensate him adequately. In lieu of his earldom of Northumberland he created him Marquis Montagu. He gave him the Courtenay honours of Tiverton, Plympton and Okehampton, with their appurtenances and nine associated manors in Devon, in crown hands by the death without issue of the Earl of Devon. They probably yielded more than six hundred pounds a year. He also gave him the custody of the lands, persons and marriages of two West Country heirs. This was authorised by a letter patent of 27 February 1470, which was based on a privy seal writ of 13 February.[22] The original warrant, perhaps oral, to the keeper of the privy seal, does not survive. It may well have been earlier. At Tiverton John's receiver collected issues from Christmas 1469, two months before the formal grant, and a jury stated that he enjoyed them from 5 November. They also said that Joan Courtenay held other estates from that date, even though her patent was dated 18 November.[23] There is reason to suppose that they were authorised together, but that the execution of John's patent was delayed.

Why should grants be made to him so early? After all they were in compensation for Percy lands, which he only surrendered a little before 21 February 1470. An anonymous observer records his creation as Marquis Montagu and Henry Percy's as Earl of Northumberland on 25 March. Certainly Percy was granted his lands on that day.[24] The distance in time between grant of estates and title was due to the need to take account not only of Percy's restoration, but also of the creation of John's son as Duke of Bedford. His charter of creation, dated 5 January 1470, had certainly been authorised on 6 November 1469.

George Neville's charter reveals that the decision was made at the Westminster great council on 6 November by deliberation of the lords spiritual and temporal and with their consent. For the better safety, tranquillity and utility of the realm, Edward had resolved to give his eldest daughter Elizabeth in marriage. It was with the aim of ending discord and rebellion and in consideration of John's own military prowess that Elizabeth was betrothed to John's son and heir apparent, George Neville. George was also created Duke of Bedford and was granted a £40 annuity from Bedfordshire, for himself and his male issue.[25] This was the final element in Edward's bid for the loyalty of John Neville, who was offered a great future for his son and perhaps even the throne itself.

Moreover Edward had secured a well-breeched husband for his daughter. George was heir to all his father's estates, not only those granted by the king but also six Montagu manors settled on him at his marriage; via his mother he was heir to the important Ingaldsthorp patrimony, which included an annuity of 500 marks (£366 13*s*. 4*d*.), and had prospects of a share of the Tiptoft earldom of Worcester; finally, and most important, he was heir to his uncle, the Earl of Warwick, of all the Neville lands which were entailed in the male line. These were the lordships of Middleham, Sheriff Hutton (Yorks.) and Penrith (Cumbs.), together worth well over a thousand pounds a year.[26] Elizabeth would be well provided for, even if she did not become queen.

By settling the crown on his daughter Edward was repudiating charges made in the summer against the legitimacy of himself and his children. The reference to rebellion and Edward's desire to allay discord alluded to the summer rebellion and to Clarence's alternative claim, which was explicitly rejected. The house of York had inherited the crown through the female line and so it would descend in future, to Edward's daughter in preference to any collateral male relative. All these points were clarified and publicly confirmed by the great council. No doubts or ambiguities remained.

Edward had done much more than merely reinforce his own position. He had introduced a clash of interests into the Neville family. Warwick was not John's only brother or George's only paternal uncle: there was a third brother, Archbishop Neville, and four sisters, the wives of Lords FitzHugh, Stanley, Hastings and Oxford. They had been Warwick's supporters during the summer. Might they not now prefer the solid prospects of a crown for their nephew to the hazardous and uncertain expectations of their niece Isabel, Duchess of Clarence? Might not Warwick feel the same way himself? According to the pseudo-Worcester, the collapse of George's earlier betrothal to the Exeter heiress had been 'to the great secret displeasure of the Earl of Warwick'.[27] Evidently Warwick had wanted George to make a good marriage, presumably because he was heir to the family patrimony and a future head of the family. Now that George was making such a good marriage and had the glittering prospect of the crown, might not Warwick regard this as a satisfactory end to his political intrigues?

The marriage should have been a master stroke. It was designed to weaken the cohesion of Warwick and Clarence's faction, to produce a conflict in which Warwick's interest corresponded less obviously with that of his relatives. There might be more to be gained by following John Neville, who enjoyed royal favour, than Warwick who did not. A weakened faction was less likely to resort to force, since it stood less chance of victory. Furthermore it had been Clarence and Warwick, who had suffered most from the restoration of Henry Percy as Earl of Northumberland: it had struck directly at Warwick's control of the north. The new Earl of Northumberland was another element in the faction that Edward was constructing for himself. Others were Northumberland's uncle, the Earl of Kent, Montagu, the Bourchier-Stafford-Blount family, the Earl of Worcester, shortly to become treasurer, the Duke of Gloucester, and other recipients of patronage such as Lords Dudley and Dynham. Edward could also count on the Wydevilles and Herberts against Clarence and Warwick. With this new party of committed supporters behind him, Edward could govern without reference to the wishes of Warwick's faction. A further rebellion was improbable, as the military balance had altered, but Edward evidently anticipated ill-feeling. He seems to have been genuinely surprised and pleased, when Warwick and Clarence offered assistance against the Lincolnshire rebels.[28]

As the Lincolnshire rebellion was to show, Edward's new arrangements were quite sufficient to secure his position, but they did not bring peace: civil war broke out again within three months. Clearly Edward had miscalculated the degree of risk that Warwick and Clarence were prepared to take. Rightly supposing that they wanted power and direction of policy, Edward had taken measures to prevent them — rather extreme measures, involving their exclusion from decision making. It is doubtful whether this could have been a lasting solution, but in any case it took no account of another element in their motivation, an element of desperation. During the summer Warwick and Clarence had not been completely free agents: they had been prompted partly by the need to stave off the designs of royal favourites on their estates. These threats had not been removed, had indeed become more pressing, and Edward offered no relief. They could not give up political intrigue, as Edward apparently thought, without submitting to the continual erosion of their resources and power. In such circumstances an unfavourable military balance might not deter them from another desperate coup. If successful, there would be rich pickings.

The summer rebellion had been designed to loosen the stranglehold of the royal favourites on royal patronage in their own favour and to obtain control of royal policy. For Clarence, with his inadequate income, access to the royal purse was the first priority. For Warwick it was control of policy, especially foreign policy, that mattered most. Both wanted to avert the dangers of the Herbert marriage programme; Warwick also wanted to marry his heirs according to their status and to realise his position as dominant magnate in South Wales. As we have seen, Edward denied them all these ends. He distributed his patronage against their interests. It is unlikely that they had any influence on policy making, nor were they likely to, in view of the new royal party. It was this which had a monopoly of patronage. It was based on the enemies that the Edgecote campaign had been designed to eliminate. The Herberts recovered their dominance in North and South Wales. More important, the implementation of their projected marriages endangered Warwick and Clarence's territorial power.

When Henry Percy was restored, Warwick had lost the Percy estates that he held. Even to a magnate of his wealth this was a grievous blow. Warwick was warden of the West March, where the Neville estates were small but where he also held those of the Cliffords and the Percy honour of Cockermouth: he had no rival. Now the largest complex of lands, the honour of Cockermouth, was to be taken from him and restored to its former owner. On 14 January 1470, for service done and to be done, the forest of Inglewood was confided to Sir Humphrey Dacre, male heir of the attainted Cumbrian barony of Dacre. This was perhaps the first move towards the reversal of the attainder of his brother and his own restoration, which occurred formally in 1473. If so, Warwick would be faced by yet another rival, albeit minor, in place of the absentee Richard Fiennes, Lord Dacre of the South.[29] Already in 1468 the bishopric of Carlisle had been conferred on the confessor of his political opponent, Queen Elizabeth.

The West March was less important than the East and Middle Marches, which covered the county of Northumberland. Since 1463 the warden had been Warwick's brother, John Neville, now Marquis Montagu. In 1461 Warwick had been the king's lieutenant of the whole marches and subsequently, with John as warden,[30] this had continued in practice. When Henry Percy was restored, Montagu was deprived of the landed power on which his wardenship was based: it was predictable that he would be replaced as warden, as he was. The return of the Percies was a serious blow to Warwick's authority on the borders.

Yorkshire was the centre of the northern Neville estates. During the fourteen-sixties Warwick had controlled the Yorkshire barony of Latimer, because of the madness of his uncle George Neville, Lord Latimer. The fruit of this was the military aid of Henry Neville, Latimer's heir, in the Edgecote campaign, during which he was killed. His father died soon after. The Latimer heir was the infant Richard Neville. His custody was given not to Warwick but to Cardinal Bourchier, his maternal great-uncle. Warwick had also held the bulk of the Percies's Yorkshire estates, which were similar in size to his own. The Percies and Nevilles had fought a private war during the fourteen-fifties and the wounds had not yet healed. When Warwick was deprived of their Yorkshire estates, he ceased to dominate the county. Henry Percy's return threatened Neville power throughout the north.

None of this was concealed from Archbishop Neville, Lord FitzHugh or Lord Stanley by Edward's settlement of the succession. The archbishop remembered the Percy-Neville feud and was hostile to any revival of the Percies. Lord FitzHugh, who had benefited from Warwick's custody of the West March,[31] would suffer from his declining power. Stanley had been threatened by Edward's clumsy advancement of Gloucester in Lancashire and Cheshire, his traditional sphere of influence. Even the betrothal of Elizabeth of York to George Neville was not an unqualified gain. Both were children: Elizabeth was born only in 1466, George in 1465. Either might die before the marriage could be celebrated a decade hence, for which a dispensation would be necessary. The queen was still relatively young — she bore her last child in 1481 — and there was a good chance that she would bear a son, whose title would precede that of Elizabeth. The comments of the chronicler Warkworth, admittedly writing with the benefit of hindsight, suggest that little faith was placed on the permanence of the betrothal:[32] certainly the parties were too young for it to be binding. The new Duke of Bedford had little more hope of a crown than the Duchess of Clarence. The match could scarcely have restrained the Nevilles and their kin; it could not have curbed Clarence at all.

Edward's settlement had made no provision for Clarence nor his supporters. Neither they nor Clarence had any reason to prefer the duchess's cousin or his own niece as sovereign in place of his brother. They had nothing to gain from Edward's settlement. On the contrary. Edward gave Clarence no share of the patronage that he had wanted from the rebellion. Instead he deprived him of the Percy estates that he held, worth about £450 a year, which he wanted to keep. The transfer of Henry Tudor to the custody of the Staffords did not reduce the risk that he would be restored as Earl of Richmond, to Clarence's loss. The mistrust that Edward's treatment engendered, the uncertainty about his intentions, are both well illustrated by the duke's refusal to accept anything but a written safe-conduct in March 1470.[33] It was unwise of Edward to try to isolate him, as it gave him no alternative means to his ends except force. He underestimated him, for he was not insignificant. Quite apart from his stature as a major magnate with a powerful connection, he was the king's male heir — an adult while Elizabeth was a minor. If he felt that he was sure to lose in any case, he had every incentive to plan another rebellion before Edward destroyed all chance of success: he had everything to gain from the usurpation of the crown.

Warwick and his associates had not wanted to depose Edward IV in 1469, any more than they had wished to depose Henry VI in 1460. The possibility was deployed as a threat, but it failed to bear any fruit: the alternative was either to abandon their aims — to submit — or to make Clarence king. It seems likely that they chose the latter course reluctantly: they can have been under no misapprehension about the chances of success. The confession of Sir Robert Welles demonstrates that in 1470 it was Clarence who took the lead, whereas the Edgecote campaign had been Warwick's enterprise.

2. The Lincolnshire Rebellion, February-April 1470

Most of our knowledge of the Lincolnshire rebellion comes from two versions of a short chronicle of official origin. One is in English; the other, in French, was incorporated by the Burgundian Jehan de Waurin in his own chronicle:[34] a sign that it was circulated by the government and represents the official point of view. Both incorporated official documents and claim to be based on other papers, such as a letter which 'is redy to be shewed', and on the confessions of certain ringleaders. These are frequently referred to, especially that of Sir Robert Welles, which still survives. It confirms the chronicle at every point, perhaps because it is not genuine but an exercise in propaganda. Thus Sir Charles Oman wrote:

> 'Why Welles should confess at all we cannot see, unless he expected to save his life thereby; and if he expected to save his life he would, of course, insert in his tale whatever names the King chose'.[35]

This is a valid argument that deserves an answer. On it rests the accuracy of the whole narrative.

The chronicle is confirmed at many points by other sources. Edward anticipated help from the Earl of Warwick, to which Sir John Paston refers; he accordingly sent him a commission of array, which is enrolled on the patent roll, surely evidence against the supposition that Edward was plotting his destruction; Polydore Vergil also records that Lord Welles was forced to write to his son, ordering disbandment and submission; the capture of certain ringleaders is confirmed by Warkworth, the Croyland chronicler and Vergil; and the disposition of the king at Doncaster and Clarence and Warwick at Chesterfield was also described by an anonymous eyewitness.[36] Such instances can be multiplied and would have to be explained away. Certainly some of the sources were not set down till much later but the authors were contemporaries, just as the correspondents were.

If the main outline of the chronicle is accurate, it suggests that this is also true of the confession, which it follows closely. The confession is specific on points of detail. Admittedly Walter Werk is unidentifiable and Philip Strangways is probably a mistake for Robert, son of Sir James Strangways, Warwick's retainer. But John Clare, Robert Strangways and John Barneby were among those whose goods the king later ordered to be seized. John Barneby M.A. (Cantab.) was presented by Clarence to the rectories of Leadenham (Lincs.) in 1466 and of Hanbury by Tutbury (Staffs.) in 1471.[37] Calceby, whose stewardship Clarence granted to Sir Robert Welles, was one of his Percy manors in Lincolnshire. One ringleader, Richard Warren *alias* Ratcliffe, was a native of Clarence's town of Boston. Warwick's messenger Henry Wrottesley was brother of a right hand man and a trusted retainer himself. Edward ordered the seizure of both Warren's and Wrottesley's chattels.[38]

It thus appears that chronicle and confession are accurate. It is not true, as Oman suggests, that Welles inserted in his account whatever names Edward chose. Those named, while certainly involved, are not of special importance; most bigger fish are omitted. The confession tells little of events in Lincolnshire or of the supporters of Warwick and Clarence, so it must be supplemented from the records. The sole concession to propaganda is the interpretation of events.

The quarrel between the Welles family and Sir Thomas Burgh, usually taken as the origin of the rebellion, occurs only in Warkworth's chronicle. The dispute resulted in an attack by the former on Burgh's house at Gainsborough (Lincs.), which was destroyed.[39] Heir of Henry Percy of Atholl and husband of the Dowager-Lady Botreaux, Burgh was a man of substance and powerful connections; a knight of the chamber and master of the horse, he was also a courtier of importance and, indeed, Edward's principal agent in Lincolnshire.[40] Understandably Edward took his side: on or after 22 February 1470, when Lord Welles was at Hellow (Lincs.), Edward summoned him to London to account for his actions. Welles stayed there until pardoned on 3 March.[41]

This narrative presents chronological difficulties. Warkworth wrongly dates the raid to March; Miss Scofield placed it in January, before the first date in Sir Robert Welles's confession.[42] She had to do this, since she accepted Warkworth's statement that the raid on Gainsborough was the origin of the disturbances in Lincolnshire.

But is this the most likely course of events? According to Warkworth the raiders included Lord Welles, his son, and their associates Sir Thomas Dymmock and Sir Thomas Delalaunde.[43] But enrolled with the pardons of Lord Welles, his son, Dymmock and other obvious clients are Thomas FitzWilliam the elder and younger esquires, both from Clarence's manor of Malberthorpe (Lincs.), and William Yerburgh gentleman, reeve of the duke's manor of Gayton.[44] Evidently the duke and Welles family were already co-operating by the raid. But Sir Robert Welles explicitly states that their alliance began about 2 February, so the raid must be later in date. This fits in with his statement that 'ne had beene the said Duc & Erles provokinges we at this tyme wold ne durst have maid any commocion or sturbing but upon their comforthes we did that we did'. Warkworth also thought that 'the Duke of Clarence and Erle of Warwyke causede alle this', including the raid on Gainsborough. The alliance was probably agreed about Candlemas (2 February), when Clarence approached Welles; the raid followed. Perhaps Welles saw an opportunity to settle old scores, but it was a fatal error: it caused his summons to London, giving Edward a weapon which he later employed to good effect, and it revealed the Welles family's involvement in the disturbances.

Some time before 2 February Clarence and Warwick resolved on another rebellion. Surprise was essential, as in the previous summer, so the rebellion could not start in any of Warwick's strongholds — the West Riding, Calais, the Cinque Ports or the West Midlands. Trouble there would be held at his account. The same may have been true of areas obviously dominated by Clarence. Warwick held few lands in Lincolnshire, Clarence rather more, but they could rely on the support of Richard, Lord Welles and Willoughby. With his two baronies and lands worth a thousand pounds a year he was a leading magnate in the county. His father Leo, Lord Welles had suffered death and attainder against Edward IV in 1461, but the sentence had been reversed. Warkworth wrongly states that in 1470 they rebelled in favour of Henry VI; Sir Robert Welles knew their aim was to make Clarence king. Indeed he wore Clarence's livery. It was Clarence who directed their operations. The precise nature of their ties with him are uncertain, but they must have been stronger than the bonds of their kinship: the rebellion is not adequately explained by the fact that one of Lady Welles's stepfathers, the shortlived Thomas Neville, was Warwick's brother!

Sir Robert Welles knew that his insurrection was only part of a 'grete rising'. This may have involved the seizure of London, where bills were posted and seditious rumours circulated.[45] The Neville retainers in Yorkshire were implicated. Warwick and Clarence were to lead their own retainers to join the Lincolnshire rebels. They counted on the support of the Earl of Shrewsbury, Lords FitzHugh, Stanley and Scrope of Bolton. Perhaps the Earl of Oxford and their Welsh retainers also figured in their plans.

As in 1469, the nucleus of the rebel army consisted of the magnates's retainers: this time they came from the estates of Clarence and Lord Welles. Once again they were to be supplemented by a popular uprising. Sir Robert Welles, as 'grete capteyn of the commons of Linccolne shire', was to act the part of Robin of Redesdale, and he

> 'had doo made proclamacions of all the churchez of that shire the sonday the iiij.day of Marche in the kinges name, the duc, erle, and his owne name, everye man to come to Ranby hawe upon the tuesday the vj.day of Marche, upon payne of dethe, to resist the king in comyng down into the saide shire, saying that his comyng thidre was to destroie the comons of the same shire' . . .

Apparently the proclamation told the people

> 'that the king was comming downe wt grete power into Lincolneschire, where the Kinges jugges shuld sitte and hang & draw grete noumbr' of the commons'.

The claim was not unjustified. Probably the proclamation also denounced the king's evil councillors. It was only once the populace had assembled that Clarence's agent Walter spread the word that the rebellion was in his support.

On hearing of the raid on Gainsborough, King Edward summoned Lord Welles and Dymmock to London. They reluctantly obeyed. In February Edward granted a general pardon, but excluded offences committed since Christmas.[46] The pardon did not cover the disturbances in Lincolnshire and so Sir Robert Welles was probably right that a special oyer and terminer commission was intended. This was the logical sequel to Edward's expedition there. He was to be joined by contingents on the way, notably those of Warwick and the city of Coventry.[47] His personal retinue was large and the company of the Duke of Norfolk was particularly impressive. It clearly impressed Clarence, who informed Sir Robert

Welles that 'the gentilmen of the contre shuld passe upon us in such wyse that nedely gret multitude must dye of the commons'. Edward decided to set out on 4 March.

Clarence had probably spent Christmas at court and then gone into the country, where he planned his revolt. Even though he steered clear of Lincolnshire and probably stayed away from Warwick, his absence excited suspicion.[48] Sometime before 3 March he informed Sir Robert Welles of the scale of Edward's preparations and of his own intention of going to London. He had two purposes there: to secure the release of Lord Welles, still waiting on Edward's pleasure, and to delay the king's departure. Welles was pardoned on 3 March and Clarence arrived next day, the date of Edward's intended departure, which was consequently put off until 6 March.[49] Had Edward left as intended, he would have reached Grantham on 12 March, too early for any other force to join the Lincolnshire rebels. It was planned, for instance, that they should meet the Yorkshiremen at Stamford.

Those two days were spent by king and duke at Baynard's Castle, their mother's London residence. Clarence said he meant to travel westwards, rather than to Lincolnshire, as Edward would probably have liked. Their stay was marked by mutual, concealed distrust. Next day Clarence accompanied Edward only as far as Ware (Herts.)[50] before returning to London. Next morning he conferred with the Prior of St. John and Lord Welles at Clerkenwell and then departed for Warwick. On the way he wrote to the king, informing him that he would join the Earl of Warwick and bring him to reinforce Edward's army. Edward received the letter next day and, understandably pleased by the change of heart, personally wrote him a letter of thanks — a gesture Clarence would have recognised — and sent him commissions to array the men of Warwickshire and Worcestershire.[51]

When mustering their forces at Warwick, the duke and earl probably received unstinted help from the commissioners picked by Edward, who were almost entirely Warwick's own retainers. But the commissions covered only two counties: they had no authority to array the North Midlands, where Clarence and Shrewsbury were so powerful, still less the Welsh marches. This may be why they raised insufficient numbers — although doubtless quite enough as reinforcements for the king!

Scrope of Bolton and Conyers had difficulty in mobilising the

Yorkshiremen. Warwick had written to his supporters, but the lack of a royal commission of array prompted some to suspect treason, and hence remain at home. This was why the Yorkshiremen could not join Welles at Stamford. Similar problems in recruitment prevented Warwick from meeting Welles as planned. He and Clarence wrote to both Edward and Welles that they would be at Leicester on 13 March: they asked Welles to meet them there and to keep Edward to his north. To Edward their plan offered an opportunity to encircle the rebels; to the rebels it was a chance to combine against him: Warwick may still have hoped for northern assistance. It was a good plan. But whereas Welles knew of it on 12 March, Edward was informed only on the evening of 13 March, too late to avoid a battle.

There were several reasons for the breakdown of the plan. From the start, although ignorant of the plots of the duke and earl, Edward was well informed of the plans of the Lincolnshiremen. One day after the muster at Ranby hawe Edward had a copy of the proclamation. Next day he intercepted a letter only two days old, which told him of the scale of the rebellion and that the immediate objective was Stamford. He was henceforth unlikely to underestimate its size or purpose. Early on 7 March, aware of the participation of Sir Robert Welles, he ordered the arrest of Lord Welles: he and Dymmock may have been captured on the same day as their Clerkenwell conference with Clarence. Brought to the king, guilty of fresh treasons since their pardon, they admitted to their role but not to that of Warwick and Clarence. Edward made Welles write to his son, instructing him to desist. Instead Sir Robert tried to rescue his father and was defeated at Stamford on 12 March. But for this change of plan, the Lincolnshire chronicler thought that the rebellion might have succeeded: the other chroniclers agree.[52]

His victory enabled Edward to destroy his adversaries in detail. He despatched commissions of array to Montagu and, considering his own force quite adequate to deal with the Yorkshiremen, he ordered Warwick and Clarence to disband their levies and join him. On 16 March he sent the sheriff of York a proclamation, which reassured the populace about his intentions, extended the general pardon until 25 February, and enjoined them to submit.[53] He arrived at Doncaster on 18 March and at York on 21 March.[54] Evidence of Warwick and Clarence's complicity was found on the battlefield and more emerged from the confessions of captured insurgents.

On hearing of the battle, Warwick and Clarence remained at Coventry or withdrew there: their army was too small to take on Edward by itself. They promised to disband their forces and join him as instructed. Instead, however, they wrote to their Yorkshire supporters (and perhaps to Lord Stanley too) to meet them at Rotherham (Yorks.) and marched via Burton-on-Trent and Derby to Warwick's town of Chesterfield (Derbys.), arriving on 19 March. Probably they recruited from Clarence's estates along the route. Meantime they maintained the fiction of disbanding and joining Edward, informing him that they would meet him at Retford (Notts.).

On 17 March, however, Edward commanded them to disband and summoned them to answer charges of complicity in the rebellion. He rejected successive requests for guarantees of clemency and decided on military action against them. He considered it unseemly to treat subjects as though they were equals.

The duke and earl promised obedience if they 'have suretie for theyme and theire felaship, pardonnez for theym and alle the lordes and othere that had take theire partie'. This would have restored the status quo and left their capacity to rebel unimpaired. One cannot tell whether they were sincere or would have settled for less, as Edward refused to treat. Instead of disbanding, they looked for reinforcements. This was probably why they proceeded to Rotherham, as originally planned, rather than fighting Edward when he emerged from Doncaster, ready for battle: not, as an anonymous observer thought, because of the king's might, nor even because of the desertion of the Earl of Shrewsbury.[55] Shrewsbury's defection was serious: possibly he took with him Clarence's North Midlands retainers as well as his own. The reinforcements waiting at Rotherham may have been disappointing. It was apparently trusting in Stanley's aid that Warwick and Clarence advanced into Lancashire, but he failed them. The king, at York, was well placed to watch their routes to north and south.

Warwick and Clarence withdrew to the south-west. At Rotherham on 26 March, they reached Exeter on 3 April. Such precipitate haste did not stem from close pursuit, for Edward was far behind. It is unlikely that flight was intended. At Bristol, where Warwick left his artillery, they still had five thousand men.[56] They probably hoped to join Clarence's western retainers, notably the Courtenays of Powderham.

Until 1461 the head of the Courtenay family was the Earl of Devon. Should the three sons of Earl Thomas I die without male issue, the heir would be Sir Hugh Courtenay of Bocannoc. By 1470 two sons were dead and the third was an exiled traitor. On the death of Humphrey Stafford, Earl of Devon in 1469, Sir Hugh may have hoped to receive the estates, but they were divided instead between Lord Montagu and Joan Courtenay of Powderham. Lord Dynham was appointed steward. Perhaps Sir Hugh tried to make good his title by self-help and came into conflict with the Courtenays of Powderham. On 16 March Edward ordered Lords FitzWarin, Dynham and the sheriff of Devon to arrest Sir Hugh, five of the Powderham Courtenays and three others.[57] As a sequel Sir Hugh besieged the city of Exeter from 22 March until 2 April,[58] which he could surely only have attempted with the resources of the senior Courtenay line. His aim was to capture the gentlemen within, who included Lords FitzWarin and Dynham. The city was only relieved on the arrival of Warwick and Clarence.

It seems unlikely that Sir Hugh's behaviour was connected with the northern risings. On 22 March, when the siege began, Warwick and Clarence were still the king's lieges. The statement that Sir Hugh 'then favoured and was on the partie of kinge Edwarde' must be a gloss on the missing city receiver's account, based on the presence of the Duchess of Clarence in the bishop's palace. Dynham and FitzWarin were loyal to Edward. Earlier, when Clarence had sent his duchess westwards,[59] he must have thought it would be outside the fighting zone.

Only now that affairs were going badly did Clarence and Warwick come west. On gaining admittance to Exeter, they stayed five days. Though joined by some leading local gentry, they found that the disturbances in Devonshire could not readily be turned to their advantage. They were too weak to fight a pitched battle, so on 9 April — before Edward had reached Wells — they embarked from Clarence's town of Dartmouth.[60] They had accepted defeat, at least temporarily.

Although numerous, their retainers were scattered and difficult to unite. Some idea of who they were emerges from a list of those whose goods were declared forfeit.[61] They came from every part of England, but predominantly from Lincolnshire, Yorkshire, the North and West Midlands, and the West Country. During the Edgecote campaign Warwick's forces had been drawn from Calais and the Cinque Ports, the West Midlands, and the north. In 1470 Calais, Kent and Sussex furnished only four names on the list. Lord FitzHugh, the Carlisle garrison and most even of the Middleham retinue stood aside this time: Scrope and Conyers submitted, leaving only the younger Conyers and six others to be outlawed. Of Warwick's Midlands retinue, only two councillors, Sir Edward Grey and Sir Walter Wrottesley, their brothers and three others are listed. Many prominent retainers were absent. This supports the official chronicler's statement that Warwick had difficulty in mustering his followers.

In 1470, unlike 1469, Clarence's retinue was important. His chancellor John Tapton and his secretary William Molyneux were involved. The most numerous group was from the West Country, consisting of four Courtenays of Powderham and eight or ten others. The elder and younger Welles and six others from Lincolnshire were his men, directly or indirectly. Yet only two of his Midlanders rebelled. His influence was vital in recruitment in Lincolnshire and the south-west, almost the only areas where the rising made any appeal.

The sixty-one names comprise seven ecclesiastics, thirty-eight laymen below the rank of knight, twelve knights, and three peers. Lords Scrope and Shrewsbury, who rebelled but later submitted, should be added. Oxford, Stanley, FitzHugh and St. John may have intended to participate. If united, this represented a formidable faction: Warwick, Clarence, Shrewsbury, Welles and Stanley were all important magnates. It was partly geography, partly Edward's patent military superiority, that prevented all from turning out. Edward's military might certainly discouraged Scrope, FitzHugh, Stanley and Shrewsbury from action.

On leaving London Edward was certainly accompanied by the Dukes of Norfolk and Suffolk, the Earls of Wiltshire and Worcester, Lords Hastings and Howard, and Henry Percy.[63] Other magnates were probably with them. All these presumably fought at Losecote field, after which Worcester was appointed constable to try the insurgents: Gloucester, the usual constable, was absent. This was not because he did not support Edward, but because Edward had not foreseen the need for mobilising all his supporters, adequate though his army proved to be. From York he was able to issue commissions of array to twelve trusted magnates elsewhere in England.[64] Before leaving London he had asked the Earl of Kent to guard the Tower of London and despatched Lords Dynham and FitzWarin to the West Country: Gloucester and Ferrers were probably still in Wales. Doubtless others, such as the Bourchiers, were legitimately occupied in counties that were not arrayed. Montagu joined him at Doncaster.

Edward's army grew on the march southwards. He left Montagu and Northumberland behind, but on his arrival at Exeter on 14 April he was accompanied by two dukes, four earls and ten barons.[65] These presumably did not include three magnates deputed to arrest Archbishop Neville, which they did, or another three who fought Warwick at sea. Almost all the nobility, certainly all the politically important ones, were involved, mainly on Edward's side. His newly created faction made an outstanding contribution; the role of the Herberts and Wydevilles was marginal. There is a clear contrast with the situation in 1469: this time Edward enjoyed not only the active support of the bulk of the nobility, but the loyalty of many of the rebels's own retainers. Such extensive support for the king should have made Warwick aware of the isolation of his own faction.

3. Exile, April — September 1470

Neither Warwick nor Clarence accepted their defeat as final. Edward had refused to treat with them when they were strong, so he was unlikely to compromise now that they were weak. There was little to be gained from negotiation with him. But if they could only mobilise it, they still had considerable support in England on which to base another insurrection. After all, their principal forces had escaped defeat. Moreover Warwick had lived through a similar exile before, in 1459-60, which had ended with a successful invasion. He therefore had some idea of how to arrange an invasion. Probably their actions in 1470 were based on his experience then: the resemblance is marked. The same three elements were necessary: a secure base which would supply the nucleus of the invading force; communication with their supporters by sea; and active foreign assistance.

In 1459 Warwick had withdrawn to Calais, where he was captain, and the Duke of York had gone to Ireland. The duke had been the greatest Irish landowner, a former lieutenant of Ireland,

and it was there that his son Clarence had been born. In 1470 Clarence was lieutenant of Ireland and might have been able to exploit pro-Yorkist sentiment. So Edward thought: on 23 March he appointed the Earl of Worcester as lieutenant and ordered Sir Edmund Dudley, deputy of Ireland, not to receive Clarence and Warwick.[66] Instead they made for Calais, where Warwick was still captain. As warden of the Cinque Ports, his position there was stronger than before. It had been with an army recruited from Calais and the Cinque Ports that he had invaded England in 1469.

As captain and warden Warwick had needed ships. He had placed them under the command of his cousin Thomas Neville *alias* Fauconberg, bastard son of the late Earl of Kent. His ships were valuable, first as a means to evacuate his army and later for an invasion of England; as a means of communication with friends at home and abroad; and for piracy, by which Calais could be supplied, Edward's allies harried and diplomatic pressure exerted.

In 1459-60 the two factions had enjoyed the support of France and Burgundy. These two powers were generally hostile throughout the fourteen-sixties, when Warwick favoured the French. Edward IV himself preferred Burgundy, to whom he bound himself by treaty and marriage, and in 1467 he had announced his intention of invading France with Burgundian help. It was thus logical for Louis XI to look for help to Warwick and for Warwick to turn now to France for support. The two states of France and Burgundy were temporarily at peace, following the treaty of Péronne. Warwick needed to terminate the peace by engaging in hostilities with Burgundy and by showing himself a useful ally. Consequently he committed acts of piracy against Burgundian shipping.

This plan failed, largely because of Edward's foresight. As well as sending to Ireland, he ordered the Calais garrison to resist: Lord Wenlock refused them entry. An attempt to recover Warwick's ship the Trinity at Southampton was repulsed, with loss of ships and men. Without a base the pirates were exposed to retribution from a squadron commanded by Lord Howard and from the Burgundian fleet. It was a battered force that took refuge in the Norman ports on or about 1 May 1470.[67]

Beginning on 5 May Charles, Duke of Burgundy bombarded Louis XI, his council and the Parlement with a stream of letters. He complained of the acts of war committed by Warwick and Clarence against his subjects. They were his self-declared enemies. He warned that to harbour them was to infringe the treaty of Péronne. He emphasised that he was hostile only towards them,[68] which suggests that he contemplated a cutting out expedition in French waters. Later Charles was more concerned about the threat to his ally Edward IV and tried to prevent the invasion by force and diplomacy. The Bretons added their complaints, rather less vociferously. There was also opposition within France to granting asylem to perjured traitors: the constable of France, a relative of the Wydevilles, objected strongly.[69]

In this quandary Louis tried to appease both sides. He wanted to help the exiles, so they could return to England, but he had no great expectation of a successful invasion or faith in Warwick.[70] He was therefore inclined to restrict his aid and get rid of them as rapidly as possible. This was essential, if war with Burgundy and England was to be avoided: the exiles appeared to be a very weak ally. Louis's ambivalence emerges from the very first set of instructions that he sent on 12 May to Jean de Bourré and William Monypenny, respectively sieurs Duplessis and Concressault. Tell Warwick and Clarence that the treaty of Péronne precludes him from speaking with them or favouring them. They must leave France and go to the Channel Isles or somewhere else, although they might enter French ports on pretext of revictualling. Louis would meet them, but only in remote places and in secret. Such terms cast doubt on Louis's accompanying promise that he would help them with all the means in his power. However, as friendly gestures he offered hospitality to the Countess of Warwick and Duchess of Clarence and sent a length of silk to Clarence himself.[71]

By 19 May the exiles had made Louis accept their continued presence in France, but otherwise he was adamant. They could not remain where they were: they must proceed to other ports, preferably without letting the Burgundians know. Measures must be taken to restore prizes to appease Burgundy: this was done about the middle of June with Fauconberg's co-operation.[72] To relieve his embarrassment, Louis wanted them to invade England as soon as possible. Already on 15 May the Milanese ambassador believed that Louis was encouraging them to depart.[73] On 22 June Louis told Bourré to urge Warwick to go: he was to present it as in their own interests. A month later he instructed Bourré to satisfy all Warwick's needs, so that he might have no excuse to remain. In mid-June Louis lamented that so short a passage required so much time and expense.

On 29 June Bourré explained why the expedition was unready to depart: Warwick and Clarence would spend all without any profit.

Louis was certainly influenced by the cost of their presence. The letters between him, Bourré and other subordinates are full of difficulties about money, often quite small sums. Louis told Bourré only to disburse money on receiving a signed instrument from himself or his secretary, a measure that ensured that expenditure was constantly being referred to the king. Sometimes approval was quick but often the device was used to delay or obstruct payment. Louis's attitude was fully understood by Bourré: once he pretended that he had only twelve thousand livres tournois, when he actually had thirty thousand and on 29 June he suggested moving two days journey away because of importunate demands for cash. In one letter Louis told him to pay no more than a stipulated sum, unless it would cause the expedition to be curtailed. A near mutiny was needed for the sailors to be paid. This reluctance to spend money was not based on any realistic assessment of the sum required. Tanguy de Chastel asked Bourré to discover if Louis would allow the distribution of 3-4,000 écus among the sailors at Barfleur, who refused to serve without it. Three French officials reported that Warwick had asked them to pray Bourré to pay for a ship, which he had already bought: the earl's acquittance was enclosed and they promised that the seller would be paid. From Barfleur five officials complained about the failure to pay for some ships, which were essential.[74]

The Frenchmen assisting Warwick thus found themselves at odds with their king. Neither Louis nor Bourré showed any understanding of military matters: they were willing for Warwick to sail unprepared. Louis's letter of 23 June,[75] in which he urged Bourré to encourage the exiles to depart, was written long before they reached any agreement with Queen Margaret of Anjou. Louis was content for Warwick to sail without her Lancastrian supporters, or alternatively, with them but without any agreed programme in the event of success. Bourré's correspondence reveals that he expected the invasion to be defeated, as earlier ones had been defeated, and was averse to supporting it. Louis also anticipated failure and guarded against it, but he hoped for success. He achieved both his aims: war was averted until after the invasion succeeded. He deserves full credit for supplying the resources that alone made it possible, but at the time he seemed less conscious of the 'alluring possibilities'[76] than of the risks he was running. His fears created extra obstacles for Warwick and Clarence. It was almost in spite of his efforts that the expedition was adequately prepared and that the dynastic revolution took place.

It is Warwick and Clarence, who deserve the credit for this. Their best course of action was much more obvious than Louis's. They needed his committed support, and were determined to extract it: they could not afford to sympathise with him in his diplomatic impasse. They compelled Louis to accept their presence in France, then in ports where he did not want them, to receive them publicly, to give them more money than he wished, and to await their convenience on the date of departure. They decided Louis's conflict of interest in their own favour and, in the process, succeeded in extracting far more material help than had been forthcoming for earlier Lancastrian expeditions. The Lancastrians also tried to persuade Louis of the advantages of assistance: hence certain memoranda submitted to Louis by Queen Margaret's chancellor.[77]

From the moment of landing in France, Clarence and Warwick realised that Lancastrian support was required. Louis's first set of instructions of 12 May refers to the subject as one already broached: he had sent to Queen Margaret.[78] It is therefore almost certain that the idea originated with the magnates. It would give them the extra support in England that their recent defeat had shown to be essential. They would recoup their losses in return for restoring Henry VI as king. The project to marry Anne Neville to Henry's son Prince Edward was an early development. It was a guarantee of good faith and political peace once in England.

Two sources are usually employed to describe the course of negotiations with the Lancastrians. Sforza de Bettini, the Milanese ambassador, reported their progress from the French court. On 29 June he wrote:

> 'Up to the present the queen has shown herself very hard and difficult, and although his Majesty [Louis] offers her many assurances, it seems that on no account whatever will she agree to send her son with Warwick, as she mistrusts him. Nevertheless it is thought that in the end she will let herself be persuaded to do what his Majesty wishes'.[79]

On 20 July he wrote:

> 'The Queen of England, wife of King Henry, has been induced to consent to do all that his Majesty desires, both as regards a reconciliation with Warwick and the marriage alliance'.[80]

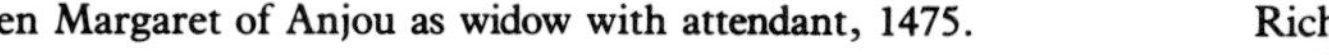

Queen Margaret of Anjou as widow with attendant, 1475.

Richard Neville, Earl of Warwick and Tewkesbury. Contemporary portrayal from the Tewkesbury Chronicle.

The other source is the document entitled *The Maner and Gwidinge of the Erle of Warwicke at Aungiers from the xvth. day of July to the iijth. of August, 1470, which day he departed from Aungiers* and known as the *Maner and Gwidinge* for short. Concerning reconciliation with Warwick, it states that the 'Quene was right dificyle', but eventually gave way and pardoned him in return for his oath of allegiance. It continues that,

> 'Towchinge the second poynt, that is of mariage, trew it is that the Quene wolde not in any wise consente thereunto for offer shewinge, or any maner request that the Kynge of Fraunce myght make her . . . and so the Quene persevered fifteen dayes or she wold eny thynge intend to the seyd Treatie of Marriage'.[81]

At first sight the two accounts agree closely. But do they? The ambassador's first report does not refer to any disagreement over the marriage but over the proposal that Prince Edward should accompany Warwick to England, as the original Italian wording demonstrates. The second report refers to the marriage alliance, but later says that the prince will not accompany the earl to England. The *Maner and Gwidinge* is concerned with a different disagreement to that mentioned by Sforza de Bettini.

Moreover Bettini's account casts doubt on the whole chronological framework of the *Maner and Gwidinge,* which purports to describe Warwick's activity at Angers from 15 July, although he did not arrive until 22 July. It tells how the queen opposed the project to Warwick's face, even though agreement was reached by 20 July, before either of them had arrived. The reconciliation described in the *Maner and Gwidinge* was a pure formality for Bettini. The *Maner and Gwidinge* claims that Margaret resisted the treaty of marriage for fifteen days, yet already on 25 July Louis was writing of its successful conclusion.[82] In view of such discrepancies, can the *Maner and Gwidinge* be regarded as reliable?

Much depends on the nature of the document. It exists only in copies in manuscripts containing other proclamations and manifestoes issued by Warwick, Clarence and Prince Edward on their return from France in 1470. Among them are instructions from Prince Edward to Henry VI's Readeption council, which suggests that all have a common official source.[83] It is not a formal instrument. It contains neither the text of the treaty of Angers, nor a detailed description of the negotiations leading up to it. As its title suggests, it concentrates on the role of Warwick to the exclusion of Clarence, who made terms with Queen Margaret that it does not mention. It lacks the detail that might have made it useful to Warwick himself. Written in English, it was obviously destined for an English audience. Taken together, its official origin, language and selective content indicate that it was designed to give a favourable account of the treaty and Warwick's part in it. Any unfavourable elements were omitted.

This explains why it presents the treaty as Warwick's work, at his initiative. It is true that the Yorkist exiles had the idea first, but the Lancastrians did not oppose it. On the contrary. A memorandum by Margaret's chancellor, Sir John Fortescue, which was presented to Louis XI, reveals that it was the view of 'the council of the king and queen of England' that[84]

> 'the marriage will take place between the Prince of Wales and the daughter of the Earl of Warwick. By means of which marriage the said Earl of Warwick and his friends will live in security and the said earl will have the principal role in government of the kingdom; and by favour of him and the friends and loyal subjects of King Henry, the queen and the prince will be able to enter more easily into the kingdom'.

Nor was this entirely new. In 1467 the Duke of Calabria, Margaret's brother, had suggested that the Lancastrians should ally with Warwick to dispose of their common enemy, Edward IV.[85] There may have been more to the suggestion than a mere outburst of rage. Moreover, on Warwick's flight abroad, Margaret saw that it could work to her advantage: she wrote at once to the diet of the Hanseatic League at Lübeck, urging it to support her against their common enemy, Edward IV.[86] The advantage of alliance with Warwick was obvious to the Lancastrians: even the marriage alliance, which bound him and his supporters to the Lancastrian cause, had its attractions.

It has usually been said that, in addition to preventing her son from accompanying Warwick to England, Queen Margaret delayed the completion of the marriage until after Warwick's successful invasion. This is based on a statement in the *Maner and Gwidinge* that Anne Neville

> 'shalbe put and remayne in the hands and kepinge of Quene Margaret, and also that the seyde marriage shal not be perfyted to th'Erle of Warwick had bene with an army over the Sea into England'.[87]

'Perfyted' normally referred to the consummation of the marriage, not the wedding ceremony itself. Bettini's despatch of 31 July, six days after the treaty, reveals that it contained no such clause:

> 'The Queen of England and the Earl of Warwick left this morning together for Normandy to celebrate the nuptials of their children, as Warwick wishes to see them united before he proceeds to England. Immediately afterwards he will proceed with his enterprise'.[88]

The decision to put off the marriage was that of Warwick himself, as the despatch of 7 August demonstrates:

> 'The Earl of Warwick departed, as your Excellency has heard. He did not wish to lose time in waiting for his daughter's marriage. The ceremony will take place at Amboise, according to what they say'[89] . . .

They were still unmarried at his embarkation on 9 September. Why was there this delay? It is highly improbable that Warwick wanted to go back on his agreement or that he felt the marriage to be unnecessary security. His motive was almost certainly shortage of time, as Sforza de Bettini says. He could not afford to wait. The marriage was delayed because no dispensation could be obtained at such short notice. One was obviously needed as the young couple were cousins. It would take months to obtain a dispensation at the Roman curia. Louis tried other means: he sent a messenger to the Bishop of Beauvais

> 'to know of him if he had power to dispense for the marriage of the Prince of Wales and the daughter of the Earl of Warwick' . . .

About the same time, on 2 August, he had sent similar messages to the Archbishop of Rheims and the Bishop of Laon,[90] probably without receiving any satisfaction. So Warwick could not attend his daughter's wedding.

The marriage was vital for Warwick, which is why he gave it such prominence in his manifesto. His kinsmen and supporters had no reason to want Henry VI back. Even they might be exasperated by his repeated changes of loyalty. His conduct otherwise indicates a loss of control, that he was clutching helplessly at every available straw. So he portrayed the agreement as the result of his own initiative. Against opposition, he had won a marriage that would make his daughter consort to Henry VI's sole heir — a future queen. Her prospects lacked the uncertainty of those of the Duchess of

Clarence or Elizabeth of York. Control over policy and patronage would be guaranteed for the foreseeable future. The plan required the use of force, but he was no longer dependent purely on his own resources, which had been shown to be inadequate. Co-operation with the Lancastrians gave grounds for hope. As Warwick could not take his son-in-law with him, the manifesto provided an explanation for his absence.

It was useful propaganda, as much for what it omitted as for what it contained. As victors in 1461, Warwick's retainers had been granted property forfeited by Lancastrians. On Henry VI's restoration they could expect material loss. This was agreed at Angers, but no reference was made in the *Maner and Gwidinge*. Warwick and Clarence probably neglected the interests of their retainers, confining themselves to their own: indeed Warwick had authorised Louis to accept Margaret's terms on his behalf.[91] The appearance of a diplomatic triumph may have reassured his followers.

The manifesto did not mention the proposed war against Burgundy, which was incorporated in the treaty.[92] It might have been fatal had it been discovered. It fulfilled a long-term aim of Warwick's foreign policy. By the terms of the treaty he was to rule England; he would retain his offices and such lands that he would have to restore were relatively unimportant beside his great hereditary estate.

Clarence's position was ambiguous. He appeared unimportant to Louis and his practical role in formulating the treaty was small. At Amboise he was honoured equally with Warwick and he was also associated with him in proclamations, for he was important to Warwick both as his coheir and as a magnate. It was necessary that the contribution of Warwick's faction should appear essential to the Lancastrians: Clarence was a crucial member of the faction. He alone of Warwick's supporters stood to gain from reconciliation with Edward. Indeed Commines thought that he had reached an agreement with Edward before leaving France,[93] but this is contradicted by other sources and is hardly credible: he was later to help depose Edward IV. Clarence had much to give up, so he received much in return. At Angers he abandoned his own claim to the crown and the bulk of his estates: lands formerly of the duchies of Cornwall and Lancaster were to be surrendered at once but forfeited estates only for compensation.[94] He was recognised as Duke of York. He would be brother-in-law of a future king in Prince Edward; in the interim their father-in-law would rule. On the failure of Henry VI's heirs, an unlikely eventuality, Clarence was probably promised the succession, as the chronicler Warkworth says.[95] He was guaranteed a position on the edge of the throne.

Individual Lancastrians gained little from the treaty. They would recover their possessions but would not be rewarded for their loyalty. They must accept a status quo founded on their own misfortunes. Apart from Jasper Tudor, Earl of Pembroke, Louis XI's first cousin, it is unlikely that any of the Lancastrian magnates shared in framing the treaty.

There were also differences of policy. Before the treaty Chancellor Fortescue urged Louis to help, offering as inducements the location of the wool staple in France, the resumption of Anglo-Gascon trade, and a perpetual peace: very different from the offensive alliance ultimately concluded. He also hoped to satisfy Edward IV,[96] perhaps with the duchy of York. Later another memorandum was despatched by Prince Edward to England.[97] Full of Fortescue's own ideas, it provided for a continual council in which great lords would not be dominant, and for limits to patronage and its distribution. This was very different from the objectives of Warwick and Clarence in 1469-70. As the treaty did not bind Henry VI in his absence, they may have hoped to adjust the settlement on the success of the invasion, as indeed they did: Warwick and Clarence had no security against this.

It was on this basis that a united force assembled in Normandy. While its composition is unknown, most were probably Frenchmen and only a minority were Warwick's supporters and Lancastrian emigrés. Clarence, Warwick, Oxford and Pembroke were prominent in its preparation. Efforts were made to stimulate risings in England. Warwick probably sent copies of the *Maner and Gwidinge* to his supporters. The Earl of Shrewsbury and Lord Stanley, who met him at Bristol, must have been forewarned of his plans. So were his two brothers, Archbishop Neville and the Marquis Montagu. The latter had not been adequately compensated for his earldom of Northumberland. On Warwick's flight he had not been given Warwick's northern estates, of which he was heir. The promised marriage was insufficient. Edward was unaware of Montagu's change in loyalty.

The exiles also appealed for popular support, sending a proclamation in advance. Recalling their concern for the 'Comon Weale of England', it denounced the oppression, extortion and default of justice of those that 'have gieided and bene about the estate Royall of the Realme'. These were posted among other places in London, where a sermon was delivered at Paul's Cross in favour of Henry VI. On landing, the invaders issued their own commissions of array.[98]

They disembarked at Plymouth and Dartmouth on 13 September. The plans unfolded without difficulty. Pembroke went to Wales to recruit. In the south-west the combined influence of Clarence and the Lancastrian exiles elicited a ready response, rapidly enlarging the initial force of several thousand men. At Bristol they were joined by Shrewsbury and Stanley. A Kentish rising, probably based on Warwick's local supporters, rapidly became out of hand and compelled London to prepare defensive measures. Finally in Yorkshire Montagu turned his levies against Edward, who narrowly evaded capture: on 2 November he fled to the Netherlands.[99]

With his flight further resistance became futile. It appears to have been non-existent, largely because Edward was unprepared. All through the summer an expeditionary force was being prepared in Normandy, of which Edward had received continuous information from the Duke of Burgundy and his own spies. Yet there seems to have been no force to resist the landing. Of course Edward could not be sure where it would take place. He may have been unable to raise troops, because of the appeal of the invaders to the people. After ten years he may have been uncertain who still harboured Lancastrian sympathies: those willing to oppose Warwick might be Lancastrian at heart; those who would fight the Lancastrians might not oppose Warwick. Who was he to trust? In which localities should he guard against insurrections? Altogether Edward's difficulties should not be underestimated, but he did not even issue commissions of array. What resistance was offered to the invaders, such as that of Thomas St. Leger at Salisbury,[100] seems to have been independently organised. Edward's supporters had no opportunity to resist, as they were never mobilised. The Duke of Gloucester, Earl Rivers, Lords Hastings, Dudley, Say and Duras accompanied Edward into exile; Queen Elizabeth took sanctuary in Westminster Abbey, the chancellor, keeper of the privy seal and William Bourchier took sanctuary at St. Martin-le-Grand, and Thomas Howard at Colchester.[101] The remainder stayed in England and acquiesced in the new regime.

On 15 October, shortly after the arrival of Archbishop Neville,

Clarence, Warwick, Shrewsbury, Stanley and St. John, Henry VI was conveyed from the Tower to the Bishop of London's palace near St. Paul's cathedral. It was there that the first acts of Henry VI's second reign were made:[102] the Readeption had begun.

4. The Readeption, October 1470 - April 1471

Henry VI's new government dated its documents with the formula: 'In the forty-ninth year of the reign of King Henry VI and the first year of the readeption of his royal power'. On 26 November the chancellor preached to the assembled houses of parliament on the text: 'Turn, O backsliding children, saith the Lord, for I am married unto you'.[103] Both dating clause and sermon show that this was seen as the start of a new reign as well as the continuation of Henry's old one. Warwick and his faction were anxious not to turn the clock right back to 1461, as the intervening decade had been relatively prosperous for them. This emerges in the distribution of royal office, their avoidance of extreme measures, and in the terms of the treaty of Angers itself.

The new government made few inessential changes, retaining royal judges, serjeants-at-law and many other officials at their posts. Most of Edward's peerage creations and all his surviving bishops were summoned to parliament. No revenge was sought on the traitors of 1460-1. Above all, there were no, or few, attainders and hence no grants of forfeited lands, which made it easy for Edward's fellow exiles to make their peace with the new regime, should they so desire. Only the Earl of Worcester was executed.

Henry VI ratified the treaty of Angers in parliament, presumably at the beginning of the first session. It contained clauses providing for the change of dynasty, the entail of the crown after Henry's death successively on his son, the latter's issue and Clarence, and the reversion to Clarence of the duchy of York.[104] All these were relatively uncontroversial compared with the settlement of land.

If the precedent of 1461 had been followed, three measures could be expected: the restoration of the lands of the royal family and the reversal of any attainders against its supporters; the attainder of the committed followers of the deposed rival monarch; and the distribution of forfeited property among its own committed supporters, thus creating a vested interest in its own survival. This is what one would expect: what actually happened?

Unfortunately there is little suitable evidence: not only has the text of the treaty of Angers been lost, but so too have the roll of parliament and the text of its politically important acts; the relevant chronicles are sketchy and ill-informed; and even the chancery records are little use. The limitations of the chancery rolls are surprising. Admittedly much can be explained by the interruption of business by war and the short duration of the Readeption, but one suspects that they also stem in part from the nature of the settlement: no enrolments need result from mere restoration of land, from resumption, or if there were no new attainders. In spite of the inadequacies of the evidence, however, one can see that the Readeption government departed from the pattern of 1461.

The absence, or near absence, of new attainders has already been mentioned. Although the chroniclers mention them, there are no references in contemporary *records*. Neither the patent nor the fine rolls refer to the grant of property formerly belonging to Edward IV or his fellow exiles. There are not even any entries relating to the custody or administration of such property, with one exception: two appointments relating to Gloucester's lordship of Chirk made on 28 October, before parliament even met. One would expect a rash of grants and appointments relating to the estates of Gloucester, Rivers, Hastings, Say and the other exiles. Finally, if anyone was to be attainted, surely it should have been Worcester? Instead his heir was treated as a royal ward, whose lands were in royal custody during his minority.[105] Indeed, the only lands that were seized by the crown were the dowers of Queen Elizabeth and her mother the Duchess of Bedford and certain leasehold properties: these may have been resumed, not forfeited.

One can only speculate why Edward's supporters escaped attainder. Was it already considered wrong to attaint the supporters of a de facto monarch, as in 1485? Perhaps. But if this argument really carried weight in 1471, as it did not in 1485, it was because other factors militated against attainder. Worcester could hardly be attainted when the probable loser was Montagu himself, as next heir to his infant son: Montagu obtained custody of the inheritance during the minority.[106] Warwick, Montagu, Stanley and FitzHugh had similar objections to the attainder of Hastings, their brother-in-law, and so had Clarence about his two brothers. In fact their faction had too many points of contact with Edward IV and his supporters to favour extreme measures, which could only obstruct attempts at reconciliation.

Had the Readeption lasted longer, abstention from attainders might have produced desertions from Edward IV to Henry VI, but none are known. In the short term, it meant that there were no new forfeitures. Henry VI lacked the extensive estates enjoyed by Edward IV in 1461 and consequently lacked Edward's advantages. He had to recover alienations from the duchy of Lancaster, crown lands, his consort's dower and the estates of the Prince of Wales to support his government and family. He could not create a vested interest in his survival by judicious distribution of patronage; he could not compensate anybody forced to surrender lands to the returning Lancastrians.

The treaty of Angers had provided

> 'for the recovery of the state and possessions of our aforesaid consort [Queen Margaret] and son [Prince Edward] and of other nobles and of our land of old inheritance'.[107]

'Our land of old inheritance' referred to the duchy of Lancaster and apparently certain crown lands; Prince Edward's lands were the principality of Wales, duchy of Cornwall and county of Chester. The reference to the lands of the nobles demonstrates that attainders against Lancastrians were to be reversed, for reasons that were succinctly expressed:

> 'Of which possessions and hereditaments certain will have pertained . . . to the aforesaid lords, who have long lost the profits and revenues of their possessions because of the fealty and allegiance they felt and displayed towards us and for our true and just title'.

Henry confirmed the treaty[108] and presumably its terms were executed by parliament. The reversal of attainders is implicit in the use of hereditary titles by attainted Lancastrians and their heirs, in their attendance at the Readeption parliament, and in their appointment to royal office. A clear illustration concerns Henry, Lord Clifford: his father had been attainted in 1461, yet he was now a royal ward and his lands were in wardship during his minority.[109] Finally, it is clearly stated in a grant of 24 February 1471 to Clarence. By the treaty of Angers he was entitled to keep any forfeited estates until he had been fully compensated, but now, under a new arrangement, he was

> 'disposed and agreeable to relinquish his title, interest and estate in all possessions and hereditaments, which la.e were . . . of the said lords, against whom any act of forfeiture or attainder was had during the usurpation of Edward, lately acting by force as King of England' . . .

The wording shows that such attainders were no longer considered to be valid. It is unlikely that anyone successfully retained forfeitures, when even Clarence's special provision was waived and when even Warwick gave up land. If a minor like Clifford, who could not speak for himself, could recover his lands, there can have been few or any exceptions. Since so many returning Lancastrians were commoners, their attainders must have been reversed as well as those of the nobles and peers explicitly mentioned above. All of Edward's attainders were probably reversed, not merely those of Lancastrians who had actually returned to England.

Less could hardly have been done, but the land settlement was nevertheless revolutionary. Edward had created a vested interest in his regime by the lavish distribution of forfeited property: all the recipients were potentially losers. The Readeption may have been too short for all Lancastrians to recover possession of their estates, but they now had the right to do so, a right they were bound ultimately to exercise. Some forfeited property lay vacant because of the flight of Gloucester, Rivers and Hastings, but most was occupied by Edward's grantees. The restoration of Lord Clifford was at the expense of Warwick himself, Sir William Stanley, Sir John Huddleston, John Pilkington, Nicholas Gaynesford, Henry Pierpoint and William Harrington.[110] The return of John Courtenay as Earl of Devon would hurt Lord Mountjoy and Lord Dynham, that of John Butler as Earl of Ormond would dispossess the Earl of Essex and Lords Audley and Ferrers of Chartley. Even the return of Warwick and Clarence was at the expense of those given their possessions, especially George Neville, later Lord Abergavenny.[111] Even for those with a long lineage and great inheritance this was no trivial matter.

The blow was heaviest for Edward's new creations. The Herbert family possessions were drastically reduced by the return of Jasper Tudor as Earl of Pembroke: he recovered his own lands, such as Pembroke and Haverfordwest, and was given offices and custody of estates of the Herberts.[112] Lord Ferrers of Chartley may have lost the Courtenay, Butler and Vaux estates given to support the estate of baron. Lords Mountjoy and Howard, whom Edward had endowed, might sink into the ranks of the gentry. Some changes altered the whole political map of England: Warwick returned in place of Arundel as warden of the Cinque Ports; in East Anglia the greatest magnate — the Duke of Norfolk — sued to the Earl of Oxford for favour; the new Earl of Northumberland, warden of the East March, was supplanted and overshadowed by the Marquis Montagu.[113]

It was not only the great who were affected, but it was they who mattered most. If the loyalty of Edward's affinity or magnate supporters faltered, this loss of patronage, often of longstanding, would have strengthened it. None of the great were unaffected. For some the losses sufficed to ensure their hostility. The remainder could not be enthusiastic buttresses of the regime. Without new attainders, Henry VI had no patronage to offer as compensation. Of all the former Lancastrians who had reconciled themselves to Edward IV, only Lord Sudeley committed himself to the new regime, though hopes were nourished regarding others.

In 1461, as in 1470, parliament had contained members of the defeated party when endorsing the change in dynasty and proscribing its enemies. Then, however, the ousted party had been vanquished in battle and the ruling party had confirmed its control by force. The situation was different in 1470: Edward had fled without a battle, so most of his supporters had acquiesced in the dynastic change. They had not been exterminated, and their power was still in being and potentially available for use against the government.

Probably there were forty-six magnates present in England and eligible for summons to parliament, namely five dukes, a marquis, twelve earls, a viscount and twenty-seven barons: only fifteen — less than a third — belonged to the ruling faction.[115] Among those summoned, the Earl of Kent and Lords Howard, Mountjoy, Cromwell, Ferrers of Chartley, Audley, Strange and Grey of Codnor were removed from the commissions of the peace. Only the last three did not owe their present titles to Edward IV's creation. All but two had campaigned against Clarence earlier in the year. Several magnates were in custody, others in sanctuary. So weak was support for the Readeption, so strong the potential hostility. Reconciliation was necessary, but was rendered almost impossible by the material losses occasioned by reversals of attainders of former Lancastrians.

On his return several of these peers joined Edward; none defected to Henry VI. They imposed an immensely difficult problem of control on the Readeption government.

If the ruling faction was weak and had to place reliable supporters in key offices, it also had to distribute them evenly among its component parts. Positions had to be found for former Lancastrians and for supporters of Warwick and Clarence. The chief offices of state and household were carefully balanced. The new keeper of the privy seal was John Hales, Bishop of Lichfield, a former servant of Queen Margaret; the chancellor was Warwick's brother, the Archbishop of York, and Sir John Langstrother was again treasurer; the secretary was Master Piers Courtenay, a servant of the Duke of Clarence, who also advanced his clerical career.[116] The secretary was one of the officers in closest personal contact with the king. The other was the chamberlain, Sir Richard Tunstall,[117] a prominent Lancastrian. The new steward and treasurer of the household were the Earl of Oxford and Sir John Delves: the latter had been treasurer of Clarence's own household. All these officers could influence policy. The great officers controlled the great departments of state, subject to the written and oral commands of the king. He, in turn, could be influenced by those with access to him, his secretary, his chamberlain and other members of his household. This was the normal situation. Had Henry VI the normal freedom of action?

There survives a memorandum written by Sir John Fortescue at this time.[118] The heading states that it consists of suggestions sent by Prince Edward by way of the Earl of Warwick to be shown to the king and council, to be implemented if they thought it expedient. This does not prove that any part of it was carried out, but it shows that it represented the view not only of Fortescue but of the Lancastrian government in exile. It shows what they considered appropriate decision-making machinery for Henry VI's government. The memorandum concentrates on the king's finance and the authorisation of patronage. The first stressed the need for the king to support the ordinary expenses of government with ordinary sources of revenue, so that the need for extraordinary lay and clerical taxation might be avoided. The method envisaged was by firm assignments for each item of expenditure, which could not easily be ignored. Such an approach required some control over patronage.

Patronage was to be controlled by a continual executive council with a fixed membership. It was suggested that all grants

> 'be deferred, vnto the tyme that ther be a counseill stablisshed; and thanne the supplicacions of alle such persons mow be sende by the kyng to the seide counseile, where as every man his merite(s) may be indifferently examyned'.

In this way he might be rewarded according to his deserts. It also provided that Henry

> 'do no grete thing towching the rewle of his reaume, nor geve lande, ffee, office, or benefice, but that firste his intente therinne be communed and disputed in that counseill, and that he haue herde their advises ther upon . . . And also that no patente be made in Inheritaunce of any partie of the kinges lyveloode, by what title so ever that it be comen to hym, without thassente of his parliamente, nor for terme of lyfe, or yeres countervailing terme of lyffe, withoute thaduice of his counsale, excepte such patentes as shalbe made of fermes by the Thresour[er] of Englonde' . . .

The regulations would also apply to others in such matters. By these means, it was hoped to prevent such grants being obtained 'with Importunite of Sute, and by parciall meanes', so that nobody

> 'may grugge with the kinges highnesse nor with the lordis nor with any other manne aboute his personne as they were wonned to doo . . . And thanne shall the king not be counseled by menn of his Chambre, of his housholde nor other which can not counsele hym'.

The chancellor was forbidden to seal anything not approved by the council, on pain of dismissal and forfeiture of his temporalities. The tone shows that the Lancastrians thought it necessary to restrict Henry's prodigality, to reduce his susceptibility to undesirable influences. Several statements seem to refer specifically to King Henry. They had previous experience of his shortcomings. It was practically necessary, but it was too large an encroachment on the prerogative of the crown. This may account for the addition of a provision, that the council 'may in no thing restreyne his power, libertee or prerogatiff'.

In view of this memorandum it is surprising how many entries on the patent roll were authorised by Henry alone.[119] A couple were authorised *per ipsum regem* (by the king himself), presumably by a letter signed by him or sealed with his signet. There are no direct warrants among the warrants for the great or privy seal, but several dozen were authorised by the king by word of mouth. They relate to all periods of the Readeption. But the most important, such as the appointment of the treasurer and the keeper of the privy seal, belong to the month of October 1470. Later warrants generally refer to minor matters. Over half concern presentations to ecclesiastical benefices; there is one pardon; Henry appointed the protonothary of chancery, the clerk of the hanaper, a parker, a ranger and the constable of Shrewsbury castle. His authority is not invoked for any politically important act between October 1470 and March 1471. Apparently Henry was permitted to act independently only in minor matters close to his heart, such as ecclesiastical patronage. The absence of written warrants suggest that the secretary himself was bypassed: Piers Courtenay was able to leave Henry and visit the West Country.[120] The appointment of Sir Henry Lewis as governor of the household shows that Henry's authority even stopped short of control of his household.

Was the king's role effectively taken over by the lieutenant? From his September proclamation until at least 25 March Warwick used this title.[121] There is no contemporary evidence to support Vergil's claim that Clarence was appointed joint-protector with Warwick by parliament:[122] it is unlikely, since he did not use the title in his letters. The term protector does accord with the nature of the office: the patent granting the lieutenantcy to Prince Edward on 27 March makes it clear that his duties were purely military, to array and command troops for defensive purposes.[123] The patent mentions no civil authority. Other powers exercised by the lieutenant, such as the grant of safe conducts, emanate from conciliar delegation, not from the nature of his office. In the council, the lieutenant was merely the first among equals: Fortescue's memorandum ignores the office.

In his memorandum Fortescue provided that the chancellor should refer to the conciliar origin of a warrant either in the text of a letter patent or by a separate warranty clause. This provision was not observed. There are no conciliar bills among the warrants for the great or privy seal, among the warrants for issue, or even the writs to the exchequer barons (brevia directa baronibus). The universal mandate for action was the writ of privy seal, which at other times was the vehicle of conciliar decisions: certainly some of these writs refer to the council, but many do not. None of the patents under the great seal refer to conciliar authority, either in the text or warranty clause, but as Professor Lander has shown, this is not conclusive evidence of conciliar inactivity. Between 12 November and

7 December 1470 fourteen writs of allowance for fourteen sheriffs were sent to the exchequer of receipt. At least the eight sealed on 19 November are likely to result from a single decision, but only two mention the authority of the council.[124] Fortescue's advice on this point was apparently rejected.

The council's activity ranged from the politically important to the trivial. It was the council that thought it 'right expedient and behoueful' that Warwick should be appointed keeper of the seas. It assigned Lady Scrope to attend Queen Elizabeth in sanctuary, perhaps rather to prevent political intrigue than to help her in labour. The council agreed to Lewis's appointment. In March it issued commissions of array and in January commissions of oyer and terminer. Many of its acts were matters of minor routine: the audit of Lewis's accounts, allowances to sheriffs, presentations to benefices, the appointment of the clerk of parliament.[125] It even delegated certain powers. On 26 October the chancellor was sent a writ saying:

> 'We . . . by thauis of oure Counsail wol and graunte vnto you ful power and auctorite after youre discrecion to graunte licence vnder oure grete seal to all oure ligemen and subgettis hauyng sufficient saufconduites of the parties aduersaries and also to make saufconduites vnder the same seal for deliuerance of all maner of prisoners aswel of our ligemen taken by oure aduersaries and enemies as of the parties aduersaries taken by oure subgettis'.

It is a sign of the omnicompetence of the council that it should authorise the chancellor to perform his normal function! Similar authority to issue safeconducts was given to Warwick on his appointment as admiral: he referred to his authority when employing it.[126] On another occasion the chancellor was authorised to confirm any appointments that Clarence made as farmer of the Forest of Dean.[127] Such routine matters did not call for individual consideration by the council. Those that were not delegated remained in its hands.

Such an executive council would be expected to meet frequently — perhaps several days a week. There might be a balance of estates and a fixed personnel, perhaps confirmed by parliament, as in earlier experiments. So far Fortescue's suggestions seem to fit the bill, although there is an absence of direct evidence to show they were carried out. But his hope to eliminate pressure from individuals and groups and to return the dominant role to administrators certainly failed. It could hardly be otherwise, for politics demanded that the magnates should be well represented and that their influence should correspond to their actual power.

Petitions for this period do not survive, so we cannot tell whether they were addressed to the council. Supplicants continued to seek the support of individual councillors. The city of Exeter asked Sir Hugh Courtenay to approach Sir Richard Tunstall about the confirmation of their charter: a Lancastrian M.P. approaching a Lancastrian councillor. New Romney deferred to the Earl of Warwick, warden of the Cinque Ports, and gave him a gilt cup. Such approaches were not mere wishful thinking. The Earl of Oxford, for example, told John Paston III to 'axe and haue. I trow my brodyr Syr John shall haue the constabyllshep of Norwyche Castyll wyth xx li. of fee; all the lordys be agreyd to it'.[128] Some of the warrants tell the same story. At Warwick's instance a safeconduct was issued to three Scots; Henry VI paid for wine supplied from Gascony 'at our behove and to the behoue of our right trusty and right welbeloued Cousyns' Clarence and Warwick; and Gerard Caniziani and the Medici were taken into royal protection at the advice of the duke, earl and the Archbishop of York. Warwick gave a personal assurance regarding the treaty with France before it was concluded.[129]

So far it has been shown that the Readeption settlement, in accordance with the treaty of Angers, was favourable to Warwick, Clarence and their faction. They secured a large share of the key offices, including the valuable lieutenantcy, and dominated decision making. They took as conciliatory a line as was consistent with the change of dynasty and return of the Lancastrians. This was achieved with the assistance of such Lancastrians as Pembroke, although there were differences. As time passed, however, there were changes, which may be due to the return of further Lancastrians, who harboured resentment about their long exile,[130] were anxious to turn the clock back a decade, and were more interested in a rapprochement with former Lancastrians than with Edward IV. They pressed for revisions in the Angers settlement itself, objected to the dominance of the Warwick faction, and differed on foreign policy.

This changeover coincided with alterations in the balance of power at Westminster. Warwick and Clarence were dominant from their invasion until Christmas, obtaining the ratification of the treaty of Angers and other favourable decisions. After Christmas, however,

Warwick was generally absent at Calais and the Cinque Ports and was preoccupied with the transport of Queen Margaret and Prince Edward from France.[131] In his absence, Clarence was the faction's representative at London, residing from October 1470 until February 1471 near Dowgate in the City at the house of another councillor, the Bishop of Salisbury. After Christmas Clarence bore the brunt of Lancastrian hostility.

Up till then, he had been a powerful and influential figure, whose good lordship was widely sought and effectively employed. He had secured for his retainers the offices of treasurer of the household and secretary and at least two shrievalties. At Lord Mountjoy's desire he had issued a protection for his manors of Elvaston and Barton (Derbys.); several letters patent were issued at his instance; and some towns, such as Exeter, sent gifts to him or his duchess. At his request the dean and chapter of Salisbury had reinstated a recalcitrant vicar choral and he had induced the Bishop of Lincoln to grant a prebend to his own clerk.[132] Of course, he had also exploited his position for his own benefit. As in the previous reign, he was entitled to have his charters and patents free of fee or fine. Although the patent was not sealed until 18 February, he was issuing protections as lieutenant of Ireland from December. He apparently made good his claim to the duchy of York, issuing a quitclaim to grantees of his father.[133]

The first point of disagreement concerned his lands, none of which were held by hereditary right: all had been granted to him by Edward IV. As they were originally parts of the crown lands, the duchies of Lancaster and Cornwall, the dower of Queen Margaret, or the estates of attainted Lancastrians, he stood to lose them all by a Lancastrian takeover. Hence a clause in the treaty of Angers allowed him to retain them all except Tutbury honour until he had been fully compensated.[134] Since he held so much of these lands, since Queen Margaret's dower was larger than that of Queen Elizabeth, and since there were no new forfeitures, the Readeption government was quite incapable of compensating him. He seemed assured of indefinite tenure of these estates, but in fact he gave them up by 24 February. His retention of these lands was unacceptable to returning Lancastrians. Ultimately he gave way, perhaps to save the rest of the Angers agreement, perhaps to ease co-operation against Edward IV. What he surrendered were the honours of Tutbury (Staffs.) and Duffield (Derbys.), the lordships of High Peak

(Derbys.) and Castle Donington (Leics.), formerly parts of the duchy of Lancaster and Queen Margaret's dower; crown lands and feefarms in Nottinghamshire and Derbyshire,[135] the Gournay lands and part of the feefarm of Coventry, formerly of the duchy of Cornwall;[136] and all his forfeited property. In return he received such dowerlands and feefarms in southern England late of Queen Elizabeth that had not been previously held by Queen Margaret, a quite inadequate substitute, and the promise of ultimate compensation equal to what he gave up: in the interim he did not even receive an annuity to maintain his income at its former level. True, he acquired the duchy of York, but the lion's share was held in dower by his mother, who still had two decades to live, and it was concentrated mainly in Wales, a region that he may not have visited since 1459. He was thus deprived of the concentrations of land, on which his military power had formerly rested. Alone of the leaders of the ruling faction, he had no sphere assigned to his influence.

One exception to the surrender was his honour of Richmond, which had not belonged to either of the categories so far mentioned. This had been granted by Henry VI to his half-brother Edmund Tudor, Earl of Richmond (d.1456), but had been resumed by Edward IV and granted to Clarence. In 1470 Edmund's heir was his son Henry, still a minor. Henry Tudor's stepfather was Sir Henry Stafford, younger son of the first Duke of Buckingham: Stafford's household accounts speak of 'dominus Richemound' and Stafford's will describes him as 'my sonne in law Therle of Richemound'.[137] Sir Henry secured the custody of some of the Duchess of Bedford's dowerlands, to which Earl Edmund had held the reversion, but not the part he had actually secured.[138] It was probably in pursuit of his stepson's claim that he visited Clarence six times between 6 October and 16 December 1470. He also contacted two other councillors, the Bishop of Winchester and the Earl of Essex,[139] perhaps to secure their support. As Henry Tudor was cousin of the Duke of Somerset and nephew of Jasper Tudor, Earl of Pembroke, it is not surprising to find that Stafford was on good terms with the Lancastrians. On 28 October the Earl of Pembroke and Sir Richard Tunstall were his guests at dinner in London, returning afterwards to Westminster. As Tunstall was Henry VI's chamberlain, Henry Tudor may well have had an audience with his uncle the king on his visit to Westminster two days previously.[140] It was thus a formidable connection with which Clarence had to contend. In the short run

TABLE V: LANCASTRIAN TITLES TO THE CROWN IN 1470-71

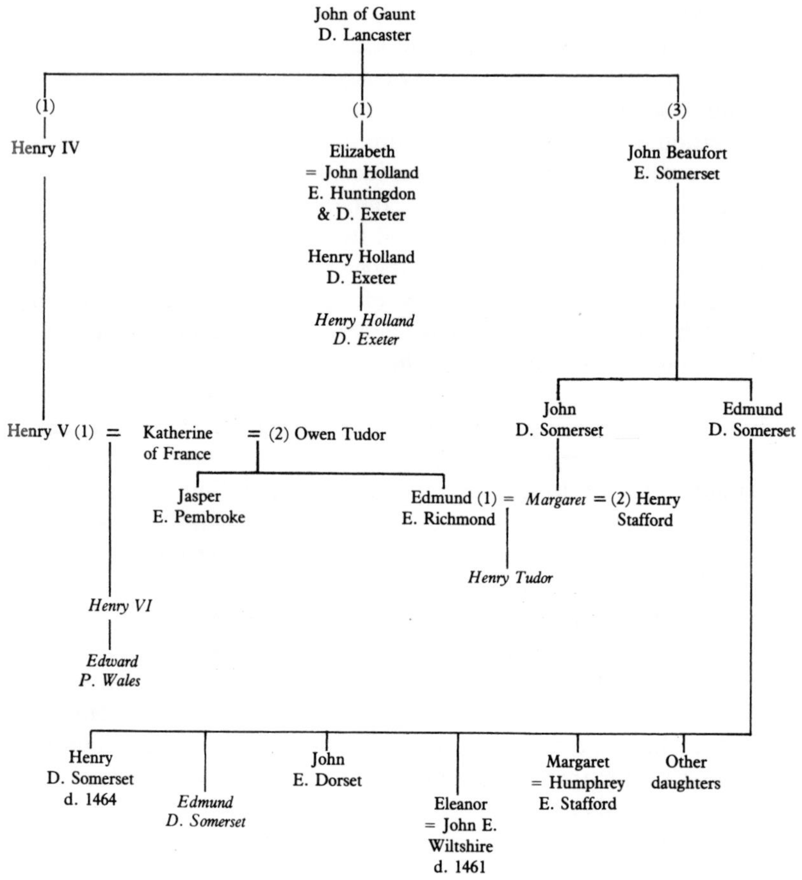

Clarence won, as he was granted the honour on 24 February 1471, presumably to the annoyance of Stafford, Pembroke and other Lancastrians; however, his title was only for life,[141] a blow to Clarence and a victory for Henry Tudor, if still a rather distant prospect. This compromise probably failed to satisfy either party.

Friction was not confined to Richmond honour. Henry Tudor and his mother Margaret Beaufort, heiress of John Beaufort, Duke of Somerset, were among the representatives of the Beaufort claim to the crown. This had been a live issue during the 1450s[142] and certainly Jasper Tudor and the Beauforts must have been aware of it. When — if — Henry Tudor was received by his uncle Henry VI, it was probably in people's minds. Indeed Polydore Vergil, who was admittedly writing after Henry Tudor's accession as Henry VII, records that on seeing him Henry VI said before witnesses: 'This trewly, this is he unto whom both we and our adversaryes must yeald and geave over the domynion'.[143] The story itself may be apocryphal, but it was obvious that, in the event of failure of Henry VI's issue, the succession would devolve on either the Beaufort or the Holland families. Henry Holland, Duke of Exeter was the grandson of Elizabeth of Lancaster, sister of Henry IV and like him offspring of John of Gaunt and his first wife Blanche of Lancaster. Exeter was aware of his claim.[144] The Beauforts were descended from the eldest son of John of Gaunt's third marriage: Edmund, Duke of Somerset was the heir male, Margaret Beaufort and Henry Tudor the heirs general. Only the life of Prince Edward separated Henry Holland, Henry Stafford or Edmund Beaufort from the lieutenantcy of England during Henry VI's lifetime and the crown on his death. Their claims were mutually exclusive, but all were set aside by the ratification in parliament of the entail of the crown on Clarence in default of Henry VI's issue, for which the duke secured an exemplification.[145] If he struggled for it as he did for Richmond honour, it was no wonder that they held him in 'great suspicion, despite, disdeigne and hatered'. As *The Arrivall* observes, they still wished the title to remain to Lancastrians.[146] Clarence could not expect their help to implement his claim.

Clarence therefore had some reason to feel that they broke 'theyr appoyntementys made with hym' and were hostile.[147] Yet this was while Warwick was still lieutenant. When his title was superseded by the arrival of Prince Edward, they were bound to lose some of their influence. Even decisive victory over Edward IV would bring no advantage here: it would render his support unnecessary. Clarence could not view the future with equanimity: his position offered less security and certainly less material advantages than when he was Edward IV's brother. He was probably also dissatisfied with the misfortunes that beset his family. Two brothers were in exile. The return of the Duke of Exeter must have been uncomfortable, materially and personally, for his sister Anne, Duchess of Exeter, who had been living with Thomas St. Leger. The war projected against Burgundy threatened his sister Margaret, Duchess of Burgundy. So when reconciliation was proposed by his mother, his sisters, his uncles Essex and Cardinal Bourchier, and Edward's former chancellor and chamberlain, he was ready to listen. The Duchess Margaret put him in direct contact with Edward, so that 'a perfecte accord was appoyntyd, accordyd, concludyd and assured, betwixt them'.[148] The details are unknown, but it must have included assurances about his future position, which his family and the others involved could guarantee. It must have been completed before Clarence's departure for the West Country in February 1471.

He was not alone in disillusion. When agreeing to the restoration of former Lancastrians at Angers, Warwick was agreeing to give up his share of their forfeited lands. Presumably he thought it the lesser of evils, and comforted himself with the vast size of his own inheritance. Even so, the restoration of Lord Clifford, which deprived him of the Clifford estates in Cumberland and Westmorland and eroded his territorial base in the West March, was serious. He may also have lost Butler estates in Northamptonshire and Buckinghamshire.[149] As a great marcher lord he had ambitions in South Wales, where he now had to resign himself to the preeminence of Jasper Tudor, Earl of Pembroke: for example, he had to share with Pembroke the custody of the Stafford lordships of Hay, Huntington and Brecon, which he had held since 1461.[150] Warwick's brother, the Marquis Montagu, failed to recover the earldom of Northumberland which he had lost in 1470, nor any part of the Percy estates except Wressle (Yorks.). Instead he had to surrender the Courtenay estates that he had received in compensation. He was indeed appointed once more to the wardenry of the East March, for which he no longer possessed the territorial resources. His grant of the custody of the Tiptoft and Clifford inheritances in the minority of the heirs was no substitute for lands of his own.[151] No wonder Edward had hopes of winning over Montagu. Even Warwick proved open to negotiation, but understandably wanted more than just his life, which Edward regarded as 'apoyntement unresonable' and not in accord with his honour. At least Warwick could console himself with what he had saved.

Few of his retainers can have felt that way. Many must have suffered serious losses, like those faced by Sir Walter Wrottesley, who held seven Butler manors in Dorset and Staffordshire.[152] This cannot have improved their relations with the Lancastrians. After Warwick's death, few of his supporters joined the Lancastrian army that fought at Tewkesbury. Some, like Lord Stanley, were unwilling to fight. Others, like Sir William Stanley, who had lost Skipton-in-Craven (Yorks.), and Sir William Parre deserted to Edward IV.[153]

Returning Lancastrians had secured little more than reversal of their attainders and recovery of their estates, no doubt often wasted. Their exile gave them a claim on royal patronage, but their bloodless victory and the absence of new forfeitures meant that the government had little to give. What there was had to be shared with Warwick's own connection. Thus they received only a share of the offices of state and household; there is no sign of wholesale changes in the personnel of king's and queen's households.[154] Three Lancastrian knights, Tunstall, Plummer and Tresham, became respectively master of the mint, keeper of the great wardrobe, and speaker of the commons, and Pembroke recovered his former lands and offices and secured several grants and custodies.[155] Most Lancastrians had to content themselves with mere restoration.

Instances of this include the Dukes of Somerset and Exeter, the Earls of Devon and Ormond. As Henry's half-brother, Pembroke could justifiably expect special consideration, which he in fact received. Similar consideration, however, was also appropriate for the cadet Lancastrian house of Beaufort and for the Duke of Exeter. All had claims to be king's lieutenant, but in fact this office went to Warwick. It was Clarence who was nominated as residual heir of Henry VI and his son, which, apart from offending those whose claims were overlooked, was certainly not for what Lancastrians had fought and suffered attainder and exile. His success on this point and in retaining possession of Richmond honour suggested to Lancastrians that the interests of Warwick's connection were receiving unduly favourable treatment. In addition to obtaining a share of the forfeited offices, Warwick and his associates recovered those that they had previously held. Warwick himself was captain of Calais, warden of the Cinque Ports and West March, admiral and great chamberlain of England. One brother was chancellor, another warden of the East March, his son-in-law was lieutenant of Ireland, a brother-in-law constable of England and steward of the household, and a retainer was treasurer of England. Servants of Clarence were king's secretary and treasurer of the household. It was clear that they had more than their share of offices. The new regime appeared as much in danger of Neville domination as had the government of Edward IV in 1461-4.

Neville support had certain disadvantages. Warwick had many enemies and may have added them to those of the regime. Many Lancastrians had preferred to make peace with Edward rather than continue resistance. When they failed to join the Readeption, one possible explanation was hostility to Warwick. Even his defeat at Barnet was not regarded as wholly disastrous, as the Milanese ambassador reported:

> 'There are many who consider the queen's prospects favourable, chiefly because of the death of Warwick, because it is reckoned she ought to have many lords in her favour, who intended to resist her because they were enemies of Warwick'.[156]

This was presumably what *The Arrivall* means when stating that, after Barnet, the Lancastrian 'partye was nevar the febler, but rathar stronger'.[157] According to Commines, the Duke of Burgundy let the Dukes of Somerset and Exeter go to England, for he saw that they had no friendship for Warwick. Clarence, too, was unpopular with the Lancastrians. Even John Butler, Earl of Ormond, an exile with everything to gain from returning to England, needed persuasion to make his peace with Warwick:

> 'You know how the Earl of Warwick has been the cause of the restitution of the goods of very many people. I, who love you, advise you to put out of your heart all shame and rancour towards him and bear him love and benevolence and friendship'.[158]

Perhaps this is why Somerset and Devon did not assist Warwick in 1471.

The Lancastrians hoped for the support of Henry Percy, fourth Earl of Northumberland. He had been ill-treated by the Readeption government, replaced as warden of the East March by Montagu, who dominated the north with Warwick at his expense. Rivalry between Nevilles and Percies had culminated in private war in the fourteen-fifties. Several Percies had died at Neville hands and, from a contemptuous reference to Montagu in his will, it seemed the fourth earl shared the hostility.[159] Otherwise he seemed a natural Lancastrian, as his grandfather, father, three uncles and a brother-in-law had died for Henry VI in 1455-69. In fact he did not commit himself, his conduct on balance favouring Edward IV.

Of the others of whom hopes were nourished, the most promising was Sir Henry Stafford. Son of the Duke of Buckingham killed on the Lancastrian side at Northampton in 1460, he had married Margaret Beaufort, whose claim to the crown was an incentive to support the Readeption. His household books record cordial contacts with leading Lancastrians, suggesting that he was willing not only to accept the new dynasty but to support it. He might have won over or neutralised the entire Stafford, Blount and Bourchier kinship network. His own will and those of the Bourchier widows of of Sir Aubrey de Vere, Sir Robert Welles and Sir Henry Neville illustrate the close family ties.[160] On 16 July 1470 Stafford and his uncle Lord Berners lunched together at Guildford. On 11 December he visited the Earl of Essex. The Duke of Buckingham came to supper on 28 October.[161] On 16 November the dowager-duchess and Lord Mountjoy obtained the custody of most of the ducal estates,[162] a clear sign of conciliar favour. Essex himself may have been a councillor, since he was assigned to treat with the French.[163] Such support would have strengthened Henry VI and weakened Edward IV. It depended on Stafford's satisfaction regarding Richmond honour and the succession, but neither was forthcoming. At Barnet Sir Henry Stafford fought for Edward IV.

Two other potential allies were the Duke of Burgundy and Edward IV himself. In the event Edward had difficulty in surviving his first days in England, even with Burgundian help; without it, he could not have succeeded. His brother-in-law, Duke Charles of Burgundy, was disinclined to help him: he had little faith in Edward's chances of recovering his kingdom and wanted to avoid offending Henry VI's government.[164] Without help, perhaps Edward might have been willing to come to terms. Chancellor Fortescue had hoped to satisfy him and on his arrival in England Edward won more support for his claim to the duchy of York than to the crown.

Henry VI's government had good reason to seek good relations with Burgundy. In proposing good relations with France rather than an offensive alliance, the Lancastrian government in exile was wise. But Louis XI and Warwick had agreed on a war of aggression against Burgundy and Warwick secured the ratification of the treaty in parliament.[165] Probably there was serious opposition: the London merchants tried to arrange an agreement between England and Burgundy. While in Burgundy the Dukes of Exeter and Somerset had tried to secure Charles the Bold's support:[166] in England they could hardly act differently. Warwick, however, reinforced Calais and commenced hostilities against Burgundy.[167] This was a fatal mistake, since it compelled Charles to support Edward's invasion of England. Once in England, Edward easily exposed the weakness of the Readeption government.

5. The Return of Edward IV, March — June 1471

The second session of the Readeption parliament opened at Westminster soon after 24 January 1471.[168] Much of the session was occupied by negotiations with France. The truce and treaty were sealed on 16 February, but already three days earlier Warwick had informed Louis XI that the Calais garrison had been ordered to commence hostilities against Burgundy.[169] With the conclusion of the alliance, parliament disbanded. By 21 February the barons of New Romney had returned home.[170]

This was not because of lack of business, but because the government was preoccupied by defence, as Edward was about to invade. The measures taken were of two kinds. Firstly, magnates of suspect loyalty were summoned by writs of privy seal from the localities to London, where they were held in custody or secured by recognisances: thus the Duke of Norfolk was removed from East Anglia and the Duke of Suffolk from Ewelme (Oxon.).[171] Secondly, commissions of array were issued and specific magnates were assigned responsibility for the security of certain areas : Oxford in East Anglia, Montagu in the north, Pembroke in Wales, Warwick in the West Midlands. On 30 January 1471 Clarence, Warwick and Pembroke were appointed commissioners of South Wales and the adjacent marches.[172]

Clarence's duchess arrived in England late in 1470 and was well-received at Exeter.[173] Probably she had joined her husband by Christmas. He and Warwick assisted the passage of the treaty with

France.[174] It was probably the last meeting of the earl, his daughter and son-in-law. The duke and duchess left Westminster before the end of the session and arrived at Salisbury before vespers on 17 February, lodging in the episcopal palace in the absence of the bishop, and proceeding westwards on 20 February.[175] They may have gone as far as South Wales, for they next appear at Bristol on 15 March and arrived next day at Wells. Clarence remained there until at least 23 March, again residing in the bishop's palace.[176]

Henry VI had commissioned Clarence to array troops. Clarence used this commission himself in Somerset, where until lately he had been a leading landowner, and employed agents elsewhere: he assigned the task in the North Midlands to Henry Vernon of Netherhaddon (Derbys.), who was instructed to despatch those arrayed to join him.[177] Magnate retainers and allies, like the Earl of Shrewsbury and Lord Stanley, were capable of independent action and were suspected of disaffection, so Clarence asked Vernon to discover their views. He also wanted to know the demeanour of the Earl of Northumberland.[178] As one of Henry VI's officers, Clarence could easily communicate with others in all parts of England. The force that he arrayed, although nominally for the benefit of Henry VI, was ultimately to be used against him. There was a risk that this might prove impossible, even though Clarence could probably rely on his own men. In any case premature discovery would be fatal, so he concealed his intentions even from Vernon.

Edward IV landed at Cromer (Norf.) on 12 March, but found Oxford's control to be too effective and therefore re-embarked. He proceeded to Holderness, where he landed on 14 March. Attended by only 1,000 men, he was fortunate to survive the first few days, but afterwards his force grew rapidly. Montagu could not take effective action against him, at least partly because of the inactivity of Northumberland, who persuaded the local gentry to 'sit still'.[179] Evidently the Nevilles had relied heavily on the Percy estates and retinue to dominate the north. Edward proceeded via Newark (Notts.) to Warwickshire, where the Earl of Warwick was to be found. Edward's forces increased as he advanced, the most important accretion consisting of three thousand men of Lord Hastings's connection who joined him at Leicester. Most important of these was Lord Grey of Codnor.[180]

By the time Edward reached Coventry he led a formidable army. It did not need Clarence's letters to persuade Warwick to avoid battle until he could concentrate his forces. Immediately after repelling Edward at Cromer, the Earl of Oxford arrayed the men of East Anglia and Cambridgeshire, and advanced to Newark. There he joined the Duke of Exeter and Viscount Beaumont, who had been recruiting in Huntingdonshire and Lincolnshire. As their united levies of four thousand men were too small to ensure victory, they let Edward pass and followed him.[181] As early as 16 March Clarence knew of the Cromer landing and he had news of Edward's invasion of Yorkshire by 23 March. Assembling his forces, Clarence marched northwards: he was at Malmesbury (Wilts.) on 30 March and at Burford (Oxon.) on 2 April. On his arrival at Coventry he led a force of over four thousand men. As Montagu was also advancing on Coventry, Henry VI's supporters had a clear numerical superiority, but had to combine their forces to exploit it fully.

This did not happen, because Clarence joined the army of Edward, not that of Warwick. The meeting of Clarence with Edward and Gloucester was marked by formal reconciliation and public rejoicing. Even though Edward failed to stop Exeter, Montagu, Oxford and Beaumont from joining Warwick at Coventry, Clarence's defection had destroyed their numerical advantage, so they declined to fight. Clarence meanwhile used his influence with both Edward and Warwick to try to arrange terms. Although successful in extracting a more favourable offer from Edward than originally envisaged, there was no agreement, according to *The Arrivall* because of Warwick's intransigence.[182] This was a serious rebuff for Clarence.

Since Warwick would not fight, Edward marched on London. Warwick counted on it being held against him, but the Lancastrians Somerset and Devon had left it almost denuded of men. A procession by Henry VI, Archbishop Neville and Lord Sudeley failed to rally the citizens, who admitted Edward and his army. He immediately took firm control and placed Henry and his ministers in custody. Oxford and the other magnates had stripped the surrounding region of their supporters, so there was nothing to stop other lords from joining Edward. He was already accompanied by Gloucester and Clarence, Earl Rivers, Lords Hastings, Say and Duras and perhaps by Lords Dudley and Grey of Codnor. He was now joined by his former chancellor, treasurer and keeper of his privy seal, respectively Bishops of Bath, Ely and Rochester; by the whole Bourchier-Stafford-Blount connection, namely Cardinal

Bourchier, the Earls of Essex and Wiltshire, Lords Berners, Cromwell and Mountjoy, Sir Henry Stafford and the heirs of Essex and Berners; by the heirs of the Earls of Arundel and Kent, each married to sisters of Queen Elizabeth; and by the Duke of Norfolk and Lord Howard.[183] It was an impressive turnout.

Warwick meantime followed at a distance from Coventry, apparently hoping to trap Edward between his own army and London. When London fell, he took up a defensive position astride the Great North Road north of Barnet (Herts.). Edward again took the initiative, marching out of London with his brothers and other supporters and drawing up his forces in front of Warwick's position during the evening of 13 April. Very early next morning, in a mist and before it was fully light, Edward launched his attack. The battle of Barnet was a hard fought and thoroughly confused affair, partly because of the poor visibility and partly because the two armies were not exactly aligned: for this reason Oxford came to blows with other Lancastrian units. Although probably at a numerical disadvantage, the Yorkists were victorious: Warwick and Montagu were killed and their forces were dispersed.

Although Somerset, Dorset and Devon knew of the crisis, they lent no support: it was the army of Coventry that fought at Barnet. Most of those indicted, pardoned or summoned after the battle are of uncertain affiliations: lesser men without fixed loyalties or recruited by commissions of array. About twenty came from Warwick's manors of Brailes (Warw.), Dartford (Kent), Collyweston (Northants.), Hanslope, Newport Pagnell (Bucks.), Ware, Bushey, Flamstead (Herts.) or their immediate environs. Others are familiar from earlier rebellions.[184] Wholly absent are the Calais and Cinque Port contingents, who rose too late, and the northerners, who never rose at all. The only known northerners, such as Sir John Malliverer and John Trygot of Wressle (Yorks.), were Montagu's personal retainers.[185] A substantial group from Lincolnshire, presumably recruited by Lord Beaumont, included some of Clarence's erstwhile associates,[186] the de Vere brothers and John Paston served with Oxford, but others could have accompanied any of the magnates.

Somerset and Devon left London in March on their way to meet Queen Margaret and raised an army in the West Country on the basis of their Beaufort and Courtenay retainers. Jasper Tudor, Earl of Pembroke was in Wales and there was potential support in Lancashire and Cheshire. Margaret needed to combine her resources to improve her chances against Edward, but this she was not permitted to do. Her army was probably still smaller than Edward's when he advanced through the Cotswolds to Malmesbury (Wilts.). She moved from Bristol to Sodbury, apparently intending to meet him in battle, but instead hurried northwards, aiming to cross the Severn and join Pembroke in Wales. When Edward thwarted her by securing the river crossing at Gloucester, she was forced to march up river to Tewkesbury, the next crossing, where she was brought to battle. Her Lancastrian army occupied a strong position in a ruined castle on top of a hill, up which Edward made a frontal assault. When Somerset's Lancastrian vanguard advanced down the hill, it exposed itself to attack from several directions, enabling the Yorkists to roll up each Lancastrian division in turn. Margaret was captured, her army was destroyed and all the Lancastrian commanders were killed or captured, including Prince Edward, Somerset, Dorset, Wenlock and the Prior of St. John.[187] With Henry VI's death soon after in the Tower, the main lines of the houses of Lancaster and Beaufort were extinct.

The Readeption had enjoyed the military support of the Dukes of Somerset and Exeter, the Marquis Montagu, the Earls of Devon, Dorset, Pembroke, Oxford and Warwick, Viscount Beaumont, and Lords St. John, Wenlock and Camoys.[188] Of those who had helped restore Henry VI, Clarence, Shrewsbury, Stanley, FitzHugh and Scrope had withdrawn their support; no former Lancastrians had returned to the fold and nobody had defected from Edward IV. On Edward's return to London, he was accompanied by five dukes, six earls and thirteen barons,[189] most of whom had probably fought at Tewkesbury. Lords Say and Cromwell had been killed at Barnet and other peers participated in the Kentish campaign against Thomas Neville, Bastard of Fauconberg. From this it is clear that almost the whole peerage, certainly all the greater magnates, were actively involved in the 1471 campaign. Edward's army had a strong family tinge, as it included both his brothers, his brother-in-law Suffolk, Earl Rivers and the husbands of five of the Wydeville sisters. It was not merely a faction: there were others without court connections, such as Norfolk and Cobham. Clearly Edward enjoyed the general support of the peerage and, with the annihilation of his opponents, his position was stronger than ever before. Furthermore the birth during the Readeption of his son Edward, the future Edward V, placed the succession beyond doubt and removed any lingering hopes of the throne that Clarence might still harbour. Clarence was among those who swore allegiance to the boy on 3 July,[190] recognising him thereby as heir to the throne.

Chapter III

Clarence, Gloucester and Edward IV 1471-5

1. Clarence, Gloucester and the 'Warwick Inheritance' 1471-3

In 1471 Clarence was reconciled with King Edward by the mediation of his mother and other members of the house of York, who guaranteed his future. It was agreed that Clarence should desert Henry VI and adhere again to his brother. In return Edward received him into his allegiance and restored all his former possessions to him. Obviously Edward could not forget all that had happened in the previous two years, but he seems to have sincerely tried to forgive. Clarence enjoyed his trust and Edward made a conscious effort to consult him. He was even allowed to negotiate with Warwick and to mediate between him and the king: understandably he wanted to save his father-in-law, if he could. As *The Arrivall* says, Clarence was

> 'right desyrows to have procuryd a goode accorde betwyxt the Kynge and th'Erle of Warwyke . . . The Kynge, at th'ynstaunce of his sayd brothar . . . was content to shew hym [Warwick] largly his grace, with dyvars good condicions, and profitable for th'Erle' . . .[1]

The terms that the official chronicler considered good proved unacceptable to Warwick. Edward may well have framed them with this in mind: he can hardly have supposed that any compromise could be lasting or genuine. But he listened to Clarence's advice and let him have his way.

Relatively few of those defeated in 1471 suffered forfeiture of their estates. Members of the royal family were heirs to several of them and would suffer if they were condemned. Consequently these escaped attainder and their immunity protected some of the smaller fry.[2] But this element of self-interest should not be exaggerated. Some of those captured at Tewkesbury were spared and there was a general pardon. At least some owed Edward's forgiveness to Clarence's intercession. The city of Bristol petitioned for 'his good and gracious lordschipp to be schewyd un to the Kyng oure Soveraigne lordis highnesse For his goode Grace to be hadd'. *The Arrivall* states that he tried 'to reconsyle . . . unto the Kyngs good grace many lordes and noble men of his land, of whom many had largely taken part with th'Erle',[3] and ascribed this conciliatory approach to a desire to avoid bloodshed, but Clarence was primarily anxious that his followers should escape punishment for acts committed in his service. He also needed to protect Warwick's retainers, if he was to enjoy their loyal service as Warwick's heir. He was obliged to exercise his influence in their interest as their lord.

In the same way he had sued for Edward's pardon in 1470 not only for himself, but also for the participants in his rebellion. At that time Edward had refused: negotiations with subjects were derogatory to his royal dignity. Necessity had made him renounce this principle in 1471 with reference to Clarence and his immediate adherents. After his decisive victory at Tewkesbury, Edward could afford to be lenient towards the Lancastrians. With the destruction of Henry VI, Prince Edward and the Beauforts, the Lancastrians had no further reason for resistance: their cause was dead. Among those who submitted to Edward were Sir John Fortescue, the chancellor in exile, Master Ralph Mackerell, Queen Margaret's chancellor, and Sir Richard Tunstall, Henry VI's chamberlain. He admitted them to his grace, their attainders were reversed, and their possessions were restored. Similarly the Neville faction ceased to be dangerous with Warwick's death. Instead of executing the Kentish rebels, Edward preferred fines. He could even afford to trust his former enemies and draw them into his service: Lord Stanley became steward of his household and Master John Morton, the future cardinal, became master of the rolls.[4]

Edward's readiness to forgive and reluctance to condemn meant that there were few forfeitures for him to give away. Most of the Lancastrians were already attainted: their estates merely reverted to those, who had been given them before. Some, however, were restored to Lancastrians when their sentences were reversed, to the loss of the grantees. Edward's own priorities were to provide for his son Prince Edward and his brother of Gloucester. Prince Edward's endowment meant loss for some — among them Clarence and the Herberts — but was relatively straightforward. He had more difficulty in providing for Gloucester and very little was left for anyone else: the Wydevilles, for example, went without any reward. True, the great offices of the Nevilles were distributed: thus Clarence added the great chamberlainship of England to the lieutenantcy of Ireland; Gloucester, already constable, became admiral of England, warden of the West March, and chief forester north of Trent; and other offices passed to Hastings, Arundel, Essex and Wiltshire.[5] But these offices did not stretch far and were poor substitute for land. Clear though their claims on his generosity were, few who had shared Edward's exile and victories received anything. Those who were dissatisfied were naturally jealous of Clarence.

He was immediately restored to his former eminence. So rapidly was he recognised as lieutenant of Ireland, that protections were issued in his name on 19 and 23 April 1471.[6] With the exception of the Gournay lands, all the estates he had held in 1470 were restored, even some lost during the Readeption. For those Percy lands surrendered in 1470 were substituted the Courtenay patrimony in Devon: a more than adequate exchange. Furthermore Edward promised that if Clarence or his heirs should ever be dispossessed by act of resumption or other means, they would be compensated in full.[7] He gave Clarence all those parts of Warwick's estates to which his duchess had any hereditary right. Taken together these acquisitions made Clarence into the wealthiest of contemporary magnates. When he petitioned to Edward for the cancellation of Gloucester's patent as great chamberlain of England, so he could be granted it himself, he received his desire.[8] Relations with Edward were so cordial that it seemed as if the king would refuse him nothing.

There seems to have been little contact between the Dukes of Clarence and Gloucester since 1464. Between 1469-71, when Clarence was repeatedly unfaithful, Gloucester was consistently loyal. They were formally reconciled in 1471. As a result of Clarence's machinations, Gloucester had been driven into exile and perhaps attainted, and therefore possessed a genuine grievance. To instil cordiality into their relations, Clarence needed to act in a conciliatory fashion, but this he did not do. Instead he opposed

Gloucester's interests. Unlike himself, Gloucester had never been adequately endowed, yet Clarence competed with him for patronage and secured the most important grants. Far from being friendly, he persuaded Edward to make Gloucester disgorge one of his offices.[9] Not surprisingly Gloucester was jealous of the lavish favour bestowed on his brother in reward for less devoted service. When their interests conflicted, Gloucester was not restrained by any brotherly affection and acted with ruthless disregard of Clarence. Their quarrel arose over the Warwick inheritance.

Had Warwick died a natural death, his vast inheritance would have been divided three ways: the Neville patrimony itself, entailed in the male line, would have passed to Warwick's brother John, Marquis Montagu and the latter's son George, Duke of Bedford; the rest would have descended to his daughters Anne and Isabel, Duchess of Clarence, to be divided equally between them. But both Warwick and Montagu fell in battle against the king and thus incurred the penalties of treason, including confiscation of their estates. An oyer and terminer commission indicted them posthumously of treason.[10] Such forfeitures took effect even without confirmation in parliament. The whole inheritance thus belonged to the king: Warwick's daughters and nephew were disinherited.

Such a vast windfall was attractive to the king, but he could not exact his full legal rights. Clarence was helping him recover his throne: he could hardly respond by depriving him of his wife's inheritance. Perhaps some provision for this eventuality had been made at their reconciliation; certainly Edward could not afford to alienate Clarence again before the war was won. Accordingly, he granted him all those lands to which his wife had hereditary expectations: the whole of what would otherwise have been divided between the two sisters, or double Isabel's natural share. She had never had any claim to the Neville patrimony, so Edward granted it to Gloucester.

This meant that the estates had not been inherited by the Duchess of Clarence. All had been forfeited and had been given by Edward to his brothers. This enabled them to set aside the entitlement of Warwick's countess to a third share of the Salisbury and Neville estates in dower. It took no account of the fact that her jointure and the Beauchamp and Despenser lands, together quite half the total, were her property, not Warwick's: they could not be forfeited by his treason, but only by her own. The title of the royal dukes was thus extremely shaky, as she pointed out in repeated petitions to them and others about the king. For the moment, however, she could be ignored.

Warwick's other daughter Anne was youthful widow of Edward, Prince of Wales, son of Henry VI. She was also a minor in Clarence's custody. In view of her claims to his estate, he had good reason to keep her single. Gloucester, however, abducted her, apparently with the intention of marrying her. They were well acquainted, for he had lived with her father during the fourteen-sixties, but it was obviously not her person but her property that attracted him. He hoped to secure a half share of the tail general estates, in addition to the tail male estates that he already held.

What Gloucester wanted was a legal impossibility. Anne could only inherit the Salisbury estates if Warwick avoided forfeiture. Could this be arranged, they would be encumbered by the dower and jointure of her mother and the Neville lands would pass to George, Duke of Bedford. This eventuality could be averted by attainting Montagu, but as he was less guilty than Warwick, this was an affront to natural justice. Anne could only inherit her mother's estates when she was dead, not while she was living, but Gloucester wanted immediate seisin. He could not have it all ways.

Moreover Gloucester was defying canon as well as common law. To enjoy Anne's inheritance he must marry her. They were related several times over within the prohibited degrees, so this might be impracticable. Clarence was cousin of Isabel Neville, who was his mother's godchild: it had been difficult to obtain their dispensation. Their marriage itself constituted an additional impediment in Gloucester's case. The refusal of a dispensation was predictable. In 1474 it was agreed that, should the marriage be declared void, Gloucester would keep Anne's estates. Any offspring would then have been illegitimate.

Clarence's anger at Gloucester's attempt to disturb the settlement was perfectly understandable. He had been given lands in return for services rendered; he had entered and enjoyed them; he was bound to lose heavily if Gloucester had his way. Besides, his title was based on a royal grant, against which no hereditary claim was valid. Gloucester had no legitimate interest in Anne's inheritance until he had contracted a legal marriage with her. Clarence's case was perfectly logical; Gloucester's so hopelessly illogical, that the conflicting elements could only be reconciled with royal support.

Edward could force Clarence to disgorge, either by making him surrender his patent or through an act of resumption. Understandably Gloucester appealed to Edward, who responded favourably. His gift to Clarence had undoubtedly been influenced by Isabel's hereditary expectations, so it was not difficult for him to take those into account. Partition of the estates would enable him to provide for Gloucester at no cost to himself. For Edward these considerations evidently outweighed the quarrel with Clarence that irrevocably followed. Presumably he calculated, rightly, that Clarence no longer represented any threat to him. But why was he willing to permanently sour their relations?

The chronology of the Croyland chronicle is hazy, largely because it glosses over the various stages of the dispute. The first stage reached a head in February 1472. On 17 February John Paston II wrote to John Paston III:

> 'Yisterdaye the Kynge, the Qween, my lordes off Claraunce and Glowcester wente to Scheen to pardon, men sey nott alle in charyte. What wyll falle men can nott seye. The Kynge entretyth my lorde off Clarance for my lord off Glowcester, and as itt is seyde he answerythe that he maye weell haue my ladye hys suster in lawe, butt they schall parte no lyvelod, as he seythe'.[11]

During these discussions Clarence conceded both points. A warrant executed on 18 March reveals that a partition had been agreed and that Clarence had given up some lands, receiving greater security in others. He was also created Earl of Warwick and Salisbury and granted four manors, two parks and a messuage in London. Taken together these documents reveal that the whole inheritance was to be divided, leaving Clarence with lands in the West Country and West Midlands. The tail male estates granted to Gloucester were included in the new settlement, which indicates that Gloucester's case was not accepted without reservation. One can only speculate whether Edward as arbiter sought to allay bitterness and prevent perpetual enmity.

Clarence capitulated to political pressure. A warrant of 18 March, which guaranteed compensation to him and his heirs in the event of future losses of land, refers specifically to the Courtenay estates and to acts of resumption: an indication that he was threatened with the resumption of his estates, which posed a choice between rebellion and submission. The ultimatum enjoyed powerful backing. Queen Elizabeth attended the conference. She was back in London by 23 February, when she renewed a grant to Gloucester of a stewardship carrying £100 a year in fees: a sign that he enjoyed her support. Wydeville hostility towards Clarence probably persisted in spite of their formal reconciliation: litigation certainly did. In response Clarence appointed the king's chamberlain, Lord Hastings, to key offices on his estates on 20 March, in spite of differences on national and local affairs. Evidently recent events had convinced him of the urgent necessity of strengthening his influence with Edward. He hoped to achieve this by gaining the support of those around him, of whom Hastings was outstanding. Although the Croyland chronicle refers to a debate in council, it indicates that the dispute was highly personal.[12] No committee or council could threaten the king's brother in this way without the king's direct instructions: the warrants were authenticated not by the council, but by Edward's own signature.[13]

Gloucester's marriage to Anne Neville, already decided by 18 March, was probably concluded soon after, even though no dispensation was to arrive for at least two years. Only the principle of division was resolved, not the detailed partition, and it had probably not been resolved how to make it stand up in law. Certain lands were surrendered by Gloucester to Clarence, who apparently did not reciprocate. He had good reason to delay: should Gloucester fail to obtain a dispensation, he might not have to surrender anything. Such Fabian tactics contributed to a gradual deterioration in the brothers's relations.

In the short run Clarence's submission resulted in his return to favour. Some of the lands given him had been held by Warwick by royal grant and not hereditary right. Their grant to Clarence was a generous gesture of re-assurance and a reward for obedience. In March Clarence's term as lieutenant of Ireland was extended for a further twenty years, even though his previous commission still had two years to run. On 7 April he and his retainers were granted the custody of lands in Somerset, in spite of the opposition of the Herberts. Clarence also attended the celebrations surrounding the creation of the Burgundian Lord Gruthuyse as Earl of Winchester at the opening of parliament in October 1472. The speaker complimented him on his part in securing Edward's restoration and the king himself nominated him a trier of English petitions.[14]

It was not until the summer of 1473 that the dispute of the two dukes broke out afresh. On 3 June 1473 Sir John Paston informed John Paston III

> 'that the Countesse off Warwyk is now owt of Beweley seyntwarye, and Syr James Tyrell conveyth hyre northwarde, men seye by the Kynges assent, wherto som men seye that the Duke of Clarence is not agreyd'.[15]

His opposition was predictable. Her release endangered the 1472 settlement and threatened to dispossess him of his wife's estates in Gloucester's favour. A rumour to this effect was indeed reported on 1 June:

> 'Sir also the king hath restored the countes of Warwick to all hir inheritaunce, and she have graunted itt unto my lord of Glowceter with whom she is'.[16]

Both correspondents agree that Edward favoured Gloucester. Her inheritance had been mainly held by Clarence in 1471-2, so it seems that he retained lands provisionally allocated to his brother. This is supported by the resemblance of the ultimate partition to that projected in 1472 and by Clarence's subsequent surrender of lands to Gloucester. In February 1474 the Milanese ambassador to France summarised the trouble in these terms: Gloucester, he added, 'was constantly preparing for war with the Duke of Clarence'.[17]

The removal of the countess from sanctuary failed to bring Clarence to heel. Instead he was reported on 6 November to be preparing to 'dele wyth' Gloucester, while Edward tried to restrain him. Sixteen days later Sir John Paston trusted in God that the king would arbitrate the dispute.[18] Eventually he did.

Sir John was not satisfied that Clarence's conduct was adequately explained by a dispute over land. Several times he voiced suspicions that there was more to it than this, namely treason. His fears have been accepted by Miss Scofield and other modern historians.[19] What justification is there for this charge?

2. Clarence and Treason 1471-3

Sir John Paston's own letters are the main source connecting Clarence and the seditious movements of the early 1470s. Sir John wrote fully and reliably on matters with which he was acquainted — family business, for example. He was well placed in London to collect political news and particularly that relating to the royal dukes, whom he knew personally: both had supported his family against the Duke of Norfolk in 1469; Clarence and William Paston, Sir John's uncle, were associated as litigants; Sir John's brother Edmund served in Gloucester's retinue in France in 1475, perhaps evidence of a more permanent tie.[20] He was thus likely to be well-informed about the dukes's quarrel. As prospective husband to Anne Haute, he may also have known the views of her Wydeville kindred. A former associate of the traitor Earl of Oxford, who tried to base his conspiracy on his old connection, it is probable that he could follow developments accurately. His letters show that he did.

But when he connects Clarence with treason he is less explicit and has no concrete information. The comment in his letter of 6 November is a mere inference from his speculation about the nature of the quarrel: 'som men thynke that vndre thys ther sholde be som other thynge entendyd and som treason conspyred, so what shall falle can I nott seye'.[21] Regarding his letter of 3 June 1473, Miss Scofield discerned in the confused ordering of events the belief that Clarence and Oxford were in collusion, but this is not what he says. Miss Scofield rightly remarked that 'Paston's meaning is not always as clear as could be wished'.[22] This may be because he lacked reliable information. It is not that he was less interested, but that his sources were less circumstantial. This is not surprising, as treason requires secrecy, but it renders Sir John a defective witness.

Other contemporary observers, the Milanese ambassadors, were hampered because they were not resident in England but in France or Burgundy. For information on English affairs they relied on the reports of chance travellers and the disclosures, often biased and selective, of the potentates to whom they were accredited. When Aliprandro warned that Edward might be overthrown, he added that 'certainly things are doubtful and changeable in that realm, owing to its nature and for reasons that it would take too long to write': not the words of a well-informed man. He was writing on 25 November 1472, six months before Oxford's expedition. Bollati wrote on 6 July 1473 that Oxford had sent King Louis the seals of twenty-four lords and knights, who had pledged their troth, including one unnamed duke. If the story is true, this may just as well refer to Exeter as Clarence; but Louis thought that the seals were counterfeit, forged by Oxford to extract further support from France.[23] Nothing else known about Oxford's activities suggest that he enjoyed significant independent support.

George Neville, Archbishop of York still hoped for a rising to depose Edward. In March 1472, at le More (Herts.), he discussed it with his household officials and receiver-general. A month later he was arrested and imprisoned, first in the Tower, later at Hammes by Calais.[24] He was still there during Oxford's expedition. There is no evidence that their plots were connected, although they were brothers-in-law and closely related to Warwick. European observers assumed that the basis of any disturbance must be the disgruntled remnant of Warwick's connection,[25] to which Clarence himself belonged, but there is no suggestion that they would make Clarence king. There was no longer a credible Lancastrian claimant. Louis was content to use Oxford to harrass Edward and prevent him from invading France. There seems to have been no concrete plan of action in the unlikely event of success. In 1471 *The Arrivall* singled Oxford out as irreconcilable,[26] perhaps ultimately because of the execution of his father and brother in 1462. The same desperate hostility apparently marked him, the archbishop and their motley supporters.

On 14 July 1474 fourteen men were pardoned treasons, insurrections and other offences. These were Oxford's adherents in 1473. Apart from two Welshmen and one man each from the counties of Worcester, Wiltshire, Lincoln and Cambridge and from London, all were natives of Essex, most of them from Oxford's own estates. Some must have joined him during his landings in Essex and the south-west, others had shared his exiles: these included his two brothers, the Lancastrian Viscount Beaumont, and Sir Thomas Clifford.[27] Oxford does not seem to have discovered new sources of support.

Clarence held few manors in Essex, but he was a major landowner in the south-western counties. Yet on Oxford's arrival in the West Country, he received no support from Clarence or anyone else. He was besieged at St. Michael's Mount, though not sufficiently closely to starve him out. Nothing that King Edward did before or after the siege points to the involvement of Clarence or his retainers. One native of the duke's manor of Hanley (Worcs.), one John Hanley, was among those pardoned,[28] but there is no evidence of any other connection between him and the duke.

Edward delegated the task of suppression to others. Oxford was besieged in turn by Sir Henry Bodrugan and by John Fortescue, an esquire of the household. Edward evidently regarded this as sufficient to cope with the earl. His confidence was justified by the capitulation of the Mount the following winter.[29] Apparently he did not fear any substantial reinforcement for Oxford from within the realm.

This is significant. For Edward was acting in a manner that would surely have driven Clarence into Oxford's arms, if any understanding had existed between them. He had already authorised the release of the Countess of Warwick by 1 June 1473 and let her take refuge with Gloucester. This endangered Clarence's hold on his wife's inheritance. Then, in December, he refused to exempt him from an act of resumption, which destroyed his title to all his lands. Once again Clarence had to choose between rebellion or submission on whatever terms Edward chose. Again he submitted. It is reasonable to deduce that he had no understanding with Oxford; that Edward was confident that drastic measures would not cause him to rebel; and that he therefore did not regard his brother and Oxford as accomplices.

Arguments from negative evidence are speculative, but hardly more so than those based on the doubts and suspicions of Sir John Paston. Why, if Paston's reports were accurate, did not Oxford's presence lead to full scale rebellion? Records do not support Sir John's fears. In times of disorder the characteristic reaction of King Edward's government was to issue commissions of oyer and terminer. This occasion was no exception, but none of the resultant proceedings implicate Clarence or his retainers in insurrection or treason.

Chronicles are equally uninformative. No contemporary annalist links the duke with treason during these years. In particular, the well-informed Croyland chronicle describes the quarrel of the royal dukes without hinting at treason.[30] Historians have been unduly influenced by the duke's later execution as a traitor. His indictment, the act of attainder, portrays him as an incorrigible plotter without referring to any treason in these years. He was probably innocent of treason in 1473.

The arms which Clarence acquired were apparently intended for use against Gloucester. There is no evidence whether either duke did resort to force. Doubtless Edward endeavoured to restrain them, but it is not clear whether he gave their quarrel priority among his problems. Throughout the summer of 1473 he was at hand to cope with it, but it did not absorb his full attention.

In 1471 King Edward had created his newborn son Edward,

Prince of Wales, Duke of Cornwall and Earl of Chester, and had appointed a council to manage his affairs. Late in 1472 he decided to strengthen royal control of Wales. Following precedent, the prince's household was to be established in Wales and was to be financed by the issues of his estates, which were granted to him in November. An enlarged council nominated on 20 February 1473 was to be responsible for the principality of Wales, for Chester and for any marcher lordships in the hands of the crown. Councillors were appointed to the border commissions of the peace. In the rest of the marches, where his writ did not run and he had no authority to delegate, Edward sought the co-operation of the independent lords.[31]

The queen and prince were at Ludlow on 30 April 1473.[32] In March and April a judicial commission was active in the borders, headed by Earl Rivers and Lord Ferrers of Chartley. Edward himself arrived in the early summer and held a conference of marcher lords at Shrewsbury on 3 June. With their assent, he made ordinances for the restoration of law and order. Each lord agreed with the king to implement them. They could have been pressurised through the lands they held elsewhere, but probably this was unnecessary. Their independence was temporarily restricted, but the indentures did not represent a dangerous precedent, as Edward acted not as king but as Earl of March.[33] They were otherwise in the interests of the lords, several of whom were councillors. Among those certainly present were the Duke of Buckingham, the Earl of Shrewsbury, Lord Strange of Knockin and Lord Maltravers, heir of the Earl of Arundel.[34] After the conference the prince's authority was firmly established. Queen Elizabeth remained after Edward's departure until at least September: her second son Richard was born at Shrewsbury on 17 August.[35]

Parliament had been prorogued on 8 April. Before going to Wales, Edward went to Nottingham, where he held a council on 12 May. It arbitrated the dispute between the Duke of Gloucester and the Earl of Northumberland, deciding in the latter's favour.[36] This quarrel and the disorder in Wales partly explain why Edward lingered in the Midlands throughout the summer of 1473. He was in easy reach of Clarence's Tutbury and Warwick estates, not far from Gloucester's lands in Yorkshire, ready to prevent conflict. He was well accompanied to enforce order. At various times — perhaps continuously — he was attended by his chamberlain and steward, by Gloucester and Shrewsbury, and by the queen's connection. Apart from Elizabeth herself, these included her brother Rivers, her brothers-in-law Buckingham and Maltravers, and Dacre of the South and Ferrers of Chartley.[37] Rivers was collecting arms. The Wydevilles were hostile to Clarence, so it is not surprising that Gloucester was allowed to seize the Countess of Warwick during the Shrewsbury conference. This conference was evidently ignored by Clarence, himself an important Welsh magnate as lord of Glamorgan and Abergavenny. His failure to co-operate may have reinforced Elizabeth's support for Gloucester. The council of Wales was to be dominated by her family and would provide them with a new power-base. There were obvious advantages in transferring the disputed lordships to the more amenable of the two brothers.

3. Clarence and the King 1473-75

Clarence was not exempted from the act of resumption of December 1473. This was observed by Dr. Gairdner in 1898 and by later writers, including Miss Scofield and Professor Kendall, but its significance has not been appreciated. Miss Scofield merely mentioned it. Dr. Gairdner believed that Clarence's excessive pride prevented him from seeking a proviso of exemption in his favour. Kendall saw it as a purely accidental complication.[38] Their views were influenced by the belief that Yorkist government was inefficient, which has recently been discounted. Modern historians have begun to look behind events for common aims and royal policies. Professor Lander connected the 1475 act of attainder to divisions in the royal family, particularly between Clarence and Gloucester. Dr. Wolffe placed the resumption in the context of the Readeption and Clarence's continuing sedition. For him this act had two functions:

> 'to undo the considerable rearrangements of crown lands and revenues which the advisers of Henry VI managed to effect in the short six months of his Readeption, and, with parliamentary authority, peacefully to curb the power of George duke of Clarence, who, a traitor to his royal brother, had been intimately concerned in those rearrangements'.

He observed that the inheritance dispute and resumption coincided in time and he linked them in a description of royal policy:

> 'While stubbornly hanging on to all the king had given him he [Clarence] was at the same time avidly pursuing every scrap of the vast Warwick inheritance, in spite of the king's great anger'.[39]

There are errors in this analysis, which is hardly surprising since Dr. Wolffe was writing a history of royal landholding rather than a political history, but it is a starting point for an examination of resumption and partition as aspects of the same royal policy.

Exemption from acts of resumption required the express consent of the king, who personally signed every proviso. It follows that the absence of a proviso for Clarence resulted from a deliberate decision by Edward himself. There is certainly no indication that Clarence was too proud to seek one: he had obtained others for acts of the same parliament and most of his patents originated as petitions.[40]

The obvious stimulus for Edward's action was the feud between his brothers. The release of the Countess of Warwick from sanctuary had threatened Clarence with the loss of his estates. Doubtless Edward had expected this to bring him to heel. When it did not, Edward was unwilling to implement the threat: why one cannot be sure. Most probably the countess would not surrender her estates to Gloucester, who had yet to marry her daughter. Such difficulties were predictable: perhaps Clarence had foreseen them and called his brothers's bluff. Edward, however, was not nonplussed; instead he introduced a bill of resumption into parliament, which quickly became law. Almost everybody except Clarence was exempted from it. This deprived Clarence of all his estates, not just the Warwick inheritance, as all his lands were held by royal patent. It was not even necessary for his exemption to be considered in parliament, where he was well-represented. Simply by denying a proviso, Edward deprived him of his lands. Dispossessed entirely and without a case at law, Clarence was again faced by a choice of rebellion or submission.

As he did not rebel, subsequent events are the fruit of his submission. In May 1474 an act of parliament authorised both dukes to acquire the lands of the Countess of Warwick as their wives's inheritance and to divide them, as if the countess had died. This gave force of law to the 1472 settlement, which had first given Gloucester a share in her estates. It protected both dukes from future acts of resumption and restored Clarence's title in those estates to be allocated to him. Both dukes must have already accepted an outline agreement and probably the transfer of lands to Gloucester had begun. The act of resumption was used to settle the division of the inheritance.

The next stage followed in July. A final indenture of partition, containing full details of the lands assigned to each duke, was drawn up on 20 July. Seisin had probably been transferred already. On 18 July Clarence was granted the bulk of his former estates. This was in response to a petition, but the initiative certainly came from Edward and the lists were settled by prior consultation. What Clarence should lose and what he should keep was already determined by March 1474.[41]

The final stage of the agreement, not completed until 1475, excluded the heirs of the Marquis Montagu from the Neville lands in favour of the two dukes. A result of this was the exclusion of Warwick and Montagu from attainder with other rebels of 1471. Probably no lands changed hands at this stage: the dukes's titles were merely confirmed in those they already held. The logical corollary of submission was to accept resumption in the localities, but Dr. Wolffe believes that Clarence resisted this process.

Wolffe refers to difficulties encountered in collecting the issues of resumed lands. His specific example of the Gournay lands[42] is inapplicable, as Clarence had not held them since at least 1471. Elsewhere he is probably right that little was collected, but this was not due to Clarence's resistance. Before collecting the revenues from resumed lands, Edward had to discover which they were, and for this purpose sheriffs in every county prepared inquisitions. These accurately describe Clarence's property. But writs authorising them were only issued on 12 July — a mere week before Clarence's recovery of most of his estates — and the inquisitions were held even later. Few of these lands can have left Clarence's hands. As Edward also granted him the issues from 21 December 1473 to the new patent,[43] nothing was due from them to the king and nothing should have been paid.

However, some duchy of Lancaster and crown lands in the four counties of Stafford, Derby, Nottingham and Leicester were permanently resumed and of course the issues of these should have been paid to the king. Apparently they were. One of Edward's receiver-generals dated his account from Michaelmas 1473, before the resumption took effect, and another succeeded in collecting two-thirds of the usual revenues from over forty ministers by Michaelmas 1474.[44] The rest may have been collected next year. Apparently nothing was paid to Clarence. Edward himself visited the area between 30 March and 2 April 1474, staying at Burton Abbey. Then and in the following months he issued three commissions and made twenty-four appointments. In spite of this apparent upheaval, there were relatively few changes: many of his acts merely modified old grants, substituting annuities for offices; others apparently confirmed Clarence's nominees in office.[45] This continuity in office demonstrates that Edward had no need to crush resistance. Altogether it cost a commission less than five pounds to recover the Tutbury estates.[46]

Edward had been prepared for resistance, issuing a commission on 9 January 1474 with powers to expel Clarence by force and take possession of the estates on his behalf. By confining its scope to the North Midlands,[47] however, he had given Clarence an incentive to submit, before the remainder of his lands were seized. Clarence had no real alternative but to submit, as he lacked allies among the magnates on whom he could count in rebellion or at the royal council. Shrewsbury was dead; the loyalty of Warwick's retainers was due to both daughters, not just Isabel; and Hastings could not be expected to resist the king, especially as he was the principal beneficiary, succeeding to Clarence's power in the North Midlands. The Stafford-Bourchier-Blount connection was no longer an effective moderating force: several members had died and the young Duke of Buckingham, now of age, had married a Wydeville.

By submitting Clarence had to accept Edward's terms. Edward had no desire to destroy him — he still had to live with him — so he restricted his losses. Clarence had to give up some of his wife's inheritance, but not as much as had been feared, as the Neville lands were taken into account. The loss of the Welsh lordships was a blow to his prestige and purse rather than his power: there is no sign that they interested him or that he ever visited them. He kept those in the West Midlands and south. But Edward resumed lands worth £1,350 a year,[48] which had been a major element in Clarence's power, perhaps the most important: Tutbury had been his principal seat. It was Edward's intention to end this: perhaps partly to punish him; perhaps partly to prevent him from being too powerful, as lord of the West and North Midlands; perhaps partly to assign Hastings a sphere of influence, but this was secondary, as he was not granted the land but only the 'rule' for life.

Clarence was not ruined but remained one of the wealthiest English magnates. Gloucester failed to obtain all he wanted and had to accept certain terms that he disliked. Edward had wisely arbitrated the dispute with moderation, hoping to appease Clarence and avoid giving him grievances that might make him an intolerable nuisance in the future. Even so Clarence grudged the loss of Tutbury, which had been freely given to him, had not been disputed, and had meant so much to him.

Edward gave Clarence a few minor estates to round off existing holdings and occasional marks of favour. He was godfather to Clarence's heir, gave him his name and created him Earl of Warwick. In 1475 Clarence was allowed to alienate lands in mortmain to Tewkesbury Abbey and was among the founders of a chapel at Ashwell (Herts.) in 1476. He obtained numerous writs to the exchequer concerning income due from York and was pardoned offences relating to his wife's inheritance and any debts due.[49] These minor concessions may reflect Edward's affection, but there is no sign that Edward trusted him on more important issues.

Clarence had submitted only when the sole alternative was ruin. Such grudging obedience gave Edward little pleasure and did nothing to restore his confidence in him. After the 1472 settlement, Edward had appointed Clarence as lieutenant of Ireland for twenty years,[50] a notable sign of favour. Clarence had exercised the office, directing warrants for safeconduct to the chancellor and filling offices with his nominees. This ceased in August 1474. On 2 August Edward appointed Sir Gilbert Debenham as chancellor of Ireland 'by the advice, assent and consent of our most dear brother'. He employed a similar formula in appointing the master of the mint (11 August) and the steward of the liberty of Meath (21 August). On 2 August he appointed Thomas Danyell Lord of Rathwyre and on 13 August pardoned Marcel of Rome for offences committed in Ireland. The change was clearcut. Subsequent protections do not even mention Clarence by name, and the king even indented directly with subordinate officers. On some date before 22 August Edward indented with Clarence: the duke would retain the title of lieutenant, but all responsibilities and revenues would belong to Debenham.[51] Why was Clarence deprived of his powers as lieutenant? The situation in Ireland had deteriorated so much by 1473 that the Irish parliament had petitioned for military assistance, preferably under

Clarence's command. But 'it was thought to vs necessarie for the ease of oure said brother him not to labour in his owne persone into the said parties of Irland'.[52] Why then did he not nominate a deputy, the normal expedient, as he had done before? He can hardly have wished to deny himself the emoluments of office. Edward, however, preferred to relieve him of his authority. Possibly Clarence wanted to go personally. Clearly Edward would not trust Clarence in charge of any military expedition, directly or indirectly.

Meanwhile others were becoming more powerful, notably the queen's family in Wales and Gloucester in the north. Edward, it seems, wanted regional power to be divided, and was against its concentration in just a few hands. In practice, however, both Gloucester and the Wydevilles succeeded in dominating their neighbours. Recognising this, Edward gradually conceded other lands or powers to them.[53] As the Wydevilles and Gloucester became ever more powerful in their regions, Clarence was denied any governmental responsibility. His declining influence with Edward probably accounts for his infrequent attendance at council, referred to by the Croyland chronicler.[54] Gradually his distaste for Edward, who had broken his promises to him, grew. With no other outlet for his energies, he became increasingly pre-occupied with his local estates and power.

Chapter IV

Treason and Trial 1476-78

1. The Death of the Duchess of Clarence and its Consequences

On 22 December 1476 Isabel Neville, Duchess of Clarence died at Warwick at the age of twenty-five. Her body was removed for burial to Tewkesbury Abbey, the mausoleum of her Despenser ancestors. It was received there on 4 January 1477 by Abbot Strensham and other prelates. A service of nine lessons was conducted by suffragans of the Bishops of Worcester and Lincoln with the assistance of the dean and chaplains of Clarence's chapel. Members of his household stood vigil for a whole night. On the morrow the bishops and the abbot conducted three masses, one in honour of the Virgin Mary, a second for the Holy Trinity, and a Requiem mass. At the latter a Franciscan friar, Dr. Peter Webb, made an oration. The duchess's body lay in state in the middle of the choir until 25 January 1477, when it was placed in a vault newly constructed behind the high altar, where probably Clarence himself was later laid to rest. In the meantime masses were celebrated daily for the duchess's soul.[1]

Although he was not mentioned in the foregoing account, there can be little doubt that the Duke of Clarence was present. Perhaps he himself kept vigil. The chronicler seems awed by the magnificence and solemnity of Isabel's obsequies. It is probable that the marriage of the duke and duchess had been happy. In a period of seven years she had at least four pregnancies: there is no evidence that he was ever unfaithful to her. Six months later when he and their surviving children were admitted to the gild of the Holy Cross at Stratford-on-Avon (Warw.), she was enrolled posthumously:[2] perhaps this was a sign of his continuing sense of loss.

In 1474 the act of parliament governing the Duchess of

Clarence's brother Richard III. Copy, *c.*1590.

Clarence's sister Margaret of York, Duchess of Burgundy. Painted *c.*1525; part of a larger work and probably based on a lost original.

Clarence's estates had guaranteed Clarence possession of them for life. Her death therefore affected neither his power nor his wealth. But as heirs to their combined possessions Isabel left him only a son not yet two years of age and a daughter not yet four. Two other children had died in infancy.[3] In the circumstances of the fifteenth century it was likely that neither Edward nor Margaret would reach maturity. Clarence's awareness of this situation had prompted the changes made to the estates that he held in his own right. These had been granted to him and his male issue. In 1475 some were regranted to him and his heirs, thus making them heritable in the female line, and others were conveyed to trustees, who could settle them according to his command. His own estates were of equal value and importance to those of his duchess.

As Clarence was only twenty-seven in 1477, it was quite logical for him to contemplate a second marriage. He was unlikely to remain single for the rest of his life. The trust governing the bulk of his own estates ensured that he could provide for a second family even if his next wife was not an heiress. There were two factors that might be expected to influence his choice: the woman must be of childbearing age and of rank commensurate with his own. Neither requirement could be easily satisfied in the England of 1477. In fact there is no evidence that Clarence ever contemplated marriage to another Englishwoman. His rapid involvement in matrimonial intrigue, without even a decent interval for mourning, was perhaps initially the result of fortuitous circumstances and the promptings of others.

On 5 January 1477 Charles the Bold, Duke of Burgundy was killed in battle at Nancy. His heir was his only daughter Mary. She inherited the duchy and county of Burgundy and the majority of the provinces that now comprise the Netherlands and Belgium. Charles also left her at war with Louis XI of France and his allies, against whom her inheritance required defence. It was consequently expedient for Mary to marry at once someone capable of bringing to her defence substantial additional resources. Such a vital choice could not be made lightly.

Only two European powers, the Empire and England, could provide sufficient assistance. Although only recently bound by treaty to France, England had the more pressing motives to aid Mary. If Louis XI conquered all her inheritance, he would upset the diplomatic balance in his own favour. Almost all the coastline facing southern England would be in his hands. Calais would be endangered. The effects on English trade with the Netherlands of such a conquest, or even a prolonged war, would be serious. Moreover, in the late duke's widow, Margaret of York, there was a dynastic tie: it was natural for her to appeal to her brothers for help. To such concrete arguments can be added the traditional antipathy of the English for the French — a hostility shared by King Edward himself[4] — that less than two years previously had been expressed in an invasion of France.

Edward IV's alarmed reaction to Louis XI's attack on Burgundy was to call a great council, which met at Westminster on 13 February 1477. On 14 February Sir John Paston wrote to John Paston III:

> 'I suppose the cheffe cawse of thys assemble is to comon what is best to doo n[o]w vppon the greet change by the dethe off the Duke of Burgoyne, and for the kepyng off Caleys and the Marchys, and for the preseruacion off the amyteys taken late as weell wyth Fraunce as now wyth the membrys off Flaundrys; wher-to I dowt nott ther shall be jn all hast both the Dukys off Clarance and Glowcestre . . . Itt is so that thys daye I heer grett liklyhood that my Lorde Hastyngys shall hastely goo to Caleys wyth greet company'.

The selfsame day Sir John Paston had spoken with Lord Hastings, in whose garrison of Calais he expected to serve. He was also involved that day in negotiations concerning his prospective marriage to the queen's cousin Anne Haute.[5] It is therefore likely that his account reflects the views and desires of the king's chamberlain, of the Wydevilles, and perhaps also of the king's two brothers. Gloucester had previously revealed his enmity to France by refusing to be a party to the treaty of Picquigny. Such an attitude may have been prevalent in the council: it agrees with Philippe de Commines's general impression of English feeling at this time.[6] One cannot tell how well attended the council was, but, on the evidence of the Garter chapter of 17-19 February, it attracted a representative cross-section of English magnates. Clarence was certainly there and so were both archbishops, four bishops, two other dukes, the Marquis of Dorset, four earls and five barons:[7] the Duke of Gloucester and Earl Rivers were the principal absentees. The results of the council conflicted sharply with Sir John Paston's expectations. Probably they emanated from Edward IV's personal will rather than the advice tendered by the council.

For the council was followed not by military but by diplomatic activity. Edward IV used the war to bring pressure on Louis XI to modify or amplify the Picquigny settlement in England's favour. He also sought guarantees regarding the Duchess Margaret's jointure. He reinforced the Calais garrison, but for the purpose of defence alone.[8] The treaty of Picquigny had given him a French pension and the prospect of the marriage of his daughter Elizabeth of York to the dauphin Charles. For these gains he could apparently contemplate the conquest of Burgundy with equanimity.

One other fact may have caused Edward to abstain from helping his sister the Dowager-Duchess Margaret. She had suggested that Mary of Burgundy should marry their brother George, Duke of Clarence, whom she preferred to any of her kin.[9] This proposal may have been considered by the February council. The king opposed and thwarted it. It was probably dependent on military support that Edward refused to provide: but later in the year he was willing to supply such assistance in support of the bid by Earl Rivers for Mary's hand.[10] This lends credence to the statement of the Croyland chronicler that the king's opposition to the marriage was prompted by personal motives:

> 'So great a contemplated exaltation as this, however, of his ungrateful brother, displeased the king. He consequently threw all possible impediments in the way, in order that the match before-mentioned might not be carried into effect' . . .[11]

Edward's hostility to the marriage would be difficult to reconcile with support for Burgundy.

Edward's personal feelings were natural. So was his reluctance to sacrifice his daughter's marriage for that of his brother. But the marriage might have been to his advantage at home. No offspring of Clarence and Mary of Burgundy could have inherited the possesions of Isabel Neville: their claim to the crown would have been inferior to that of children of the first marriage.[12] Edward and Margaret would have become royal wards. As security for helping his brother, Edward might have demanded the custody of lands held in England, whatever the duke's title. It appears that Edward's hostility was due not only to policy but to their personal relationship, in which the king's distrust for Clarence was prominent. Apparently Louis XI hinted to Edward that Clarence sought Mary's hand with the ultimate intention of making himself King of England.[13] Whether one believes this or not, it indicates what sentiment those around Louis felt that he could exploit. Even after the breakdown of the marriage negotiations Edward may have feared some conspiracy between Clarence and the Duchess Margaret: in his attainder the duke was charged with the intention of sending his heir to Burgundy,[14] where, by implication, he would be received.

During this same period King James III of Scotland suggested that his sister Margaret should wed the Duke of Clarence. As England and Scotland were bound by treaty and the king's daughter Cecily was betrothed to the future James IV, this project did not conflict with English policy. King Edward declined it on the grounds that Clarence was still mourning his first wife and could not contemplate another.[15] It is difficult from this to envisage a marriage that Edward would have approved. Isabel Neville's death had introduced a new instability into relations between the brothers. These rapidly became acrimonious:

> 'The indignation of the duke was probably still further increased by this; and now each began to look upon the other with no very fraternal eyes'.[16]

Clarence's attitude is understandable. Either marriage was advantageous. As Mary's consort he would be a European power of the front rank and, moreover, removed from subjection to his unfriendly brother. Any designs he may have had on the English crown would certainly have been shelved while he attended to Mary's problems. Margaret of Scotland was Clarence's equal in birth and of childbearing age. Marriage to her would have been accompanied by a substantial cash dowry rather than lands, so Clarence would have continued to live in England. Instead Edward thwarted his every move. Their anger was fed by 'flatterers', who conveyed their angry remarks between them.[17] Yet it is not clear that their mutual distrust would have resulted in any further developments but for the execution of Thomas Burdet. The Croyland chronicler is the main source for the political background, while records in the court of King's Bench supply detail about the trial itself.[18] Both are contemporary, an advantage not shared by the account of the Tudor historian John Stow.[19] This conflicts with both other sources and must be rejected.

The trial resulted from a confession extracted under torture from Master John Stacy, in which he incriminated himself, Thomas

Blake and Thomas Burdet of imagining the king's death by sorcery. Both Stacy and Blake were attached to Merton College, Oxford, the former as a fellow and the latter as chaplain. They collaborated in the study of astronomy and metaphysics.[20] On 19 March 1473 the king granted an annuity of £40 to Stacy, then an acolyte, until he should provide him with a benefice of equal value. He accompanied Edward to France in 1475, for which he was paid £80 in reward and recompense.[21] These substantial sums were Edward's payment for unknown service on which he placed a high value, perhaps within his household. This would explain why Stacy's wife Marion was described as 'of London'.[22] In Easter 1473 Blake was acting as financial agent of Richard Fowler, chancellor of the duchy of Lancaster, when he paid money to the king in his chamber.[23] Each therefore had access to the king.

Thomas Burdet of Arrow (Warw.) fell into a different category. He was a prominent esquire with substantial lands in the West Midlands, who had served as M.P. and undersheriff for Worcestershire and was an active Warwickshire J.P. He was violent and litigious, a man with many enemies: the indictment for a riot of 23 March 1477 states that he would have been murdered had he been present. Several times he was involved in lawsuits over events at Alcester (Warw.), where he held land.[24] Alcester was the home of Richard, Lord Beauchamp of Powicke, which may account for his connection with Stacy and Blake, who were suspected of plotting the death of Lord Beauchamp by sorcery at the desire of his adulterous wife. This, however, appears insufficient explanation for their association, since the indictment reveals that they were acquainted before Richard Beauchamp succeeded to the barony.

All three conspirators came from the West Midlands. Stacy is described as a native of the diocese of Worcester. Blake may be the Thomas Blake who had been granted an annual fee of four marks and reward of two marks from Brailes (Warw.) in 1454 by Richard Neville, Earl of Warwick. The same earl gave Burdet a fee of ten marks from the same manor in 1451.[25] Both were still being paid in 1460. No later connections of Blake and Stacy with the area are known. Burdet's family had traditionally served the Earls of Warwick and he himself had deputised for Earl Richard Neville as sheriff of Worcestershire in 1459 and was later surveyor of his estates. After the earl's death Burdet served Warwick's son-in-law, the Duke of Clarence, with whom he developed a close personal relationship.[26] It was this tie with Clarence that made the trial politically explosive. However disturbing that men with access to the king and whom he had trusted should plot his death, Stacy and Blake were small fry. The participation of Burdet in a conspiracy to destroy the king and his son, which could only benefit Clarence, cast suspicion on the duke himself.

Burdet was charged with approaching Stacy and Blake with treasonable intent in April 1474. At his request they calculated the dates of birth of Edward IV and Prince Edward and foretold their early death. In May 1475 they revealed their findings to Alexander Rushton and others,

> 'to the intent that by the revealing and making known these matters, the cordial love of the people might be withdrawn from the King; and the King, by knowledge of the same, would be saddened thereby, so that his life would be thereby shortened'.

Furthermore, the indictment runs, on 6 March and 4-5 May 1477 at Holborn in Middlesex, the accused

> 'seeking the death and destruction of the King and Prince . . . by exciting war and discord between the King and his lieges . . . did . . . falsely and treacherously disperse and disseminate divers seditious and treasonable bills, rhymes and ballads, containing complaints, seditions and treasonable arguments, to the intent that the people should withdraw their cordial love from the King and abandon him, and rise and make war against the King, to the final destruction of the King and Prince'.

The jury returned a true bill. Subsequently the trial jury convicted the defendants, who were sentenced to death. Burdet and Stacy were hanged at Tyburn: Blake was pardoned.[27]

One may doubt the efficacy of necromancy but presumably sorcerers do not. The actions described in the indictment certainly indicate treasonable intentions and their attempts to implement the predictions also constitute treason. There are no suspicious circumstances about the trial, except that the indictment was based on a confession extracted under torture. How much reliance should be placed on such evidence? The Croyland chronicler makes it clear that it was the confession which implicated Burdet, not any of the other charges. There is no reason to doubt the chronicler's statement that Stacy admitted committing treason while being examined for another offence. This makes it difficult to believe that the trial was engineered by the government as a means of striking at Clarence through his friend. There seems to be no justification for doubting the honesty of the jurors. At least one of the charges, the posting of bills at Holborn only eleven days previously, was within their experience. The indictment mentions witnesses, who may have been summoned to testify at the trial. With six professional judges on the quorum, the forms of law must have been observed. Altogether the evidence suggests that the accused, including Burdet, were tried in accordance with justice: they were therefore guilty of at least some of the offences attributed to them.

The discovery of treason was a serious matter for Edward, requiring urgent measures to discourage any recurrence. Recognising the possible political repercussions of the trial, Edward was anxious that the verdicts should not be impugned. Consequently he appointed a particularly strong commission to try the case. Of eleven adult magnates at the chapter of the order of the Garter on 10 May, only Clarence was not on the commission. Seven other magnates were also nominated, making a total of seventeen, almost a third of the English nobility. Since the Dukes of Gloucester, Suffolk and Buckingham, the Earl of Northumberland and Lord Hastings were excused from attending the Garter chapter,[28] they were probably not available for the trial. The commission was therefore as authoritative and as representative as possible. In view of the proximity of the trial to the Garter chapter, it is likely that most of the commissioners attended, although the formal record is silent on this point.

Before their execution at Tyburn on 20 May, both Burdet and Stacy declared their innocence. Their protestations were recorded. On 21 May, or shortly afterwards, the Duke of Clarence took Dr. William Goddard, a Franciscan friar, to a meeting of the council at Westminster. The king was then absent at Windsor. Goddard read the declarations of innocence of Burdet and Stacy to the council. Then he and Clarence departed.[29]

The motives behind this strange act are unclear, for it is difficult to see what purpose it could serve. It was natural that suspicion should fall on the duke when his close associate was tried for treason, but it is clear that neither the disclosures at the trial nor the confessions of Stacy and Burdet implicated him directly. It is credible that Burdet acted independently. Nevertheless it was dangerous for Clarence to identify himself too closely with Burdet, especially once he was convicted. It was probably because Clarence opposed the trial that Edward omitted him from the commission. Perhaps Clarence thought them innocent, perhaps not, but he registered his belief that they were convicted in error. This may have been for their posthumous benefit, to clear their names, or because he feared his own implication in treason. If the latter was the case, his approach was wrong, as he identified himself with convicted traitors.

This aspect has been obscured by the constitutional implications of his action. Miss Scofield thought it particularly significant that Clarence's spokesman had publicly expounded Henry VI's title in 1470. In fact Clarence's spokesman was one of two brothers, both friars minor, both doctors of theology, and both called William. Either of them, or the Dr. John Goddard who preached several times before Edward IV, may have been the Dr. Goddard of 1470, whose christian name is not known.[30] Thus it is not clear that the preacher of 1470 was Clarence's spokesman and, if he was, there is no evidence that any contemporary linked the two or thought the connection significant. Moreover Miss Scofield thought that 'the duke had appealed from the king to the king's council'. Her view was coloured by the belief that the executions were Edward's 'revenge on Clarence', which 'was intended as a warning for him'.[31] The legal records, however, indicate an orderly legal process before an authoritative commission. Of course the council had no authority independent of the king, so Clarence's act was not an appeal. It is inconceivable that Clarence expected the verdicts to be reconsidered. His stance threw doubt on the justice and validity of the king's courts, the expression of the king as fount of justice. On this issue there could be no compromise, as Edward realised. When he arrested Clarence, and consigned him to the Tower, he accused him not of treason but of

> 'conduct . . . derogatory to the laws of the realm and most dangerous to judges and juries throughout the kingdom'.[32]

This statement may also refer to another trial, conducted at the Warwickshire quarter sessions on 15 April 1477. It was with this trial in mind that Miss Scofield regarded the Burdet case as Edward's revenge on Clarence. But the Croyland chronicler does not specifically mention it and there is no evidence that Edward knew of it until after Burdet's trial. The first indication of royal interest was the issue of a writ of *certiorari* — an order to the Warwickshire J.P.s to hand over the records of the trial — on 20 May 1477.[33]

The three defendants were Ankarette Twynho, John Thursby and Sir Roger Tocotes. Ankarette, a servant of the Duchess of Clarence, was accused of poisoning her mistress on 10 October 1476, with the result that she died on 22 December following. John Thursby was accused of poisoning Isabel's baby son Richard Plantagenet, so that he died on 1 January 1477. Sir Roger Tocotes was charged with aiding, abetting, and subsequently harbouring them. All three were indicted. Ankarette Twynho and John Thursby, who were present at the sessions, were tried, convicted and executed. Tocotes was elsewhere.

The process was later reversed and annulled on the grounds that

> 'the jurors for fear gave the verdicts contrary to their conscience, in proof whereof divers of them came to the said Ankarette in remorse and asked her forgiveness, in consideration of the imaginations of the said duke and his great might, the unlawful taking of the said Ankarette through three several shires, the inordinate hasty process . . .'

Certainly the trial was summary: the record indicates that all the stages were completed in a single day. Ankarette Twynho was brought to Warwick by force, having been seized at Cayford (Soms.) on 12 April by Richard Hyde and others.[34] A native of Swindon (Wilts.), Hyde had been a prominent retainer of Clarence since at least 1471.[35] As she was alleged to have committed her crime at Warwick, it was logical that Ankarette should have been tried there, but the methods to secure her attendance at court were irregular. The defendants could not expect a fair trial at Warwick, the seat of the duke's power, where he could influence both the jurors and the justices, if this was necessary. At least four jurors were his tenants, natives of Warwick and Solihull, and all were local men, seven belonging to the gild of nearby Stratford. They were empanelled by a former retainer of the Earl of Warwick and the justices were the county clerk, Clarence's trusted retainer John Hugford, and Henry Boteler, another former associate of Warwick.[36] Clarence himself was probably present: a petition in parliament states that he acted 'as though he had used a Kyng's power'. Altogether it is clear that undue pressure was exerted to secure the convictions.

Does this mean that there is no truth in the charges? Medically it is unlikely that Isabel died of poison so long after it was administered. Although not above suspicion, the Tewkesbury chronicler attributed the duchess's illness and death to the after effects of childbirth.[37] As Clarence wanted the trial to take place at Warwick, it was necessary for the crime to have been committed there to comply with legal forms. Perhaps it was for this reason that he tampered with the chronology of events. The charges appear to have been fabricated.

If the duchess and her son were not poisoned, why did the trial take place? To Professor Lander, 'the accusations . . . were so fantastically implausible that only a seriously disturbed mind could have produced them'.[38] Such a conclusion absolves the duke of responsibility and removes the need to explain any of the other extraordinary occurrences of these months. It is too facile a solution. It assumes that Clarence believed the charges, but he was sufficiently aware of the flaws in his case to see the need for maintenance. If the charges were frivolous, the consequences were not. Why did Clarence wish to destroy the three defendants?

The most important of the trio was Sir Roger Tocotes. By his marriage to Elizabeth Braybrooke, the St. Amand heiress, he was one of the leading gentry in Wiltshire. Unlike Elizabeth's first husband, William Beauchamp, he was never summoned as a baron to parliament. He was brother-in-law of Richard Beauchamp, Bishop of Salisbury, an influential prelate who was first chancellor of the order of the Garter. They were frequent associates and Tocotes was to be the bishop's executor. In 1477 Tocotes was a knight banneret, who had twice been M.P. and twice sheriff of Wiltshire. From 1468 nobody was a more constant associate of the Duke of Clarence in adversity or prosperity. His career suggests that he was the duke's friend as well as his servant and one of his leading officials.[39] A more improbable object of Clarence's hostility it is difficult to imagine.

The Twynho family are more shadowy but were the duke's adherents from at least 1470. Ankarette Twynho, the duchess's household servant, was the widow of William Twynho, a minor Somerset gentleman, who may also have served the duke before his own death in 1472. Their two sons were implicated in Clarence's rebellion in 1470 and were later involved in the management of his estates. So was their near relative, John Twynho the elder, recorder of Bristol, to whom the duke gave a silver cup.[40] This John Twynho was an important man, but his kinswoman Ankarette was of minor significance.

What had these two in common with John Thursby, a yeoman of no importance? Why did Clarence break with them? It seems that the motive must have been compelling, in view of the identity and powerful connections of the victims. These questions will be considered later, in the light of subsequent events.

In the Burdet case, in the Duke of Clarence's reaction to it, and, by inference, in the Twynho case, the Croyland chronicler saw adequate explanation for the duke's arrest. The other matters close to the king's heart, to which the chronicler refers, were of secondary importance. Clarence was summoned before the king at Westminster. He appeared on, or soon after, 10 June 1477. At an audience attended by the mayor and aldermen of London, Edward upbraided him for his misconduct, emphasising the perilous consequences of his actions for the judicial process everywhere. Clarence was arrested and imprisoned in the Tower.[41]

It would be unwise to suppose that the duke's death was certain. It is true that in September a continental observer reported his death, but he was wrong.[42] Clarence's execution was not the obvious sequel of his arrest. He was imprisoned not for treason, but for other offences. Although serious, these did not carry the death penalty. Edward may have envisaged a period of custody, during which the duke might learn discretion, followed by his release. This would explain why Edward publicly revealed his reasons for Clarence's arrest. It was normal for the king to take custody of the lands of prisoners, as Edward did at Michaelmas (29 September). He had, for example, seized the temporalities of Archbishop Neville, although he was never formally condemned. Only on 20 November 1477 were writs issued to summon parliament. The delay may have been for tactical reasons, such as the timing of the marriage of the Duke of York and Anne Mowbray,[43] but it probably also marks the decision to try Clarence. Seven days previously Edward had despatched a councillor with instructions to Coventry. All pledges, money and jewels of the Duke of Clarence in the hands of the burgesses were to be surrendered to the king, a clear indication of impending forfeiture. Instructions were also issued to keep order, evidently to forestall any resistance to the king's will.[44] This suggests that the decision to try Clarence was recent and was still not generally known. Clearly at some date between June and November 1477 Edward changed his plans regarding the duke.

Parliament assembled at Westminster on 16 January 1478.

Clarence was condemned as a traitor and was sentenced to death. On 18 February 1478 he was executed in the Tower of London.

2. The Parliament of 1478: The Political Setting

Hitherto the events of 1477 culminating in the arrest of the Duke of Clarence have been considered separately from his trial. This is not because the charges against him are unknown. They are catalogued in the act of attainder by which he was condemned.[45] As evidence of his activity, the charges have certain defects. They represent the indictment of the accused, of which it was necessary to prove only one article to invoke the penalties of treason. Because they were dependent on the voice of parliament, they may have borne little relation to the guilt of the offender or to natural justice. Acts of attainder always represent the version of events of the winning side, and thus sometimes distort the truth. A totally false picture may be represented. This is true of the statute that embodies the abdication of Richard II, for example. Great care must be taken to verify the facts before accepting the version of events contained in such acts.

This particular act has also come under criticism as a source. There are two reasons why its statements cannot be accepted without reservation. The most reliable narrative, that of the Croyland chronicler, indicates that the trial was not conducted in a manner conducive to justice. Great emphasis was laid on the testimony of King Edward himself, whose word was accepted as record in the courts of common law. He was not unbiased in his brother's case, yet he alone accused:

> 'For not a single person uttered a word against the duke, except the king; not one individual made answer to the king except the duke. Some parties were introduced, however, as to whom it was greatly doubted by many, whether they filled the office of accusers rather, or of witnesses; these two offices not being exactly suited to the same person in the same cause'.

Clearly the chronicler was shocked. He also reveals that Clarence was offered inadequate opportunity for defence. Nobody else spoke on his behalf.[46] The conviction which followed may have depended on the eccentric character of the trial. Indeed, nowhere in his account did the well-informed chronicler indicate that he thought Clarence guilty of the offences alleged against him and, indeed, he did not consider it necessary to state what the charges were.

On 20 February 1478 a royal councillor, Dr. Thomas Langton, wrote a letter which contained the following passage:

> 'Ther be assignyd certen Lords to go with the body of the Dukys of Clarence to Teuxbury, where he shall be beryid; the Kyng intendis to do right worshipfully for his sowle'.[47]

The duke was to be honourably interred in an abbey of his own patronage at the side of his wife. Near their tomb was erected a magnificent monument, incorporating their effigies, which completed the ring of Despenser tombs around the abbey choir. It was probably never finished. This was presumably financed by King Edward. Earlier work on the tomb may explain the duke's debt of 560 marks to the abbot and convent. Edward IV and later Richard III took measures to satisfy this by instalments. It was necessary for debts to be paid for the good of the soul. Consequently Edward took over responsibility for the payment of them. It cannot be ascertained whether all his brother's debts were paid, in the absence of Clarence's two books of creditors. Some payments may have been made in cash from the king's chamber; of these there is no record. Evidence does survive of the disbursement of substantial sums for a variety of miscellaneous items. Edward authorised the exchequer to pay debts to the duke's household servants totalling £325 19*s*. 3*d*., to which additions were later made. Eighty pounds due to his receiver John Luthington since 1474 were assigned to him from the revenues of his office and other sums disbursed by local officers, apparently on their own authority, were also allowed. Clarence forfeited his moveable goods and chattels and no will survives, but he was apparently given the opportunity to express his last wishes. In this way he was spared the perils of intestacy. It seems that his last wishes were exemplary. He recalled the injuries and grievances that he had inflicted on the parents and person of Earl Rivers, for which he wished to make recompense: this request King Edward faithfully performed. Later, on learning of extortion by Clarence from Lord Dynham, the king granted as compensation an annuity of £100 from the duke's lands for six years, for the safety of the soul of the said duke.[48] Are these measures to ease Clarence's progress in the afterlife inspired by guilt about the termination of his life on earth or are they merely evidence of residual fraternal affection?

Two historians thought that Edward regretted his brother's

death. Sir Thomas More wrote that 'kynge Edwarde (albeit he commaunded it) when he wist it was done, he pitiously bewailed and sorowfully repented'.[49] Another humanist historian, Polydore Vergil, was more explicit:

> 'yt ys very lykly that king Edward right soone repentyd that dede; for (as men say) whan so ever any sewyd for saving a mans lyfe, he was woont to cry owt in a rage, "O infortunate broother, for whose lyfe no man in this world wold once make request" '.[50]

Neither was a contemporary, but their accounts correspond closely. Vergil at least deserves attention, as he states that he applied for information on this matter to surviving councillors of Edward IV.[51] His statement suggests that fraternal affection was an important element. It was not on Edward's own motion that the rigour of the sentence against Clarence — hanging, drawing and quartering — was commuted. It was obtained 'by the great prayer and request of the mother of the said Edward and Clarence',[52] so it is not unlikely that the Duchess Cecily sought also to save Clarence's life. It is remarkable how early Edward's concern for his brother's spiritual welfare emerges. He had decided to take measures for the good of Clarence's soul as early as 20 February, only two days after his brother's death. Did Edward's vacillation lie behind the delay in Clarence's execution, a delay against which the commons remonstrated through their speaker?[53] Richard, Duke of Gloucester may also have lamented his brother's demise. It seems that King Edward had second thoughts. Evidently he did not regard Clarence's guilt so seriously that he could not contemplate the duke's continued existence. This is the second reason for doubting the justice of Clarence's trial. If Edward approached it so reluctantly, it suggests that he undertook it at the instigation of others. Yet the proceedings in parliament indicate considerable preparation on the part of the crown.

One cannot follow day to day events in medieval parliaments, with a few exceptions, but sometimes light is cast on them by other contemporary events. This is true of the parliament of 1478. The trial of the Duke of Clarence was only one of two important events concerning the royal family in January 1478, and it is the one about which we know least. The marriage of the king's second son Richard, Duke of York to the Norfolk heiress, Anne Mowbray, was celebrated during and immediately after the parliament. A full account by a herald survives.[54] In addition to sending writs of summons to parliament, 'the kinge directed his letters to diuers nobles of his Realme to come and appire at his palays of Westminster' for the wedding. When Sir John Paston wrote to his brother John Paston III, M.P. for Great Yarmouth (Norf.), he asked for tidings not of the trial but of the marriage.[55] The same order of priorities may have been observed by some at the parliament itself. The wedding was celebrated in St. Stephen's Chapel, the parliament chamber, on Thursday 15 January 1478. A banquet followed. Prominent at it were King Edward, his queen, his eldest son Prince Edward, three of his daughters, his mother the Duchess of York, his brother the Duke of Gloucester, his stepsons the Marquis of Dorset and Lord Richard Grey, his sister's son the Earl of Lincoln, and two brothers-in-law, the Duke of Buckingham and Earl Rivers. On Saturday 17 January parliament convened for the first session, at which the chancellor preached on the text 'Not without cause does the king carry a sword': an ominous text which foreshadowed Clarence's death. On Sunday 18 January Edward created twenty-four knights of the Bath, including his brother-in-law Thomas St. Leger and four sons of peers. On the following Thursday (22 January) jousts were held at Westminster in honour of the newly wed couple. Two of the queen's brothers and two of her sons participated: they were attended among others by the Earl of Northumberland and three brothers-in-law of the king. The tournament ended with the presentation of prizes.

Even the herald was dazzled by the splendour. Of the banquet on 15 January he wrote that 'the presse was soe great I might not see to write the names of them that served; the abundance of the noble people were so innumerable'. The members of both houses of parliament were probably no less impressionable. The dominant feature of the herald's account is the full and active participation of members of the royal house, whether related in blood to the king or kindred of the queen, that demonstrated their solidarity and unanimity. It is scarcely credible that this observation would not colour attitudes to events in parliament. It is equally difficult to accept that parliament and marriage were not intended to coincide or that their concurrence was not planned to stress family unity at the time of the trial of a defaulting member, George, Duke of Clarence.

The herald's description reminds one how extensive the king's kin had become. Apart from more distant ties, there were the husbands of the king's sisters, Sir Thomas St. Leger and the Duke of Suffolk, his mother, his sons and his daughters. There were the queen's kin, of which two other sons, four of her brothers and six sisters survived. The latter had married Lord Strange, the Duke of Buckingham, the Earl of Pembroke, and the heirs of the Earls of Kent, Arundel and Essex respectively. Through these and other ties she had a huge family. All her sisters's husbands were now adults, although not all were yet peers, so the process of integration of the Wydevilles into the higher nobility was nearing completion. Family ties can conflict with one another, but the marriage celebrations of the Duke of York indicate harmonious co-operation. The future second Earl of Essex, son of William Bourchier and Anne Wydeville, was knighted. Earl Rivers, Lord Richard Grey, and the Duke of Buckingham, husband of Katherine Wydeville, were prominent at the wedding. The latter and Lord Maltravers, husband of Margaret Wydeville, attended two of the queen's brothers and her two elder sons at the tournament. Other relatives attended parliament and were therefore at the wedding. Within the royal family the Wydeville connection played the dominant part.

There was an active council at Westminster during Michaelmas term 1477. For at least part of the time there was a great council. On All Saints' Day (1 November) 'the moste Parte of the nobles of his Realme bothe Spirituell and Temporell' accompanied Edward to St. Stephen's Chapel. The council was concerned with foreign affairs, for two foreign embassies were present, and with plans for the marriage and parliament. In addition to seeking its advice, the king required a representative assembly of magnates to discover the climate of opinion regarding the trial of his brother. Within the council the Wydevilles stood out, for their numerous connection was present in strength. The marriage of Prince Richard was very much the queen's affair, as he lived with her, so she was present, together with her household. So was Edward, Prince of Wales, together with his Wydeville dominated household and council, including the Marquis of Dorset and Earl Rivers. Rivers, indeed, presented the king with his translation of *Les Dictes des Philosophes*.[56] On 9 November Prince Edward entertained the lay magnates to a banquet. After dinner those holding lands of Prince Richard as Duke of Norfolk did him homage, including the Dukes of Gloucester and Suffolk, the king's brother and brother-in-law. This event reveals the central importance of the Wydevilles. They also stood out as individuals, for Dorset was given £40 in reward and his father-in-law, Lord Hastings, was paid £50 for attendance at the council. After the decisions had been made, on 12 November 1477, Rivers and Dorset joined in proclaiming the articles of the jousts.[57] They had been involved at every stage, from Clarence's arrest to his execution, which was true neither of the Duke of Gloucester nor Lord Hastings, who were also influential with the king. Their prominence in the Westminster council, where the decision to try Clarence was formally determined, is significant, for if any could influence Edward to act against his better judgement it was the Wydevilles.

The narrative sources suggest how the Wydevilles exercised their influence. Dominic Mancini speaks of the longstanding hostility of the Duke of Clarence to the queen,[58] a hostility which she returned, if earlier events in the fourteen-seventies are any guide. Towards his death the duke regretted the wrongs that he had done to Earl Rivers, especially his treatment of the earl's parents, an indication that their injuries still rankled. Sir Thomas More, not a reliable source, states among other explanations of the duke's death that it ensued 'were it by the Queene and the Lordes of her bloode which highlye maligned the kynges kinred'.[59] Dominic Mancini, a visitor to England in 1483, analysed the political situation at that date partly in the light of events in 1478. In the intervening five years both the Duke of Gloucester and Lord Hastings broke with the Wydevilles, which Mancini reads back in time. His detail, however, is accurate, and his statement agrees with the record evidence:

> 'The queen then remembered the insults to her family and the calumnies with which she had been reproached, namely that she was not the legitimate wife of the king. Thus she concluded that her offspring would never come to the throne, unless the duke of Clarence were removed; and of this she easily persuaded the king'.[60]

Although Polydore Vergil's information was partly derived from Edward IV's councillors, his comments are often his own. Of Edward's regret at Clarence's death, he remarks astutely that the king was 'affirming in that manyfestly, that he [Clarence] was cast away by envy of the nobylytie'.[61] All three accounts agree that the king was persuaded, perhaps reluctantly, to consent to Clarence's death. Two of them cast the queen in this role. She could influence the king; her kin could dominate the council; but could they control parliament so no dissentient voice was heard? The answer lies in an examination of the elements that comprised the parliament of 1478.

3. The Composition of the Parliament of 1478

Parliament now consists of two chambers, the House of Lords and the House of Commons, but this was not so in the fifteenth century. It then consisted of three estates, the lords spiritual, the lords temporal and the commons, although the latter already met separately. The personnel of the commons varied from parliament to parliament, but the members of the other estates, if of age, were entitled to an individual writ of summons. Occasionally barons failed to receive writs, sometimes episcopal sees or abbacies were vacant, but summonses were not subject to royal whim. Instead of selecting for attendance those who were amenable, the crown was faced with the task of influencing the lords on their arrival. Not all those who were summoned were necessarily present at parliament. Sometimes the discrepancy was substantial and occasionally, as in 1478, even the list of those summoned is lost.

It is therefore necessary to determine which lords were eligible to attend. Six additions should be made to Lord Wedgwood's list.[62] Altogether two archbishops, eighteen bishops, twenty-four abbots and priors, three dukes, a marquis, seven earls and thirty barons were eligible, making a total of eighty-three. More difficulty is involved in establishing who actually attended, for apart from the parliament roll and the account of the wedding one must rely on chance references. Others certainly attended of whom there is no record. The heads of religious houses, the abbots and priors, are worst documented: only the five triers are known to have sat, but others probably did. They were normally the least assiduous category and were less politically important than other lords. Both archbishops and ten bishops attended: of those whose attendance is not demonstrable, four came from remote Welsh sees. Among the lay lords, three dukes, a marquis, four earls and twelve barons were present. Probably others were there: the case is particularly strong for Lords Dudley, Howard, Grey of Wilton and Dacre of the South, whose sons played a significant part.[63] Of those for whom there is no direct evidence, Lord Stourton died during the parliamentary session. Six others were northerners. Nothing is known of over half the barons. Their presence is more easily overlooked, as Edward chose the triers mainly from the greater magnates, on whom the herald concentrated in his account of the wedding. Omitting the heads of religious houses, of fifty-eight peers eligible to attend thirty-four did. With more complete knowledge, it would be surprising if there was not a response from over two-thirds. The relatively high rate of attendance among the great magnates, coupled with the presence in the commons of five sons of peers and the titular Lord FitzWalter, indicates a lively interest. The assembly was representative of the magnate class and contained the bulk of those who were politically important.

According to Mr. Knecht, one effect of the political upheavals of the period was to produce an episcopate subservient to the crown.[64] Already by 1478 there survived only seven bishops appointed before Edward IV's accession. Two of these had held royal office, two had received advancement from Edward, and the Bishops of Winchester, Salisbury and Coventry and the Archbishop of Canterbury were triers at this parliament: a sign of royal confidence. Already they were integrated with the rest, who had been elevated by Edward, mainly for administrative service. Such a background did not preclude political independence, but a high proportion remained in royal service after their elevation to the episcopate. Four of them had acted as chancellor since 1471 and three others as chancellors of the queen and Prince Edward during the same period. At least seven bishops attended meetings of the royal council during 1476-8.[65] From such a group resistance to the crown could not be expected.

Edward had also recruited new men to the nobility: in 1478 sixteen bore titles conferred since 1461.[66] They had been selected from those in whom Edward had confidence, but they were more powerful and less malleable than the bishops. Those on whom Edward felt he could rely were nominated as triers of petitions, to vet them before they came before parliament. Five of these were among his closest supporters. His uncle, the aged Earl of Essex, was a former steward of his household and currently treasurer of England. Lords Hastings and Stanley were respectively chamberlain and steward of the household. Lords Dynham and Ferrers of Chartley, both of Edward's creation, had been devoted adherents since before his accession. All of them were councillors. There were others in a similar mould of loyalty and service, such as Lord

Audley, a member of the council; Lord Howard, another councillor and a former treasurer of the household, whom Edward had ennobled; Edmund Grey of Ruthyn, briefly treasurer, whom he had created Earl of Kent; and Lord Dacre of the South, once controller of the household and 'gretest abowt the Kyngys person'.

Increasingly Edward gave his confidence to his Wydeville relatives. Their connection was extensive. Edward's reliance on it is shown by the presence among them of four triers.[67] Earl Rivers was one. The queen's ties with the Earl of Essex had been reinforced since he first supported her. The nomination of the Earl of Arundel is attributable to the marriage of his eldest son Lord Maltravers to Margaret Wydeville, with whose family he was a constant associate. The greatest of them was Henry Stafford, Duke of Buckingham, who had been out of favour since 1474.[68] During Michaelmas term his wife Katherine Wydeville had borne him an heir, to whom the king acted as godfather and gave his name. The duke's attitude is marked by his willingness to act as steward of England solely for the purpose of sentencing Clarence. This was a small price to pay for restoration to favour, which was expressed on 11 February 1478 by the alienation to him and his heirs of a manor in Wales for his good and laudable service.[69] The queen's son, the Marquis of Dorset, was a peer, and so were the husbands of her sisters, Lord Maltravers and Lord Strange of Knockin. Since the marriage of the younger William Herbert to Mary Wydeville, the two families had been political allies. Although this league was shortly to break down, it probably still existed. Alone of the queen's brothers-in-law, William Herbert, Earl of Pembroke is not known to have attended the parliament, but his uncle Lord Ferrers was a trier. Another of the queen's kinsmen, as stepfather of the Marquis of Dorset, was Lord Hastings. First and foremost a servant of the king, he enjoyed amicable relations with the queen. Also among the parliamentary peerage were her past and present chancellors, the Bishops of Durham and Carlisle, and her chamberlains Lords Dudley and Dacre of the South.[70] In 1478 Dacre may still have been steward of the Wydeville dominated household of Prince Edward. The Bishop of Worcester was president of it and the Bishop of Hereford had once been the prince's chancellor.[71] The marriage of the queen's son to Anne Mowbray drew Lords Berkeley and Howard, the bride's coheirs and her closest paternal relatives, into the Wydeville orbit. Both obtained provisoes of exemption from the acts settling the

Mowbray inheritance.[72] Individually the members of the Wydeville connection were influential with the king. In parliament, if all attended, they were equally formidable and constituted the most powerful faction.

What of Richard, Duke of Gloucester, brother of both Edward IV and Clarence? It is scarcely credible that Clarence could have been executed had the king's only other brother objected. Yet two chronicles refer to his resistance. Dominic Mancini mentions violent emotions:

> 'At that time Richard duke of Gloucester was so overcome with grief for his brother that he could not dissimulate so well, but that he was overheard to say that he would one day avenge his brother's death'.

Sir Thomas More speaks of the duke's sorrow, which he thought simulated. Later, as king, Richard himself told the Earl of Desmond of his sadness at his brother's death,[73] a statement which may have been shaped to meet a political need. It was certainly expressed with a political end in view. All three references were made after Richard's usurpation in 1483, when he may have wished to make his actions appear consistent. Certainly Mancini is the victim of hindsight.

Mancini's interpretation is wholly unsupported by Gloucester's actions. If the duke regretted his brother's death, he nevertheless allowed his support to be bought. Nobody benefited more from Clarence's death. He secured his spoils before parliament was dissolved: some of them were recorded on the parliament roll. Three acts seem to reflect his desires. One degraded George Neville, Duke of Bedford and heir of the Marquis of Montagu from the peerage. In 1475 he had been disabled from inheriting the Neville lands, of which he was male heir, mainly to the advantage of Gloucester. He was demoted, the act says, because he lacked the resources to support any estate, but this was patently untrue. Probably Gloucester, anxious to retain the Neville inheritance, wished to deny him a forum where his complaints could be heard, as they would be if he was a peer in parliament. Later Gloucester was to acquire his wardship. The act of 1474, which settled the division of the Warwick inheritance between Clarence and Gloucester, had prohibited alienations by either party, since these might disinherit the other. Gloucester was now exempted from this provision with regard to certain specified lands, to the ultimate loss of Clarence's heirs. A third act exchanged Gloucester's marcher lordship of Elfacl for that of Ogmore, parcel of the duchy of Lancaster,[74] which was conviently situated near his own lordship of Glamorgan.

Parliament closed on 21 February 1478. Gloucester's favour with King Edward can be traced through the dates of his grants, for which the chancery warrants are the most accurate guide. On 13 February 1478 his heir was created Earl of Salisbury, a title forfeited by Clarence; on 18 February he himself became great chamberlain of England in lieu of his brother; on 19 February he was licenced to found two colleges at Middleham (Yorks.) and Barnard Castle (Durh.); on 20 February he secured a grant for his servant, Richard ap Robert ap Ivan Vaughan; and on 3 March he was granted Clarence's Yorkshire lands, including Richmond and Helmsley, in exchange for others elsewhere.[75] He had been dissatisfied with the 1474-5 settlement with Clarence, which he now tried to adjust in his own favour. In addition to the act permitting alienations, he tried to secure an extra share of lands held in trust and he took the opportunity to seize some disputed property in Lincolnshire.[76] His regrets ring hollow.

Gloucester may also have participated in the planning of the trial. Without Gloucester's support or acquiescence, Edward would not have risked a public trial of Clarence. Gloucester attended the council meetings of Michaelmas term 1477. He must have pleased the king, who granted him the lordship of Ogmore on 27 November and assigned attornies to deliver him seisin at once.[77] The confirmation of this grant in parliament shows that the relations of king and duke had not altered in the meantime. Gloucester was with Edward when Earl Rivers presented his translation in December 1477; as constable, he joined with Rivers in proclaiming the articles for the jousts, which he had probably helped to draft; and on 9 November he had been among those who did homage to Prince Richard at Prince Edward's banquet.[78] These are outward signs that his relations with the Wydevilles remained cordial.

The personal support of the Duke of Gloucester for the trial was important to Edward and the Wydevilles, not only because it removed a potential centre of opposition to their plans. Gloucester was the greatest magnate in the north of England, where he enjoyed amicable relations with the majority of local magnates. Lord Greystoke, for example, was his councillor, but unfortunately it is not known if he was at the parliament. The Earl of Northumberland,

Gloucester's retainer,[79] certainly attended, and was prominent in the marriage celebrations. The predominance of the duke and earl was reflected in elections for the commons in northern constituencies.

Another was also bought, but at a less extortionate price, for he was less important. This was John de la Pole, Duke of Suffolk, husband of Elizabeth of York, sister of Edward IV, Clarence and Gloucester. He was a nonentity, ineffective in local and court politics alike, and received only one office of his brother-in-law's grant. This was conceded by a letter patent dated 10 March 1478: it was the lieutenantcy of Ireland, late of the Duke of Clarence. Furthermore an act of parliament exchanging lands between himself and the king was decidedly in his own favour: not only were the two manors which he received conveniently near his Oxfordshire centre of power, but it was provided that, should he lose them, he could re-enter those which he had given up. This was the reward for his acquiescence, which was probably secured during the Michaelmas councils. Then he had done homage to his traditional rival, the Duke of Norfolk, in the person of his nephew Prince Richard.[80]

Like other great men Clarence had enemies, but he seems to have had more than most. Apparently he had coerced Lord Dynham, or so Dynham claimed. This may have been connected with his quarrel with Dynham's kinsman, Lord FitzWarin. Lord Audley, the duke's annuitant, personally invaded Clarence's park at Canford (Dors.) and took deer there.[81] Audley's quarrel with Clarence may have influenced his nephew, Lord Grey of Powys: or did Grey keep silent during the trial because of the persuasions of his half-brother Thomas Vaughan, chamberlain of Prince Edward, or those of his wife Anne Herbert, daughter of the first Earl of Pembroke by Lord Ferrers's sister? Lord Hastings's attitude was determined by his proximity to the king. His brother was Lord Welles; Lord Mountjoy, later to be his retainer, was already deputising for him in Calais; and Lord Grey of Codnor had been in his service since 1464.[82] Were Welles, Mountjoy and Grey of Codnor influenced by his example? Such intricate bonds among magnates may be extended almost indefinitely to account for their actions, but they were complemented by others pointing in different directions. Likewise local disputes did not necessarily influence alignments in national politics. They were not meaningless, for the Wydevilles probably pulled every available string. But in happier circumstances, if ascendant, Clarence might have commanded support which in adversity he was denied.

If he had his enemies, Clarence may have depended on his friends. Most of the English nobility were related to him, in the same degree as they were to his brothers. Unfortunately his most important relatives, the king, Gloucester and Suffolk were his committed opponents. His wife was dead and, in any case, relations with her kindred were not necessarily friendly. Lords Lisle and Abergavenny, like Gloucester, had good reason to regard his fall as an opportunity to make good their claims to his estates. Other magnates were his retainers. Lord Dudley was steward of his Staffordshire estates, Lord Beauchamp of Powicke of those in Gloucestershire, and Lords Hastings and Welles had been stewards respectively of Tutbury (Staffs.) and Melbourne (Derbys.). Lord Audley was his annuitant. Lord Howard, and doubtless others, had worn his livery.[83] In none of these cases did the loyalty due to Clarence determine political behaviour. Although Richard Beauchamp had been appointed steward by the Despenser feoffees at Warwick's request as long ago as 1457, he had opposed the earl politically in 1471, and he had a grievance against Master John Stacy, whose accomplice Thomas Burdet enjoyed Clarence's support: in 1478 Edward IV trusted him sufficiently to make him a trier of petitions.[84] Lord Dudley was chamberlain of the queen. Three other royal councillors who sat in the 1478 parliament, Sir Thomas Burgh, Sir Thomas Grey and Sir Thomas Montgomery, had been granted stewardships or annuities by Clarence.[85] Another councillor, who had no seat in parliament, Master Piers Courtenay, owed his early advancement to Clarence's patronage. Like Lord Hastings, however, the prime loyalty of such men was to the king, whom they could not be expected to resist. Before the decision to hold a trial was the time for them to oppose the project: we do not know if they did. Once the decision was taken, their loyalty was to the king. Clarence could count on only a handful of M.P.s compared with the powerful faction in the previous parliament. They had secured election by their own efforts, not through his influence. As he was in the Tower, they can have enjoyed little tactical direction. They had been cowed by fear of losing offices and annuities on ducal estates now in royal hands. If the words of the Croyland chronicler are to be taken literally, none of them spoke up for Clarence.

The trial occurred in parliament, where every effort was made to control the lords and commons. The magnates must have already considered the duke's fate in the councils of Michaelmas term 1477, where the decision to try him was made. Doubtless it reflected the consensus of opinion. The evidence indicates that the councils were actively managed by the Wydevilles, who strengthened their coalition. New bonds were formed with some magnates, such as Lord Lisle, who did homage to Prince Richard.[86] Others, like Gloucester and Buckingham, were promised royal favour. As a result the magnate class was committed to Clarence's condemnation before parliament met and may well have thought it inevitable. It is difficult to believe that the commons could successfully oppose the king and magnates combined and efforts were made to ensure that they did not. The Wydevilles and their allies strove to influence elections. Professor Roskell has pointed out that no fifteenth-century parliament contained more royal servants. Miss McKisack discovered less resident borough members in 1478 than on any previous occasion.[87] It was a packed parliament.

Professor Roskell discovered fifty royal servants, a slight underestimate, comprising 17 per cent of the whole house of 295 members. Altogether fifty-six royal servants have been identified among the commons of 1478[88] and there may well have been others. In some cases, perhaps, the connection was tenuous, but in others it was close. John Elrington, treasurer of Edward IV's household, sat for Middlesex; a predecessor, Sir John Fogge, sat for Kent; the controller of the household, Sir William Parre, represented Cumberland; the treasurer of the chamber, Sir Thomas Vaughan, was knight of the shire for Cornwall; Sir John Say and Piers Curteys, successively keepers of the great wardrobe, were elected for Hertfordshire and the borough of Leicester; John Wood, under-treasurer, was returned for Surrey; Ralph Wolsley, baron of the exchequer, represented Gatton (Surrey); William Slefeld, the king's secretary, was burgess for Ludgershall (Wilts.); the speaker, Sir William Allington, sat for Cambridgeshire; and three other royal councillors, Sir Thomas Burgh, Sir Thomas Grey and Sir Thomas Montgomery, were knights of the shires of Lincoln, Cambridge and Essex.[89] Such a list could readily be augmented. In 1478, as in the Tudor period, the commons were probably guided by the king's councillors. There were plenty available to perform the task.

Their attitude may be deduced from the Wydeville connections which so many of them enjoyed. Indeed the commons contained many supporters of the queen's family: these included members of her household, blood relatives, the chamberlain, chancellor, attorney-general and controller of the household of the Prince of Wales, and the chamberlain of her second son, Richard, Duke of York.[90] Altogether they constituted a most impressive faction. How did they find seats?

An examination of those who witnessed the election returns casts little light. It does not seem that local electorates were dominated by factional groups, but there is some evidence of tampering with returns after the elections had taken place. For the six boroughs and the shire of Cornwall fourteen members were returned, including only one resident of the county. Six were lawyers and four were royal servants. All the elections are stated to have taken place at Lostwithiel on 18 November 1477. Eleven of the names are written wholly or partly over erasures. Only the names of John Chichele, M.P. for Bodmin, and the two knights of the shire are undisturbed.[91] As neither of the latter were resident, the intervention of the sheriff at an earlier stage may have achieved the desired result. He was William Carminowe, deputy of Prince Edward in his capacity as sheriff of Cornwall, on whose behalf he may have altered the returns. Prince Edward's household was dominated by the Wydevilles, notably by the queen's brother Earl Rivers, who was receiver-general of the prince's duchy of Cornwall. In 1483 Rivers enlisted the aid of Robert Courte, auditor of the duchy, to secure the election of his candidates in Cornwall:[92] in 1478 Courte sat for Truro. It is only in the light of these erasures that one can understand the election of Sir Thomas Vaughan, Sir James Tyrell and Thomas Powtrell, prominent retainers respectively of the prince, of the Duke of Gloucester, and of Lord Hastings.

The Cornish example is not typical. True, there are a handful of other erasures in returns for the city of Lincoln and the boroughs of Poole, Lyme Regis (Dorset) and Newcastle-under-Lyme (Staffs.), but these are isolated instances. New sheriffs were appointed for every county shortly before parliament was summoned but it does not appear that they were carefully selected to rig the elections, nor does it seem that they did.

There were other outlying areas like Cornwall, which were equally subject to a dominant influence. In the north the Duke of Gloucester and Earl of Northumberland held office as sheriffs of Cumberland and Northumberland for life; Sir William Parre was sheriff of Westmorland until his death, perhaps on the same terms. The results are self-evident. One M.P. for Cumberland, another for Westmorland and a third for Carlisle (Cumbs.) were Gloucester's men, while in Northumberland Earl Henry Percy secured the election of two retainers as knights of the shire and a third as burgess for Newcastle-upon-Tyne. On the borders, control over the machinery of the election, including the return of writs, combined with the military authority of the duke and earl as wardens of the Scottish marches proved irresistible. In Yorkshire, where they lacked these particular advantages, the duke and earl were leading landowners and divided the county into spheres of influence. That of the earl comprised the coastal towns of Hull and Scarborough, each of whom returned a Percy retainer. The city of York elected a supporter of Gloucester. The knights of the shire were a Percy councillor, Sir Robert Constable, and Sir John Pilkington, Gloucester's trusted retainer.

There were other ways of procuring elections. Many boroughs were controlled by magnates who were their lords. It was in this capacity that Clarence secured satisfactory returns from Plympton (Devon), Ludgershall (Wilts.), Warwick (Warw.), Worcester (Worcs.) and Newcastle-under-Lyme (Staffs.).[93] In 1478 his absence was reflected in the choice of M.P.s. In several cases his patronage was exercised by the crown: Warwick and Plympton each returned a yeoman of the crown, Ludgershall the king's secretary, and Newcastle Reginald Bray.

There was one great magnate who combined the dominance of a region, East Anglia, with the control of pocket boroughs in Surrey and Sussex. This was the Duke of Norfolk. In 1478 twelve members of the Mowbray affinity were returned for Norfolk (2), Suffolk (2), Berkshire (1), Appleby (Westmor.) (1), Ipswich (Suff.) (2), Horsham (1), East Grinstead (Suss.) (1), Reigate (1) and Southwark (Surr.) (1). Clearly the Mowbray affinity was fully mobilised, but by whom? In 1478 the last Mowbray duke was dead and his heiress Anne was a young child. She married Richard, Duke of York during the 1478 parliament. Other magnates had done him homage on 9 November 1477, but the marriage had long been arranged. Since at least 4 December 1476 the Mowbray estates had been in the hands of the king. Accounts of 1476-77 survive for those in Surrey and Sussex. The estates were nominally subject to a group of feoffees, including the queen, Bishops Storey and Dudley, the Marquis of

Dorset, the Earls of Essex and Rivers, and Lord Hastings. They made some grants. On one occasion the council acted with the queen's assent, a formula which also appears in the administration of the Prince of Wales.[94] The queen and her family controlled the affairs of both princes, using some of the same personnel. The speaker in the 1478 parliament, Sir William Allington, was chancellor of both princes, perhaps at the same time.[95] King Edward retained ultimate control, giving orders to the feoffees, sometimes making appointments without consulting them, and receiving the revenues from the estates.

By his marriage Prince Richard drew the Mowbray retainers into the Wydeville connection. Mowbray patronage was henceforth controlled by the Wydevilles, who exercised it on behalf of their dependants. This included parliamentary patronage, employed by Earl Rivers in 1483.[96] In addition to the dozen Mowbray retainers who were elected in 1478, favourable returns of Wydeville dependants were obtained in four pocket boroughs. The Duke of Norfolk's three boroughs of Horsham, Bramber (Suss.) and Gatton (Surr.) returned the queen's receiver-general and two royal servants; another Wydeville client sat for Guildford (Surr.). Only at Horsham was it necessary to tamper with the returns to secure the election of Thomas Stidolf. The total number of elections may well be underestimated, for it is unlikely that natives of the ducal barony of Lewes would be disobedient as members for the borough. Some of these M.P.s were influential locally, but it was not their local connections that determined their election. John Fiennes, knight of the shire for Sussex, was son of the local magnate Lord Dacre of the South, and his fellow, John Dudley, was feed at Petworth (Suss.) by the Earl of Northumberland. More important was that they were each sons of the queen's two chamberlains;[97] it was probably her exercise of Mowbray influence that explains their election.

Both knights of the shire for Sussex represented the same magnate interest. Does this mean that they defeated candidates from other affinities, or that there was no contest? In this parliament two important local magnates, the Earls of Arundel and Northumberland, were identified with the Wydeville interest. Perhaps they cooperated at the election. The candidates may even have been chosen by consultation with other magnates, just as six years earlier the Dukes of Norfolk and Suffolk had agreed on common candidates. Northumberland was most unlikely to oppose the election as knight of the shire of his own feed man! The attitude of the Earl of Arundel to the elections cannot be gauged without more knowledge of the composition of his retinue. It is clear that there was considerable co-operation within the Wydeville coalition. The Cornish seats of Sir James Tyrell, the East Anglian retainer of the Duke of Gloucester, and Lord Hastings's man, Thomas Powtrell, were presumably supplied by the Wydevilles. Charles Nowell, a Mowbray retainer, was elected to Appleby (Westmor.), perhaps with Gloucester's connivance. The return by Newcastle-under-Lyme (Staffs.) of Reginald Bray, a servant of the Stanleys and Staffords, resulted from the exercise of duchy of Lancaster influence.[98]

In this area, the North Midlands, duchy influence was exercised by Lord Hastings, as it had been by Clarence in 1467 and 1472. As a result Hastings's men filled seats in Leicestershire (2), Lincolnshire (1), Derbyshire (2), Staffordshire (2), Warwickshire (1) and the borough of Leicester. In all he may have had as many as ten supporters in the lower house, although it is possible that not all had yet joined his service. This was a larger number than in any earlier parliament. Apparently, when required, Lord Hastings could decisively influence elections. In 1478 he made the necessary effort.

Other magnates did the same. County constituencies were filled by the retainers of leading local lords. Thus both the Oxfordshire members served the Duke of Suffolk[99] and three of the Earl of Kent's men sat for Northamptonshire, Bedfordshire and Huntingdonshire.[100] Much the same occurred in many boroughs: at Maldon (Essex), for example, both members served the Earl of Essex. When the greatest magnates exerted their power, lesser noblemen were squeezed out and went unrepresented.

There was a high proportion of men with predetermined loyalties among the commons in 1478. They certainly comprised a third, perhaps a half of the total. Their lords, who had procured their election, were united in their attitudes. There was very little, if any, opposition. They were presented with a case to which no adequate reply was made. Like the Croyland chronicler, they may have been shocked, but this did not affect the issue. They were carefully managed, not least by the speaker, a trusted servant of the Wydevilles. Every effort had been devoted to securing a compliant commons. Their temper is indicated in the way they pressed Edward to carry out the sentence on Clarence. In these circumstances Clarence's conviction cannot be taken as conclusive evidence of his guilt.

4. Clarence's Treason

The act attainting the Duke of Clarence begins and ends with rhetoric. The king recalls past treasons and his gracious mercy in dealing with them. He states that he has learnt of further treason, yet more offensive than anything perpetrated hitherto, both because it proceeded 'of the moost extreme purpensed malice' and because it originated in one who before all others should have been true, namely Clarence. Clarence should have been loyal, not merely as a brother, but because the king had endowed him with

> 'lifelode and richesse [that] notably exceded any other within his lande . . . beyng ryght desyrows to make him of might and puissance excedyng others'.

The king had done this in the hope that Clarence would be his most faithful subject and in spite of his treason in 1469-71. There ensues a list of specific treasons committed in 1477, connected to a title to the crown dating from 1470, which the duke intended to make good. Edward argues that it is his duty to proceed against his incorrigible brother. Sentence of forfeiture duly follows.[101]

The act is not specific, but on one charge it is quite explicit. Clarence, it states, was nominated heir of the house of Lancaster while in exile in 1470, his title was ratified at the Readeption parliament, and he had a certified copy or exemplification made of the proceedings, which he had secretly kept ever since. This charge has been carefully investigated by Professor Lander, who concluded that the only source was this very act. He dismissed the charge as unsubstantiated and he declared the whole act of attainder to be fraudulent, fabricated by Edward IV to destroy his innocent, if irritating, brother.[102] There is no independent evidence for the Readeption act or for the exemplification. At an unknown date the roll of the Readeption parliament was lost or deliberately destroyed, so very little is known of its proceedings. The original exemplification does not survive either, which is hardly surprising since none of Clarence's private muniments are to be found in the Public Record Office or anywhere else. It should, however, have been copied on the patent roll, and the absence of any reference could be taken as evidence that there never was any exemplification. But this is not conclusive, for not all letters were enrolled and one class that is frequently omitted is that of exemplications or inspeximuses: some originals survive elsewhere, particularly in municipal archives, for which there are no corresponding enrolments.[103] Exemplifications were not themselves original documents but were copies of original documents certified as authentic by the royal chancery. It was less important to the crown that they should be enrolled.

Two narratives confirm that the Duke of Clarence was recognised as heir of the house of Lancaster in 1470-1: the chronicles of John Warkworth and Edward Hall. Professor Lander pointed out that both were compiled after 1478, which is certainly true, and deduced that their common source was the roll of the parliament of 1478. Consequently he rejected the independence of their testimony. Is such a conclusion tenable?

Professor Lander's attack on Warkworth's chronicle, if admitted, would destroy much of our knowledge about 1470-1, as Lander himself appreciated. Warkworth is a useful source for these years. His account confirms the detail in other sources, such as the lists of casualties in various battles. He also supplies some original material not found elsewhere. His chronicle is the only source for the text used in the sermon of the chancellor at the Readeption parliament.[104] This implies some knowledge of the parliament, which may possibly have been supplied by Warkworth's patron, William Grey, Bishop of Ely.[105] Moreover Warkworth tells us that the agreements reached in France were

> 'wrytene, indentyde, and sealede, bytwixe the seide Quene Margaret, the Prynce hire sonne, in that one party, and the Duke of Clarence, and the Erle of Warwik, one that othere party'.[106]

This bears a remarkable resemblance to the account in the document known as the *Maner and Gwidinge*. Professor Lander, who regards this as a more reliable source, has pointed out that nowhere does it mention Clarence's nomination as heir of the house of Lancaster. All it says about the duke is that

> 'in treatinge the forsayde marriege, it was promitted and accorded that aftar the recoverye of the Realme of Englande for and in the name of the seyde Kynge Henry, he holden and avouched for Kyng, and the Prince for Regent and Govarnor of the sayd Realme, my Lord of Clarence shall have all the lands that he had when he departed out of England, and the duchie of York, and many other, and th'Erle of Warwick his, and othar named in th'appoyntment'.

This reference to Clarence occurs because it concerns matters in which both he and Warwick were interested, their lands. Otherwise, as the title shows, the author was concerned only with the earl's part of the agreement. The Earl of Oxford is mentioned in association with Warwick, when both received Queen Margaret's pardon, but not otherwise. There is no mention of any pardon for Clarence or of the oaths of fealty made by him or Oxford, although there is a description of Warwick's oath.[107] Most of the account concerns Warwick alone: other matters that were also settled pass without reference. It is known that it was agreed between Warwick and Clarence on the one hand and Queen Margaret and Prince Edward on the other that full recompense should be made to Clarence for any lands that he had to surrender, with the exception of the honour of Tutbury.[108] There is no reference in the *Maner and Gwidinge*, ostensibly a description of the same agreement, of arrangements for restitution, for compensation or for reversing attainders of Lancastrians. Presumably these were omitted because they were no part of the author's purpose, which was apparently to present the treaty of Angers from the point of view of the Earl of Warwick, probably as a manifesto for consumption by the earl's supporters in England. Anxious to depict Warwick's conduct as favourably as possible, the author seems to have altered the facts to improve his case: this would account for the extraordinary discrepancies with other sources in an account apparently by a contemporary eye-witness. The *Maner and Gwidinge* is not an impartial description of events, but an exercise in propaganda. It is hazardous to argue from its silence about Clarence.

Like the act of attainder, Warkworth placed the agreement on Clarence's succession in France, but the fact that he was writing after 1478 does not in itself demonstrate that he was relying on the 1478 act, either directly or indirectly. He had no special information about the fourteen-seventies, as Professor Lander pointed out, and the Bishop of Ely, his patron, may well have been absent from the 1478 parliament.[109] There is no other evidence that he knew of the charges laid against Clarence. He is an inaccurate source for the fourteen-sixties but his account becomes full for the years 1469-71. It is therefore quite credible that he was well-informed about Clarence's exile and the Readeption. Warkworth's chronicle must continue to be regarded as an independent source until it has been proved otherwise.

The other narrative is the chronicle of Edward Hall, which refers to an act of the Readeption parliament that entailed the succession on the Duke of Clarence in the event of the failure of the house of Lancaster. Hall's chronicle, first printed in 1542, derived this information from no known surviving source. Professor Lander concluded that Hall drew the material from Clarence's act of attainder and consequently repudiated his testimony. However, he provided fuel for his own rebuttal. He pointed out that Hall did not employ the act of attainder to explain Clarence's death, but used the stories passed down by Polydore Vergil. These do not include the settlement of the crown at the Readeption. Yet if Hall took his account from the act attainting Clarence, he could hardly have failed to connect it with the duke's death and would surely have used it in this context: but Hall's account of Clarence's death is not coloured by the charges in the act of attainder.[110] Furthermore Professor Lander claims that the act of attainder itself did not refer to the Readeption parliament, although it seems to, but only to the treaty with Queen Margaret. He himself wonders whether this is going too far. Certainly the first reference appears to relate to parliament: it states that Clarence was

> 'laboryng also by Parlement, to exclude hym [Edward IV] and all his from the Regalie, and enabling himself to the same'.

This corresponds to Hall's account, but this does not mean that it was the direct origin of his reference to the Readeption act. From other chronicles something is known of the rumours surrounding Clarence's trial but there is no evidence that this story was one of them. Hall's chronicle may here be an original authority, based on an unknown source that is no longer extant.

Professor Lander has failed to impugn the independence of the chronicles of Warkworth and Hall. He has not discredited their accounts of events in 1470-1. The passage in the act of attainder relating to exemplification may be truthful, although this has not been confirmed. In the light of what is known about the Readeption the exemplification may well have existed. The mere possession of such a document was not treason, although it implies treasonable intentions.

Another charge was that Clarence sought the throne not just as heir of Lancaster but also of York. To do this the titles of his elder brother and Edward's children had to be set aside. The act states that Clarence 'published and saide, that the Kyng oure Sovereigne Lorde was a Bastard, and not begottene to reigne uppon us'. That such stories are the stock of fifteenth-century propaganda should make us cautious rather than incredulous. The story dates back to at least 1469, when it was probably disseminated by Clarence and Warwick.[111] It may have earlier origins and it was certainly current later. Richard III's title to the crown, as it was presented to the 1484 parliament, was partly based on it. It was then associated with the story of Edward IV's precontract with Lady Eleanor Butler,[112] which invalidated his marriage to Elizabeth Wydeville. This story is recounted by three independent chroniclers writing after the 1484 parliament, and by Dominic Mancini, who was writing before it.[113] He thought that the Duchess Cecily was responsible for the bastardy story, which she related at the time of Edward's wedding in 1464;[114] this may not be true but it indicates that both tales were associated with Edward's marriage. Perhaps they were inseparable from it.

Edward's marriage was clandestine and may have been invalid on these grounds alone.[115] Perhaps Clarence realised this. He was certainly careful that his own marriage should not be impugned as clandestine or for lack of sufficient witnesses. Even though there is no evidence of it, he may always have been hostile to the king's marriage, but there is no sign that he knew of the precontract story.

The only evidence that he did lies in the elusive behaviour of Robert Stillington, Bishop of Bath and Wells. He was arrested during the 1478 parliament and was later pardoned 'for violating his oath of fidelity by some utterance prejudicial to the king'.[116] This is suspicious, in view of later events. Commines held Stillington responsible for the dissemination of the precontract story by which Richard III justified his usurpation, since it rendered Edward's children illegitimate.[117] Perhaps it originated with him. If it was true, he was well placed to know about it, as keeper of the privy seal at the time of Edward's marriage. Yet, even though they must have been acquainted during Stillington's twelve years as keeper of the privy seal and chancellor, there is no sign that his relations with Clarence were other than formal. In 1471 the duke stayed at the bishop's palace at Wells, which was probably his field headquarters, and deposited his moveables there; but as Stillington was then in sanctuary in London, this does not indicate friendship. Stillington was among those who persuaded Clarence to make peace with King Edward and his deputy, the Prior of Bath, was godfather of one of

Clarence's children.[118] There is nothing to connect Stillington's disloyal utterance with the duke, even in time. He attended the 1478 parliament, where he acted as trier and, as dean of St. Martin-le-Grand, was probably responsible for securing an exemption for it from an act against counterfeiters of coins.[119] There are three letters written by Dr. Thomas Langton between 20 February and 5 March 1478 to the Prior of Christ Church, Canterbury, in which he refers to rumours current in the king's court. In the first two, of 20 and 27 February, he does not refer to Stillington's arrest, which occurs only in the letter of 5 March. It thus appears that Stillington was arrested between 27 February and 5 March, after parliament's dissolution on 21 February. This tallies with Elizabeth Stonor's observation on 6 March to Sir William Stonor, an M.P. at the late parliament, that 'the busshope off Bathe ys browthe in to the Towre syne you departyd'. At first sight Clarence and Stillington are linked in Langton's letter of 6 March, but it is so badly damaged that it is not clear whether they are mentioned in the same sentence or on the same subject.[120] In any case the bishop may have been arrested for some reference to the trial, not from evidence uncovered during it.

If Clarence is unlikely to have known of the precontract, there was quite sufficient to alarm the queen in the rumours of Edward's bastardy.[121] As already indicated, Clarence knew the story and had probably used it before, so he may well have spoken of it. Indeed, had he not, it would have been unwise of Edward to revive it. The charge may be connected with Clarence's projected Burgundian marriage, for Mary had an independent claim to the English crown[122] and another of the charges relates to Burgundy.

The act of attainder also refers to the trial of Thomas Burdet. It does not state that Clarence and Burdet were accomplices in treason but that Clarence used Burdet's sentence to foment sedition. He employed his servants to spread that Burdet was wrongfully condemned and to slander the king as a bastard. With this slander they encouraged the people to withdraw their allegiance from Edward and bestow it on Clarence, who

> 'enduced dyverse of the Kynges naturall Subgetts, to be sworne uppon the Blessed Sacrament to be true to hym and his heyres, noe exception reserved of theire liegaunce'.

Clarence planned to send his heir abroad and warned his supporters to be arrayed at an hour's warning against the king.

The act adds new points and new detail to our knowledge. The oaths described resemble indentures of retainer that lack the clause saving the loyalty of the retainer to the king and his heir. Such indentures do exist, like that between Richard, Duke of York (d. 1460) and Simon Milburn, but they are uncommon by 1478. No such indenture or letter implicates Clarence. This is hardly surprising, as few documents survive from the duke's archives. But without supporting evidence, such a charge is incredible. Any individuals forming such contracts with Clarence would be as guilty as he, but there is no evidence that Clarence had any accomplices. He was attainted alone. None of the recipients of his letters nor any bound to him by illegal indentures were prosecuted for treason. No traces of illegal retainer involving Clarence can be traced in the court of King's Bench. If his associates in crime were unpunished, they must have been forgiven by the king. Such forgiveness would be marked by a pardon, but an examination of pardons enrolled or filed among the chancery warrants does not suggest that any accomplices of Clarence were pardoned. It thus seems that there were no accomplices. If so, this charge of conspiracy against Clarence is without foundation.

The Burdet and Twynho affairs both figure prominently in the proceedings of the 1478 parliament. Ankarette Twynho's grandson Roger Twynho successfully petitioned that the process against her be annulled.[123] In its passage it was probably promoted by John and William Twynho, respectively members for Gloucester and Dorsetshire, and perhaps also by the member for Calne (Wilts.), Robert, brother of Sir Roger Tocotes. With his brother-in-law Bishop Beauchamp among the lords spiritual, Sir Roger's point of view was well represented. It was probably through him that Tocotes's grievances were first brought to Edward's notice in May 1477.[124] Moreover seventeen of the lay magnates had been on the commission that condemned Burdet. Their version of events was well-known, for it was that of the crown. It conflicted with that of Clarence, who had impugned their honesty by proclaiming Burdet innocent. He was thus identified with a condemned traitor which, if not actually evidence of treason, was liable to be interpreted in that light. The notoriety of the Twynho affair could only be damaging to his reputation.

The Burdet affair was cleverly linked to Clarence's projected marriage with Mary of Burgundy. His intentions and his resentment at Edward's prohibition were probably widely known.[125] He was accused of plotting to send his heir to his sister Margaret of Burgundy, a charge which implied that his whole motive for the marriage was treasonable. Mary of Burgundy was a Lancastrian claimant to the crown. This web of charges was connected to the events of the Readeption and Clarence's Lancastrian title to the crown, which may have been common knowledge. Certainly the act was cleverly drafted. A series of notorious events, none treasonable in the context of 1478, were combined to construct a complex conspiracy. In the absence of proof of treason, a number of acts not in themselves seditious were combined to convict him. Such an indictment, which was only put to Clarence at his trial, would be extremely difficult to rebut.

Does this impute too cynical an attitude in the framers of the act? With regard to the clause about the despatch of the duke's heir to Burgundy, there is some concrete fact. Three people are named whom Clarence approached to arrange it, but who refused his request. If there was no other specific evidence, would not these men have been called as witnesses? Indeed may it not be with this in mind that they were named in the indictment? They were Roger Harewell, Master John Tapton and the Abbot of Tewkesbury.

Roger Harewell was a prominent Worcestershire esquire, member of a family traditionally loyal to the Earls of Warwick. If the act is to be believed, he was also a member of Clarence's household.

John Strensham's abbey of Tewkesbury was in the patronage of the Duke of Clarence as Lord Despenser. He had given it the manors of Kinver and Stourton (Staffs.) and obtained licences for it to receive lands in mortmain. His son Richard was born in the infirmary, the abbot had confirmed his son Edward, and his wife Isabel had been interred in the abbey choir.[126] Abbot Strensham had a genuine tie with the duke and is a surprising traitor.

Even more astonishing is the defection of Master John Tapton, one of three brothers who had served the duke. The only layman among them, William Tapton, was bailiff of Chadlington hundred (Oxon.) and warrener of Brailes (Warw.); Hugh Tapton, chancellor of Lincoln cathedral, was surveyor of Clarence's Lincolnshire lands.[127] John himself had been Clarence's chancellor in 1462-68 and had probably remained in office subsequently.[128] He certainly remained in his service.

Why did men so intimate with Clarence desert him? It was not in the hope of reward, for Tapton received no further promotion. It is difficult to believe that it was fear that motivated them. What the Croyland chronicler describes are witnesses who appear as principals,[129] men with a bitter personal hostility to the duke which might spring from malice. This bitterness is what might be expected of men who had changed from intimates to enemies of their lord. To produce such a result Clarence must have treated them badly, for Tapton at least had stood by him through all the crises of 1469-71. The break with the abbot — and presumably with the others — occurred after February 1477.

One is reminded of another of the chronicler's observations. This time it concerns the relations of king and duke after the breakdown of the Burgundian marriage project:[130]

> 'You might then have seen (as such men are generally to be found in the courts of all princes), flatterers running to and fro, from the one side to the other, and carrying backwards and forwards the words which had falen from the two brothers, even if they had happened to be spoken in the most secret closet'.

Were Tapton, Strensham and Harewell talebearers? It is unlikely. Certainly, as members of Clarence's household or council, each might have something to repeat, but as far as one can tell none of them had access to the king or his circle and none had the divided loyalties necessary to curry favour with both king and duke. Talebearers told tales to the king in spite of their ties of loyalty to the duke. What Clarence uttered in private might well be unsuitable for Edward's ear. It might even constitute treason by words. From his intimates exclusive loyalty was required. If it was not forthcoming, vengeance might be swift and drastic. The Twynho case is an example of Clarence's revenge, apparently for reasons not disclosed by the indictment. Were these the flatterers?

Such an explanation connects an otherwise unrelated trio. Ankarette Twynho and John Thursby belonged to Clarence's household, Tocotes was his intimate. Even before the Duchess of Clarence's death relations between the king and duke were strained. Afterwards it was apparent that Clarence's service no longer offered great prospects of advancement. The Wydeville star was rising, as the queen's sons grew older and their establishments expanded. John Twynho the elder, recorder of Bristol, became attorney-general of the Prince of Wales.[131] It is unlikely that he severed his links with other lords, though henceforth their service would take second place. With the death of her mistress, Ankarette Twynho probably lost her employment and may have been glad for any patronage her influential kinsman could offer her. Since 1473 Tocotes had been constable of Devizes (Wilts.) and master of game in the queen's Wiltshire estates,[132] which were more closely situated to his own sphere than the offices bestowed by Clarence. The revival of the Bonville and Hungerford peerages rendered the service of the Wydevilles, especially of the Marquis of Dorset, increasingly attractive. Both Twynho and Tocotes were faced by an irreconcilable conflict of loyalties. Any information they supplied to the Wydevilles was likely to be used to influence Edward against Clarence.

If this assessment is correct, one can readily understand why Clarence sought revenge. But talebearing did not constitute petty treason, so it was necessary to concoct false indictments. Sir Roger Tocotes, who escaped, and John Twynho had influence with the Bishop of Salisbury and the Wydevilles, who may have brought the affair to Edward's attention. The indictment of Tocotes may account for the defection of Strensham, Tapton and Harewell, whose testimony was of real value to the Wydevilles. These witnesses may have been employed to persuade Edward to prosecute Clarence, as well as testifying at the trial itself.

The prominence of the Twynho and Burdet cases at the trial probably reflects their importance in the events of the previous year. Individually and as a group chroniclers did not understand why Clarence fell, nor did their informants, but their accounts reveal the issues with which it was associated when they wrote. Polydore Vergil mentions necromancy, which he connects with the Burgundian marriage. Sir Thomas More knew about Thomas Burdet. By a reference to the death of the Duchess Isabel by poisoning, the author of the *Great Chronicle of London* reveals his knowledge of and belief in Clarence's version of the Twynho affair. To explain the inexplicable, other tales were circulated, such as the story that the duke died because his name began with the letter G (for George), the initial that a soothsayer foretold to be that of Edward's successor.[133] This tale would have been more rapidly rejected, if it was not held to have been fulfilled by Gloucester's accession in 1483. None of the chroniclers had anything to say about Clarence's projected rebellion in 1477. Certainly there were disturbances. Placards were posted and an imposter masquerading as the Earl of Oxford was active in

Cambridgeshire and Huntingdonshire,[134] counties where neither Clarence nor the de Veres had significant possessions. There is nothing to suggest a substantial conspiracy. Clarence was condemned alone, without accomplices. The ease with which he was arrested at Westminster, in answer to a royal summons, does not suggest that he plotted rebellion. Without further evidence the plot remains only a tale, perhaps fabricated by his enemies.

One cannot wholly eradicate doubts about his attitude. In the last analysis, it was Edward IV who made decisions. However unfriendly he felt towards his brother, it was a big step to bring him to trial. If his delay in making decisions and his guilty conscience are any guide, it was a step that he did not wish to take. His reluctance suggests that his ultimate decision was based on more than mere irritation with Clarence as a nuisance. Wydeville hostility to Clarence was a constant factor, so something else was needed to persuade him. This may have been supplied by the flatterers, particularly if these were Tapton, Strensham and Harewell. It is perfectly credible that in private Clarence uttered words that could be construed as treasonable and the incident casts some hints of what they were. Apparently he spoke of Edward's bastardy; he considered shipping his son abroad, without deciding between Burgundy and Ireland; he said that 'the Kyng entended to consume hym in lyke wyse as a Candell consumeth in brennyng, whereof he wolde in brief tyme quyte hym'. He spoke of Edward's resumption of his lands and his belief that the king would dispossess him further; this resentment is also mentioned in the Croyland chronicle. He may have thought them true, but such comments indicate a lack of faith in his brother and a fear of his malevolence, which indicates how far away was the normal relationship of king and subject. No act of royal mercy could be expected to placate him. If he was tried, there was the danger that he might be acquitted, but if he was not he would eventually have to be released. His words, if not his actions, were sufficient for Edward to withraw his protection from him.

Chapter V

Estates, Retinue and Power

The magnates of late medieval England were not selected by merit, but were born into their station and distinguished by titles of nobility. Birth and rank alone were never enough to confer political power, which stemmed from only two sources — influence at court and ownership of land — which were open only to the well-born. Courtiers like the Wydevilles enjoyed only limited and ephemeral influence in the provinces, unless or until they cemented it by acquiring lands of their own. Clarence, as we have seen, started out from court, but later based his power on his estates. To support his exalted rank any nobleman required a minimum income, ideally derived from land. With this land and the revenues from it he could attract retainers, who conferred political influence in the localities. The more land, money and retainers he possessed, the greater he became, until he could command the respectful attention of government. All followed from the tenure of land: in shorthand, land was power.

So it was with Clarence, whose political career was founded principally on his physical might. It was less his birth and title than the extent of his estates and number of his dependants that made him impossible to ignore. They also conditioned his conduct. The geographical location of his estates, for example, was reflected in his territorial influence: where he had estates, there he had retainers; where he had none, he was ineffectual. Thus his will carried weight in the Midlands and West Country but was of little account in East Anglia or the Home Counties. Changes in these territorial roots altered the geographical distribution of his power. Such matters, and still more the acquisition and retention of his estates, were fundamental, vital interests that could not be surrendered or compromised. Much of his career, as we have seen, was shaped by such matters: during the fourteen-seventies the devolution of the Warwick inheritance was the burning issue in national politics.

Clarence's political career was thus a superstructure resting on his lands and retainers in the localities and profoundly affected by them. Without reference to the base, many questions cannot be fully answered: why did Tutbury or the Warwick inheritance matter so much? Was Clarence living within his means? How did his estates, his income and his retinue compare with those of other great magnates? One could not conceivably attain a complete or balanced picture of Clarence as magnate or man. It is with these topics that this chapter is concerned.

1. Estates

Clarence was a younger son. He therefore possessed no land of his own and had no expectation of inheriting any. To obtain sufficient income to support his title as duke and to finance his political career, he was dependant on the generosity of his brother Edward IV and on what he could acquire by marriage to an heiress. Up to 1471 all his estates had been granted to him by the king; after that date he also held the inheritance of his wife. I shall discuss these two categories in turn.

Kings had a duty to provide appropriately for members of their family. The sons and brothers of former kings had generally been created earls, sometimes dukes, and had received the minimum income for their rank: 1,000 marks (£666 13*s*. 4*d*.) for an earl, 2,000 marks (£1,333 6*s*. 8*d*.) for a duke. As kings seldom had such valuable estates at hand, their brothers and sons had usually been endowed only partly with lands and partly with annuities, to be exchanged for land as this became available. In practice most of these annuities were never redeemed. Edward IV differed from this pattern in two principal respects: throughout his life he was exceptionally generous to all his relatives; secondly, he had sufficient lands to make up his endowments without having recourse to annuities. As a result, Clarence was endowed lavishly.

At his accession Edward possessed an almost unparallelled fund of patronage. Apart from his own inheritance, he held Henry VI's duchy of Lancaster and the crown lands, including the estates of the Prince of Wales. The attainder of Lancastrian nobles placed a vast pool of land at his disposal. These were supplemented by the resumption of some of Henry VI's grants. Admittedly Edward had many obligations to meet, notably to his supporters and the ten new peers he created in the opening years of his reign. So prodigal were his grants that by 1464, when he wanted to endow Clarence and his queen, forfeitures had almost all been alienated and he had to give away Lancaster and even crown lands.

Up till 1464 the only lands assigned to Clarence and Gloucester were forfeitures. As neither was of age, such grants were provisional: Edward still received the revenues and could revise the arrangements at will. Thus the honour of Richmond, originally assigned to Gloucester, was transferred to Clarence, and the Percy lands in Northumberland were taken from Clarence in 1464 to endow John Neville on his creation as Earl of Northumberland.[1]

In spite of such changes of plan, Clarence had been granted the possession or reversion of eighty manors by September 1464, the bulk from forfeitures. Twenty-one had belonged to the Percies. His share of Richmond honour lay mainly around Boston (Lincs.), but also included Swaffham (Norf.) and knights's fees elsewhere. He had also title to forty-one manors, feefarms of £229 8*s*. 8*d*. and other property in fourteen counties. Most had been forfeited by the attainders of the Earls of Devon and Wiltshire, Lord Roos, Sir Thomas Tresham and Sir Anthony Nuthill. Clarence held more forfeited land than anyone else. He had the reversions of property on the deaths of seven dowagers and on the expiry of twelve years from the death of the Earl of Kent (d. 1463). The principal concentrations were in the West Country and in Lincolnshire, South Yorkshire and Nottinghamshire.

This pattern was confirmed by the grants between August 1464 and July 1465, which made Clarence into a great magnate. Four major and several minor estates were involved. The Earl of Kent's executors were induced to surrender their title in his lands, permitting Clarence to take them over prematurely. To these Edward added a life estate in thirteen manors in Somerset and Dorset, formerly of Sir Matthew Gournay and since annexed to the duchy of Cornwall. He also gave the duke the Lancaster honours of Tutbury (Staffs.) and Duffield and lordships of High Peak (Derbys.) and Castle Donington (Leics.). The logical sequel, to complete the band of possessions across the North Midlands, was the grant of the county of Chester: however, this does not seem to have taken effect.[2]

With some minor changes, the framework of Clarence's estates had been set for the rest of the decade.

None of Clarence's estates had a completely secure title, for all fell within the review of acts of resumption and most were forfeitures. Title to forfeited property was good only so long as the attainder of the previous tenant held good. Should it be reversed, the estates passed from the current holder to the former tenant or his heirs. After 1461 there were more reversals than new attainders. The amount of forfeited lands was reduced, so Clarence as the greatest beneficiary was bound to lose. Certain losses were relative pinpricks — for example the Tailbois, Nuthill and Tresham lands;[3] more important were Richmond honour, temporarily lost in 1470, and the Percy lands. Similarly, royal grants conferred an uncertain title. There were periodic acts of resumption, which afforded opportunities to review royal patronage and to revoke former grants. Clarence suffered in 1473, when he was deprived of crown and Lancaster estates in Nottinghamshire, Derbyshire, Staffordshire and Leicestershire together worth £1,350 a year. He had already lost the Gournay lands by 1471.

We have seen in earlier chapters how fear of resumption and fear of reversals affected Clarence's political behaviour. Resumption, and to some extent reversals, resulted from royal action and reflected Edward's displeasure with Clarence. Clarence's lands suffered from steady attrition, for which he was never adequately compensated. This is somewhat obscured by figures for his income, which actually rose slightly between 1467 and 1473, as reversions fell in. The composition of his estate had changed significantly and the income which he could ultimately expect, when all reversions were realised, had been substantially cut. It was not surprising that Clarence was resentful and defensive even before 1473, when resumption reduced the yield of his estates by a third.

By then, of course, he had already acquired a stake in the inheritance of his wife Isabel Neville, daughter and coheiress of the Earl and Countess of Warwick and Salisbury. This inheritance combined the great estates of the four families of Neville, Montagu, Despenser and Beauchamp. Clarence held the lion's share from 1471 until 1474, when they were divided more fairly: Gloucester received the northern and Welsh properties, Clarence those in the West Midlands, south and south-west, while those in eastern England were shared. Altogether this inheritance was approximately equal in value to the lands Clarence already held.[4]

2. Administration

Many small properties made up a great fifteenth-century estate. The revenues of each unit, whether it was a manor, hundred or borough, were collected by a salaried minister, who was supervised by the steward, who kept the courts, and sometimes by a supervisor as well. The minister paid the receipts to a receiver, of whom there were usually several, each responsible for a manageable geographical area. Ministers and receivers accounted to auditors; senior officers and councillors dealt with other business, such as the preparation of a new rental. This simple and coherent system was universal.

Clarence faced serious administrative problems, since his lands lacked geographical unity or a common past; instead they were dispersed and formed parts of many different estates. The lands held by royal grant constituted eight principal groups, not all held at once. These were respectively former portions of Richmond honour, the duchy of Lancaster, the crown, Percy, Gournay, Butler (Wiltshire), Courtenay (Devon) and Roos lands. From 1471 on Clarence also held half the Warwick inheritance: four separate estates, united only briefly before again being divided, but on different lines. Each estate had its own management structure, procedure and traditions: for example, the salaries of local ministers varied widely. Altogether there was good reason for Clarence's estate administration to be inefficient, as Professor Hilton suggests that it was.[5] Clarence could not impose uniformity of practice or interfere effectively in the detailed work of ministers, but he could devise a rational receivership structure and ensure prompt collection and delivery of his revenue.

Unfortunately Clarence's success or failure cannot be readily established by straightforward reference to the records. The study of his estates is hampered by the absence of accounts for the period of his tenure. Fortunately ministers's accounts, receivers's accounts and receivers's declarations of account cover the whole estate immediately after his death. Similarly accounts survive for years soon after his tenure for all the principal estates that he had relinquished earlier. In many cases there are also accounts antedating his tenure. Change can be established by comparing accounts from before and after his tenure and by analysing some of the later accounts. Since the evidence is always indirect and incomplete, any conclusions are tentative.

Each of the estates was probably already divided into receiverships before being acquired by Clarence. Rather then preserve several overlapping systems, it was logical to rationalise them. Was this done?

Let us look first at Clarence's own estates. Almost nothing is known about the administration of the Percy, Gournay and crown lands. On the Lancaster estates, the two receiverships for Tutbury, Duffield and High Peak and for Castle Donington were combined. At Clarence's death, there were five receiverships: Milton and Marden (Kent); Richmond honour in Norfolk (Swaffham); Richmond honour in Lincolnshire; the Roos part of Boston (Lincs.); and the Butler, Courtenay and Montagu lands in the south-west. Certainly the first three, probably the first four, existed before Clarence's tenure. Two receivers were responsible for property in Boston and only the fifth represents rationalisation. At first sight it seems that Clarence left the situation as he found it, but three receiverships covered outlying property, that must always have been administered separately; the most pressing anomalies, in the West Country, had been resolved; and other isolated manors, in Surrey for instance, had been included in the receiverships of the Warwick inheritance.

For thirty years before 1462 the Warwick inheritance had formed two units, the Neville-Montagu (Salisbury) and the Beauchamp-Despenser estates. By 1445 there was a separate receiver for the south parts of the Neville-Montagu estate. He had been replaced by at least two in 1462: one for the six south-western shires, a second for the home counties, and presumably another for Rutland, Lincolnshire and Northamptonshire. On the Beauchamp-Despenser estate Barnard Castle (Durh.) and the marcher lordships, like Glamorgan,[6] probably had separate receivers. Several others catered for the English shires: there were certainly two for the West Midlands in 1459-61, when one was responsible for Walsall (Staffs.), Brailes (Warw.), Elmley Castle and Yardley (Worcs.), the other for Tewkesbury (Gloucs.). These four receiverships were preserved by Warwick, who included in them other lands in the same areas. Clarence inherited this pattern, adapted somewhat by the partition of the Warwick inheritance and the inclusion of his own lands. In 1478 the inheritance was divided among five receiverships: one for the honour of Gloucester; one for the Home Counties; one for part of Worcestershire, Gloucestershire, Oxfordshire, Wiltshire and Berkshire; a fourth for the rest of Worcestershire, Warwickshire and other counties further north; and the other for the south-west, which took in the Butler and Courtenay lands. John Luthington was receiver both for the Home Counties and the Warwickshire circle.

Of Clarence's nine receiverships in 1478, four covered large groups of counties and four outlying estates. There was room for further improvement in Kent and Lincolnshire, perhaps to follow the deaths of longlived receivers, but considerable reorganisation had been needed to achieve the existing system.

Another measure of efficiency was success in collecting and delivering the issues. Two aspects require consideration: the speed with which money was transmitted to Clarence following collection and the extent to which revenues were successfully collected.

To some extent speed of delivery corresponded to the earlier traditions of the estate under consideration: the southern Montagu lands had a consistently bad record, in spite of attempts at reform, but ministers of Richmond honour in Lincolnshire passed on issues quickly, in spite of disruption by floods. Individual examples of improvement or deterioration can be found, but the most notable success was the Lancaster estate. Here the level of arrears stood at not less than 40 per cent and probably considerably higher at Michaelmas 1463. By 1476 this had fallen to less than 15 per cent — still high, but much improved. Arrears had grown because ministers and lessees retained the issues that they had collected rather than delivering them to the receivers. Before Clarence's tenure the duchy administration had dismissed some offenders. Clarence also did this, but in addition he sued them for detinue at the court of Common Pleas. The damages he sought were in round figures, a sign that they were not the actual sums owed but the penalties for unfulfilled recognisances. Evidently Clarence, like other landowners, extracted bonds and sureties from new ministers and farmers as guarantees of good conduct. None of the suits reached judgement, probably because the defendants submitted: the success of the tactic is shown by the fall in arrears. Clarence sued a mere handful of individuals for arrears elsewhere, presumably because nowhere else was the situation so serious.

How much collectable income was in fact collected? Professor Hilton has pointed out that the Warwickshire accounts were fossilised, being based on rentals half a century old. The long lists of decayed rents were nearly as antique and hardly any of the tenants named in the rentals were still alive. It was difficult to determine liability for rent, to locate the holdings described, and thus to collect all that was due. New rentals were required.[7]

Certainly ministers sometimes did petition for allowance for unidentifiable holdings. One can readily appreciate the difficulties posed by obsolete rentals. But inefficiency should emerge in falling income or rising arrears, whereas rents had almost ceased to decay and arrears were low. Where arrears occur, they often relate to disallowed fees and expenses. Only falling income could justify an expensive measure like a new rental. They were part of the standard reaction to a crisis, when lost revenue was written off and what remained was consolidated in a clearer record. Within this particular receivership, Clarence's administrators thought a new rental necessary only at Essendine and Shillingthorpe (Rut.).[8] Warwick's officers had renewed those at Elmley Castle, Hanley, Redmarley, Abberley (Worcs.), Mythe, Sodbury, Fairford (Gloucs.), Cherhill, Broadtown, Sherston (Wilts.), Newport Pagnell (Bucks.), Stanford (Berks.) and Rotherfield (Suss.), but in only two cases had this increased or recovered lost revenue.[9] In 1479-80 no manors in the Warwick inheritance were in a position sufficiently serious to call for a new rental. The auditors wrote meticulous notes in the margins of accounts, which show that they held ministers liable for all sums with which they were charged. It is difficult to credit the allowance of unjustifiable sums: indeed, the fact that Edward IV allowed sums to Luthington that Warwick and Clarence had disallowed shows that the administration was extremely tenacious and unyielding.

The same pattern emerges elsewhere. The economic recession and decline in income seems virtually over: few rents were decaying and in some places, such as Tewkesbury (Gloucs.), Melbourne (Derbys.) and Agarsley (Staffs.), issues rose. New rentals occur only where revenues had collapsed for economic reasons: this was true in Lincolnshire, where the sea had invaded several manors. Both there and at Hartington (Derbys.) substantial arrears, many years old, were written off. Nowhere, on the evidence, did the antiquity of rentals significantly reduce the collection of revenue due.

Whether old rentals prevented increases in income or the

recovery of old revenues, it is not possible to say. It seems improbable, on balance, that there was much opportunity to increase rents, and certainly Clarence did not exploit new sources of income. One missed opportunity may have been the demesne of Fairford (Gloucs.), leased successively to Clarence's receiver Walter Mymmes and by John Twynho and John Tame, the clothier.[10] As the old rent was charged and as Fairford was a Cotswold wool village, the lessees may have been enjoying an increase in income that Clarence was failing to tap. However, this may have been a preferential lease, where rents were kept artificially low as a form of patronage.

Our criteria of efficient estate administration were a rational receivership structure and prompt collection and transmission of revenue. On these terms, Clarence's administration seems competent. Some improvements were desirable: given longer tenure, it is possible that Clarence would have carried them out.

3. Income[11]

Another measure of efficiency is Clarence's income. The lack of contemporary accounts has already been mentioned. For the calculation of income, earlier and later accounts can be supplemented by exchequer processes for arrears and by inquisition valuations relating to forfeited lands in 1461, to the 1473 act of resumption, and on Clarence's own death.

Such materials are difficult to use. One is often told that a single account, which may be exceptional, proves nothing: a series of accounts is required. For some estates such series do survive, but the later an account is, the further removed it is from the date and conditions of Clarence's tenure. Where accounts are available for comparision from both before and after his tenure, one cannot safely assume either consistency or a continuous trend in between. The different types of account and inquisition are not strictly comparable or of equal accuracy. Not all these problems have been solved.

The aim is to establish what has been termed the disposable surplus, the total sum remaining after essential expenses have been deducted from the gross income. This is not identical to the balance in a receiver's account after the deduction of expenses, since his income normally consists only of arrears and liveries. Liveries are that part of the local surplus, which the minister transmitted to the receiver: often money was spent locally or remained in the hands of the minister. In 1463-4 the clear value of High Peak and Winslands (Derbys.) was £266, not a penny of which was paid to the receiver. A fifth of the surplus of Duffield honour was retained by the ministers. Such sums are too large to ignore. If they had actually been collected, they represented part of the ministers's liability to their lord, which he could choose to exact. Such balances, the receiver's liveries to his lord, and the receiver's own arrears were part of the lord's resources. Fees and expenses not specifically required for administration and maintenance, like local payments authorised by the lord, were forms of disposal of the surplus and have not been deducted. The sum remaining after such adjustments is the disposable surplus, the monetary value of the estate to the lord.

Clarence's income has been calculated for three dates: 1467, 1473 and 1478. The most reliable figures are based on near-contemporary accounts, like those surviving for most estates soon after 1478. The disposable surplus of the crown and Lancaster lands in 1473 and the Richmond, Percy and Lancaster estates in 1467 are probably equally accurate. The unreliable inquisition valuations have only been used where no accounts survive, which means in practice for only a few minor properties. Where necessary, later values have been interpolated for earlier dates, a relatively safe procedure in the absence of clear economic trends affecting income. Many details would have been altered had strictly contemporary accounts survived, but the global figures would probably not have been changed substantially.

Clarence's estates were concentrated in the North Midlands and West Country in 1467. The North Midland group comprised the Lancaster estates in Staffordshire, Derbyshire and Leicestershire, the Richmond, Roos, Percy and Tailbois estates in Lincolnshire, crown lands and feefarms in Nottinghamshire and Derbyshire, and Percy, Richmond, Roos and Nuthill manors in Yorkshire. Most important were the Lancaster estates, worth over a thousand pounds a year; the Yorkshire estates were worth *c.* £520, those in Lincolnshire *c.*£330, and the whole group *c.*£2,100. The other, West Country group, consisted of five castles and fifty-five manors in the counties of Devon, Cornwall, Dorset, Somerset and Hampshire. The largest concentration was in Somerset. Altogether they were worth *c.*£850 a year. Other lands and feefarms raised Clarence's income to *c.*£3,400, rather less than the £3,733 6*s.* 8*d.* intended by

Edward. He, however, had envisaged an ultimate income of 6,600 marks (£4,400), when 1,000-marks worth of reversions fell in, but Clarence's actual reversions cannot be valued.

The Percy, Gournay and Tailbois lands had been lost by 1473, but several reversions were realised and the Courtenay lands were acquired. Clarence's income was raised to *c*.£3,500, rather more than in 1467. There were still two principal groups of estates: one in the North Midlands, now shorn of the Percy lands in Yorkshire and Lincolnshire, the other in the West Country, augmented by the Courtenay lands and now consisting mainly of property in Devonshire. In addition he held much of the Warwick inheritance, certainly including the marcher lordship of Glamorgan and much else in addition to those estates he was eventually allotted. In the absence of direct evidence, an estimate of £6,000 for Clarence's total income is probably rather conservative.

By 1478 Clarence had lost the Lancaster and crown lands and his North Midland estate had been reduced to a few isolated properties in Yorkshire and the Richmond-Roos estates, worth *c*.£400 a year, in Lincolnshire. His own estates were worth *c*.£2,100, his share of the Warwick inheritance *c*.£2,400. Nearly half lay in the six south-western counties, with twin nuclei at Tiverton (Devon) and Christchurch Twynham (Hants.); a quarter were in the West Midlands, administered from Warwick; and many other properties, some substantial, were distributed all over the home and eastern counties.

The disposable surplus available to Clarence was *c*.£3,400 in 1467, not less than £6,000 in 1473, and *c*.£4,500 in 1478. This does not compare with the income of John of Gaunt, Duke of Lancaster, the greatest magnate of late medieval England; except in 1473, it does not even match the wealth of the three greatest magnates of the fourteen-fifties, but during the fourteen-sixties, with Buckingham a minor and the Mowbray inheritance encumbered by dowagers, Clarence may have been second only to Warwick. He was certainly richer than those other parvenus, Rivers and Pembroke. Likewise in the fourteen-seventies, when the Stafford and Mowbray estates were encumbered, his income was only rivalled, if at all, by his brother of Gloucester. Clarence was the outstanding magnate at a time when nobody was of the front rank.

Clarence had a direct and immediate interest in his income because he wanted to spend it: he was certainly no parsimonious

Above: Signet Letter from Clarence to Lawrence Lowe, dated at Tutbury castle 10 April [1468] and signed G. Clarence.

Right: Details of contingents of Clarence, Gloucester and other dukes for the invasion of France, 1475, together with their badges: the top two are the bull of Clarence and boar of Gloucester.

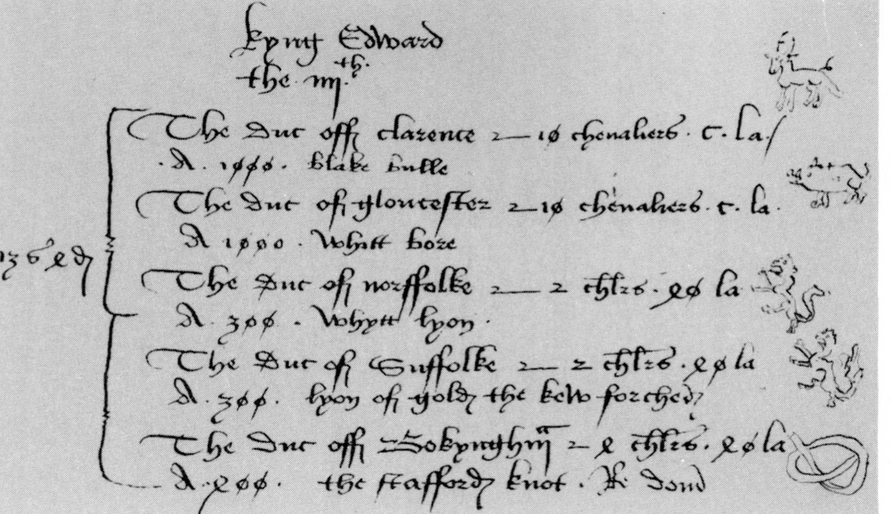

Kyng Edward
the iiij^th.

The Duc off clarence — 10 chevaliers . C. la.
A. 1000 . blake bulle
The Duc off glouceter — 10 chevaliers . C. la.
A 1000 . Whitt bore
The Duc off norffolke — 2 chlrs . 40 la
A . 300 . Whytt lyon .
The Duc off Suffolke — 2 chlrs . 40 la
A . 300 . lyon off gold the kew forched
The Duc off Bokyngham — 4 chlrs . 40 la
A . 400 . the stafford knot .

miser. Little is known of his expenditure, but there can be no doubt that his household, like that of any other magnate, was the largest item. Indeed, his household ordinance of 1468 planned spending greater than his actual income. While this can hardly have been Clarence's practice for long, there is no reason to doubt the information in the ordinance about the organisation and scale of his household. Like other similar establishments, it consisted of an upper household, comprising Clarence's personal attendants, and a lower household of menial servants in departments such as the kitchen, buttery and spicery. The scale, however, was quite exceptional: there was a staff of 188 in the riding household, 299 in all, and an anticipated annual expenditure twice that of the Stafford household in 1444. Clarence kept 93 horses at a time when other magnates had closed their stables and relied on hired transport. Annual expenditure was envisaged of 650 quarters of wheat, 410 carcases of beef and 2,700 of mutton, 365 tuns of ale and 41 tuns of wine, besides seasonal and luxury items. In spite of the splendour, there was to be no waste, for the ordinance prescribed careful accounting procedures, the sale of byproducts, fixed perquisites, and limited entitlement to meals, livery, lights and horses. Leisure activities were strictly controlled. Domestic life was to be regulated by the duke's meals and religious observances: the household was to provide him with a setting of comfort and magnificence wherever he went. Splendour and conspicuous consumption in public, economy and discipline behind the scenes, reflected the twin aims of value for money and that 'the said Duke will be well and honorabilly served'.[12] Even if the ordinance was scaled down by half in practice, relatively little can have been left for the duke's other expenditure on items such as his retinue.

4. Retinue

A magnate's military and political power was directly related to the scale of his retinue, which depended in turn on his estates and income. It is usually supposed that a magnate's retinue was composed mainly of gentry retained by indenture for service in peace and war in return for an annuity. It follows that the larger his income and the more money he could spare for annuities, the more retainers he could recruit and the more powerful he was. This argument, however, ceased to be tenable, when it was found that some leading magnates had very few indentured retainers. Indeed, even the huge indentured retinue of John of Gaunt cannot by itself account for the vast size of his total following. Where the actual turnout can be analysed, most retainers prove to be tenants of the magnate's estates.[13]

This applies to Clarence's retinue, which included a mere handful of indentured retainers and annuitants: most were recruited not by himself, but by previous holders of his lands. Yet his retinue was four thousand strong on the Barnet and Tewkesbury campaign,[14] too many to be explained either by his indentured retainers or his household. Letters to Henry Vernon, steward of his lordship of High Peak (Derbys.), show how such numbers were arrayed:[15]

> 'Overe this that ye see as well all your tenauntes and servauntes as ours in thoos parties be redy upon an houres warnyng to wayte upon us in def[ensible] array whansoevere we send for you and thaim' . . .

> 'Wyllyng and desiring you that bicause of thees tidinges ye doo the gretter devoir to arredie you as many as ye can make in defensible array as well of our tenauntes as of yours to bee redy to comme to us within an houres warnyng' . . .

Most of the four thousand were clearly tenants of Clarence or his officers. The majority were humbly born, but gently-born officers were needed to array and command them. Apart from Clarence's own household and tenants, the retinue consisted of a coalition of gentry — both officers and indentured retainers — at the head of their own tenants and servants.

This situation was repeated in different areas, on different estates, for Clarence had not one, but several retinues. One can identify West Country, West Midland and North Midland retinues: within the latter were distinctive duchy, Lincolnshire and Yorkshire elements. The degree of loyalty to Clarence was influenced by his title to the estates: his position was quite different in Warwick, where he inherited loyalty traditionally due to the Beauchamps, compared with Tutbury, long unaccustomed to any lord, or Tiverton, where he actually supplanted the popular Courtenays.[16] Everywhere, however, stewards and lesser ministers stood between him and his tenants. The stewards were generally leading county gentry, the reeves, bailiffs and parkers usually lesser local gentry, who all served him for the small salaries and fringe benefits of office.

At least some perquisites were at the duke's expense: some officers withheld the revenue they collected, others misappropriated ducal property or abused their power. At Tutbury, where they had become accustomed to treating the estate as their own, Clarence had to resort to the courts not only to secure his revenue, but also to curb large scale poaching of his game.[17] There was a fine line, however, between assertion of his authority and alienation of loyalties, since he relied on his officers to array his tenants. They were needed as a channel of communication, not a barrier, between him and his tenants. Vernon, for example, did not turn out in 1471 and presumably deprived Clarence of the support of his tenants at High Peak.[18]

Communication was a growing problem for late medieval magnates like Clarence, who had given up constant travel between their manors, allowed manor-houses and castles to decay, and lived relatively sedentary lives at a few seats: in Clarence's case, Tutbury (Staffs.), Tiverton (Devon) and Warwick. The lord was seen regularly only by the tenants of the immediate locality and depended increasingly on council, central administration and household to unite his scattered estates and retinues. This worked at both a formal and personal level. On the formal level, one can readily cite the liveries of money, the petitions and queries that passed from the estates to the duke and his council, the answers and instructions sent in reply, and the assembly each autumn of all ministers at Warwick or Tutbury for the audit of their accounts. It was the personal level, however, that mattered more to the retinue.

The household itself was recruited from all parts of the estate: thus Roger Harewell was a West Midlander, Edmund Culham originated from Stratford Langthorne in Essex, John Say was heir of Sir John Say of Broxbourne in Hertfordshire, John Curson and Francis Pierpoint were natives of Derbyshire and Nottinghamshire respectively, and the chancellor, John Tapton, seems to have started life in Lincolnshire.[19] James Norreys had served Clarence's elder brother Edmund and John Peke was already in his service before he came of age.[20] Others joined him at intervals, presumably Harewell only after Warwick's death. Some of the duke's leading councillors and confidants were members of his household. Those whose advice he sought were not a narrow clique with similar origins: among his feoffees, for example, Sir Roger Tocotes was from Bromham in Wiltshire, John Jakeman *alias* Finance from Olney in Buckinghamshire, Thomas Lygon was a Worcestershire lawyer, and Sir William Catesby was his steward in Northamptonshire.[21] Similar variety distinguishes his lawyers, his clerical staff, his receivers and auditors.

The nucleus of any retinue was the household, which contained those whom the lord trusted most, those owing him complete loyalty. They had a prime claim on his patronage. Clarence rewarded his household men with annuities, benefices and offices on his estates, some near their homes, others further afield. For example, his esquire John Curson, already parker of Posterna (Derbys.), was appointed gaoler of Worcester; his near neighbour James Norreys of Burton-on-Trent (Derbys.) held office first in Ireland, then in the Channel Isles, and was feed from Somerton (Soms.); Edmund Verney was appointed bailiff of Pipehall in Erdington, not far from his home at Compton Murdock (Warw.), and Benet Metley became bailiff of Yelvertoft (Northants.); the clerk Master John Barnaby was rector in turn of Leadenham (Lincs.) and Hanbury (Staffs.).[22] Their household wages were partly paid in this way. More important, Clarence's influence and authority was propagated by men intimately acquainted with him and attached to him, whom he could trust to array his tenants and to implement policies that they had seen formulated. His tenants knew him at second rather than third hand.

In 1468 a total household staff of 299 was projected, of whom 188 would accompany him everywhere.[23] They would be afforced on special occasions, such as sessions of parliament. His household, like that of the king himself, was the nucleus of his retinue of war in the French expedition of 1475, when Clarence contracted to take 20 knights apart from himself, 99 men-at-arms and 1,000 archers, but in fact took more.[24] To raise his retinue he subcontracted with others, two such indentures surviving: the Oxfordshire esquire James Hyde, feed after Clarence's death from Caversham (Oxon.), contracted to serve with five archers, William Floyer of Floiers Hays (Dorset) with three archers.[25] Others who obtained protections — altogether a mere fraction of the whole company — included two London mercers and gentry from Somerset, Devon, Warwickshire, Worcestershire and Shropshire. The best illustration of the geographical range of the retinue is the list of Clarence's supporters in 1469-71.

Another obvious measure of Clarence's local influence is the number of retainers who served as sheriffs, escheators or justices of the peace: five sheriffs of Nottinghamshire and Derbyshire, four of Staffordshire, were his men. But since Sir John Stanley alone was pricked five times for Staffordshire, it is questionable whether Clarence affected his appointment. All we can safely deduce is that certain retainers were leading county gentry, which was known in most cases already, and that Clarence received favourable treatment during their years of office. A few outstanding individuals are not a true measure of the strength of Clarence's retinue in a given locality. The identity of members of parliament is similarly of limited value: while their election indicates local support, it does not necessarily follow that they were elected by their fellow retainers.[26]

M.P.s call for further attention as one avenue by which local opinion and local power operated on national politics. The first question to answer is: do election returns reflect the influence of the lord or his retainer? Knights of the shire were invariably leading gentry, usually resident in the county, whether or not a magnate intervened on behalf of any candidate. Such intervention could be decisive, as in East Anglia. Can the return of Sir John Stanley for Staffordshire in 1467 and 1472 be credited to Clarence's influence, when he was elected on three occasions without such help? Was Clarence's assistance essential for the return of William Blount for Derbyshire in 1467 and of Edmund Dudley for Staffordshire in 1472, when each was son of a local baron? Influence may have been decisive in Warwickshire and Worcestershire, where four retainers of Warwick in 1467 and three of Clarence's men in 1472 were returned. On the other hand, it was surely personal initiative that secured Walter Writtle's consistent return for Essex.

All the examples considered so far relate to shire elections, but Clarence's men were also returned for boroughs.[27] Apart from the initiative of magnates and retainers, one needs to allow for the interests of the borough electorate — sometimes a relatively minor factor, often important, occasionally overriding. The election of a gently-born retainer need not reflect successful pressure by him or his lord: often he was the man best able to serve the borough, frequently one of its legal counsel. However, their choice was often a figure of local importance or persona grata with the local magnate. One can discern a variety of types among those of Clarence's retainers, who sat for boroughs. Clarence's own authority, as lord of the borough, apparently sufficed for the return by Ludgershall of the Lincolnshire knight Arthur Ormesby in 1467 and of his feoffee Robert Sheffield and local officer Richard Kingsmill in 1472, and for the election in 1472 of William Say and John Twynho for Plympton. On the other hand, the repeated election of John Boston is clearly a measure of his value to the burgesses of Bedford. Edward Hungerford, M.P. for Cricklade, was an important local gentleman, but the return of William Knyvet of Buckenham castle (Norf.) for Melcombe in 1472 was presumably the culmination of a successful search for a seat. The towns concerned range from the seigneurial borough to the corporate county town, but include none of the largest size and no major ports.

Clarence's support need not account for the election of retainers, even in counties and towns where he was predominant. There can have been few leading gentry in the shires of Warwick, Worcester, Derby and Stafford who were not his men in 1472. Even so, Warwickshire returned Richard Boughton and Warwick borough Thomas Rastell, neither known as retainers. The borough of Poole within his lordship of Canford returned none of his men, although in 1467 it had elected Warwick's servant William Kelsy. This can hardly be in defiance of the duke, whose cast-iron dominance at Warwick emerged in the trial of Ankarette Twynho. Perhaps some cases reflect variations in influence, for perhaps sometimes a nominee was defeated who was successful on another occasion: unfortunately virtually nothing is known of defeated candidates — one seldom even knows whether the election was contested. Warwick's failure to elect two recognised retainers in 1472 is more likely to stem from Clarence's nomination of a single candidate than from defiance. Could Warwick, Plympton, Poole, Ludgershall or any other seigneurial borough choose anyone hostile to their lord, even if he made no nomination? Collectively and individually the burgesses had too much to lose from his wrath, too many interests they shared with him: he could count on the support of their representatives, without needing to intrude his own men and thus risk generating opposition.

In principal towns, which returned none of Clarence's men, similar influences were at work. Such towns had sufficient strength and identifiable corporate interests to reject outside pressure and elect their own burgesses, but they recognised the need for good terms with neighbouring magnates. Whenever they were embroiled with local disputes — with a cathedral chapter for example — or required royal favour or legislation, they needed noble patronage and good lordship. Could the Coventry burgesses conceivably disregard the magnate whose estates dominated the region? Could either they or the citizens of Bristol in 1472 be hostile to a patron so recently instrumental in securing the recovery of their franchises?[28] Clarence was 'good lord' to the city and individual citizens of Salisbury and was courted by Exeter. He could count on the support, or at least the acquiescence, of such towns, which would wish to avoid alienating him.

Those of Clarence's retainers who were M.P.s in 1467 and 1472 are arranged in appendix III. The figures for 1467 exclude those, like Robert Sheffield, who probably entered his service at a later date; similarly James Blount, whose family had broken with Clarence, is omitted from the list for 1472. So too are some of the rebels of 1470, whose loyalties to Warwick and Clarence cannot be disentangled: these include Gervase Horne and George Longville, two absentees mysteriously returned by Barnstaple (Devon) in 1472. The remainder comprise fifteen names in 1467, twenty-eight in 1472, but the true total could be higher. Probably no more than six in 1467 or fifteen in 1472 owed their election to Clarence's initiative; some, like Robert Staunton, retainer to Lord Hastings,[29] owed their primary loyalty elsewhere.

There are few glimpses of events in fifteenth-century parliaments, so one cannot expect to know how Clarence's retinue behaved there. But there are two clues. The first is a charter, dated 21 October 1472, in which Clarence witnessed the demise and quitclaim of four manors to his retainer Sir Philip Courtenay of Powderham (Devon) from Edward Courtenay of Bocannoc (Cornw.).[30] The two branches of the Courtenay family were hostile. As Edward's father Sir Hugh had been killed on the Lancastrian side at Tewkesbury, his estates should have been forfeited. The conveyance of land gave Sir Philip cause to prevent Sir Hugh's attainder, so Edward may have demised them to win the support of Clarence and of Sir Philip, knight of the shire for Devon. The other witnesses were also retainers and M.P.s: Sir Nicholas Latimer, M.P. for Dorset, and Sir Roger Tocotes, M.P. for Wiltshire. This deed may thus have provided a basis for agreed action in both houses: certainly Sir Hugh escaped attainder. Another clue is that Edward IV curbed Clarence in 1473-4 by refusing him a proviso of exemption to the 1473 act of resumption, rather than by attainting Warwick. Acts of resumption were acceptable to all in principle; provisoes were added only after the act was passed and thus escaped parliamentary scrutiny. Had Edward tried to attaint Warwick, he would have been opposed by those M.P.s belonging to Clarence's retinue and doubtless by other sympathisers as well. In 1478, when elections had been carefully controlled and the duke's influence curtailed, Edward could proceed to his attainder without significant opposition.

Are the number of M.P.s in Clarence's retinue exceptional? The twenty-eight of 1472 certainly far exceed the known representation of magnates at the parliament of 1422 and are nearly three times the number of Lord Hastings's parliamentary retinue in 1478, when such a great effort was made. Of course, Clarence's resources at all times were far greater than those of Hastings. In 1472 he was at the height of his power — a great magnate in the West Midlands, North Midlands and the West Country: for any future election, minus his North Midland estates, less retainers would surely have been returned. In short, the size of the block at the 1472 parliament was exceptional, a reflection of the exceptional size of his estates and retinue, and hence unrepeatable.

The fifteen M.P.s of 1467, however, seem less remarkable: certainly Warwick had as many M.P.s at the same parliament. This may be a number that was regularly attainable by the greatest magnates, or at least the greatest southern magnates, since they could exploit the many small boroughs of southern England. The Duke of Norfolk was probably another in the same class, but parliamentary patronage on this scale must have been the preserve of very few. A handful of such magnates, acting vigorously together, might expect to influence the conduct of the commons. In 1472, when his supporters represented a tenth of the commons, Clarence may have been able to do this himself. Yet it did not enable him to frame policy, which was decided by the king and his favoured intimates, within and without the council.

Arms of George, Duke of Clarence. His Garter plate, 1461.

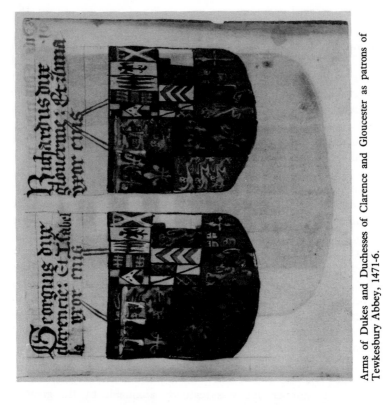

Arms of Dukes and Duchesses of Clarence and Gloucester as patrons of Tewkesbury Abbey, 1471-6.

Chapter VI

Assessment

Clarence has been traditionally dismissed by historians as an irresponsible and unstable troublemaker, whose actions defy explanation and who deservedly came to a bad end after a career of treason, folly and excess. The specific charges fall into two principal categories: one is encapsulated in Shakespeare's striking description — 'false, fleeting, perjur'd Clarence';[1] the other — more modern — criticism is that he was an overmighty subject.[2]

Shakespeare was not a contemporary of Clarence, but was writing a century later from secondhand material. What struck him were the inconsistencies in Clarence's career. As brother and heir of Edward IV, Clarence should have been a pillar of the crown, but he featured instead as leader of a series of rebellions in 1469-70, latterly to make himself king, which resulted in the deposition of his brother in favour of Henry VI. He changed sides almost at once, assisting Edward to recover his throne, yet was executed only seven years later for plotting treason. Shakespeare could see no consistency in this career, so it was obvious that Clarence was 'fleeting', inconsistent, unable to pursue the same course for long; a natural traitor, incapable of keeping faith, and hence 'false'; and of course 'perjur'd', the breaker of oaths of allegiance, not once but repeatedly. This assessment, based on a cursory survey of his career, was shared by Shakespeare's successors and is still held by modern historians. Apart from discovering evidence of further treasons in 1473, their research has generally added detail rather than broadening our understanding.

This is hardly surprising, since the narratives unknown to Shakespeare are valued primarily for their factual content rather than as guides to interpretation. Apart from the Croyland continuation, a well-informed but regrettably cursory survey, they may be classified as either official accounts of specific campaigns, or brief factual compilations, or the speculation of foreigners, or the rationalised hindsight of Tudor historians. None of these tried to explain Clarence's career, if, indeed, any of them understood it. One apparent exception is the 1478 act of attainder, which portrays Clarence as a frequent traitor, repeatedly in breach of his allegiance, ambitious for a crown, malicious and ungrateful towards the king.[3] This agreement with Shakespeare and his successors is to be expected, however, since the act was framed to convince contemporary M.P.s who, like contemporary chroniclers, lacked inside knowledge of Clarence's motives. The act was partisan propaganda, containing much that cannot be substantiated, and should be set against the following lines of verse:

> 'The duke of Clarense, that honorabill knyzte,
> Can alowe the cité notabully,
> Hym to be holde it was a goodly syzte,
> He is an excellent prynce certaynly.
> He thonckyd the cetisence of thayre fidelité
> Done to the kynge, it plesid hym soo'.[4]

Presenting an equally extreme view, commemorating a moment of triumph rather than one of disgrace, the verses, like the act, call for supporting evidence if their testimony is to be accepted.

This book, the first full life of Clarence, has not tried to condemn or whitewash, but has sought to make sense of his career. I have tried to establish precisely what happened, to distinguish Clarence's personal role, and to identify the motives for his actions. Approached in this way, his behaviour is logical and his career appears much more consistent. He was certainly not mad. His reasons for drifting into opposition *c.* 1464 are not difficult to understand. He did not enjoy the influence to which he felt entitled as heir to the throne; he considered that he was being kept short of money; he was not allowed to marry as he wished or, indeed, at all, as Edward repeatedly used his marriage as a diplomatic pawn; and he was excluded from a significant say in government by the rise of Edward's favourites. The first two grievances were satisfied by his marriage, but the government could only be altered by a coup d'état. After Edward's release, fear of his revenge forced on him unwanted expedients: the Lincolnshire rebellion, exile in France, the

Readeption of Henry VI, when they were worse off than under Edward IV. Clarence probably never wanted to depose his brother: now his enemies, the king's favourites, were dead, there was hope of a better future, so he helped Edward recover his throne. The quarrel with Gloucester was the latter's fault, since he wanted an unduly large share of the Warwick inheritance. Heated though their quarrel was, contemporaries were wrong to suspect him of treason then, or indeed in 1477, when his enemies rigged his trial. Approaching his career like this, one can see that he was justified in his dissatisfaction (but not his violent reaction) both in the 1460s and early 1470s. He only proceeded to extremes in 1469, but quickly lost control of events, reacting to them and pursuing a course not originally envisaged. Not only is his career comprehensible, but it is also more consistent: he turned his coat less often than is generally supposed.

One charge in the 1478 indictment requires more attention, the charge of ingratitude: ingratitude for Edward's generous provision for him and ingratitude for his gracious forgiveness for past treasons. The former charge reads:

> 'Wherin it is to be remembered, that the Kynges Highnesse . . . hath evere loved and cherysshed hym, as tenderly and as kyndely, as eny creature myght his naturell Brother . . . he yave hym soo large porcion of Possessions, that noo memorie is of, or seldom hath been seen, that eny Kyng of Englande hertoforn within his Royaulme yave soo largely to eny his Brothers. And not oonly that, butt above that, he furnysshed hym plenteously of all manere stuff, that to a right grete Prynce myght well suffice; soo that aftre the Kynges, his lifelode and richesse notably exceded any other within his Lande at thatt tyme'.[5]

Much of this is true. While ignorant of his moveable wealth, we know that Clarence's landed income was second only to the king, and that the gifts were greater than any other king gave his brother: although of course Edward had more to give, and was more prodigal than his predecessors. But we also know that the income from grants of £4,400 promised in 1467 was never achieved and that what was given was whittled away by reversals of attainders, by exchanges and ultimately by resumption. Sir James Ramsay was wrong to regard Tutbury as 'a mere trifle in comparison with the vast estates he was allowed to retain':[6] his principal estate yielding forty per cent of his income, its loss reduced his revenues to the level of Henry V's brothers and made him dependent on the Warwick inheritance. It may be that Edward regarded the Warwick inheritance as part of his generosity, but Clarence saw it as his right, as part of his wife's inheritance. When grants were taken back resentment understandably replaced gratitude. As for the forgiveness of 1471, this was not purely a royal act of grace — as Edward saw it — but a bargain which enabled Edward to recover his throne. The later rift was not Clarence's fault, but because Edward changed his mind, however justifiably, and took back what he had given. Clarence had plenty of reason for ingratitude, Edward insufficient cause to kill him.

Clarence has also been criticised as an overmighty subject. While certainly one of the greatest English magnates, his power by itself was no threat to the crown. In 1469-71 he was one of a number of allies who did little by himself and whose changes of side were not decisive; only in the Lincolnshire rebellion and the 1471 campaign can his contribution be detected. After 1471, when his power was greater than other magnates, it was nevertheless inferior to that of the crown: Edward curbed him twice. Clarence recognised that he could not match the king, submitting on two occasions: Edward was well aware that he posed no threat in 1473.

Of course the fact that he was consistent, that he was justified in some of his grievances, and that he was less than overmighty does not compensate for his treasons, perjury, overweening ambition, quarrelsomeness and other faults. It does cause one to doubt whether he was politically inept.

He was certainly competent to perform the military functions of his class — a proficient warrior, an adequate divisional commander, well able to organise a large retinue for use at home and abroad. The Lincolnshire rebellion and his change of sides in 1471 reveal a capacity to prepare a plan and carry it out, the mark of cool calculation and considerable nerve. Perhaps he laid these daring plans himself; certainly he succeeded in keeping them secret. The Ankarette Twynho affair shows a talent for swift and ruthless action.

These are the military virtues of a man of action: how well suited was Clarence for peacetime politics? We know that as a councillor he could make out a case and argue it with eloquence and conviction. Indeed, his impressive performance in council prompted the Croyland chronicler to lament that the 'surpassing talents' of the three brothers could not be combined:[7] of course we already know of Edward IV's and Richard III's business abilities. But Clarence had defects. He tended to adopt inflexible positions, from which retreat was difficult, and employed delaying tactics and subterfuge rather than give way. An inability to concede gracefully meant that he failed to extract full benefit from the concessions he did make: the surrender of Lancastrian land in 1470 is an example. Clearly he was unfitted for diplomacy: perhaps this was why he never participated in delicate negotiations. Another defect was his expectation that his advice would be taken, no doubt related to his exalted notion of his own importance. This defect emerges in his unwillingness to accept the decision of the majority — as in the Burdet case — or of the king. He could not accept that decisions unfavourable to him were closed. Connected with this was his attitude to the king, whom he always treated primarily as his brother, as an individual rather than an institution, distrusting his good faith and word of honour, nursing personal grievances and voicing his personal bitterness towards him. Edward could not employ a magnate who treated him as an equal rather than as sovereign and questioned his authority, the central premise of contemporary politics.

Clarence clearly possessed considerable military and political talents and one failing, which rendered him unsuitable for regular government employment and denied him the influence that his power and blood demanded. Yet it would be wrong to judge him purely on his career in national politics, for he was not often at court even before his final years. Rarely at council, he seldom sat on judicial commissions to which he was appointed,[8] attended Garter chapters infrequently and, after 1472, was never at court for Christmas. National politics was a small part of a life spent as a great country magnate.

Clarence's life was spent in a succession of great households: his parents's, his brother's, and finally his own. As we have seen, the latter provided a setting of luxury and magnificence that proclaimed his greatness to all around.[9] He lived in princely style at Tutbury, Warwick and Tiverton, his three principal residences. A sedentary life demanded more convenient and comfortable residences than these old-fashioned castles, more like the interlocking suites and well-lit rooms in the great towers at Warkworth, Tattersall and Raglan. Clarence may well have become a 'grete bylder' at Tutbury and Warwick[10] in order to update his accommodation. At Tutbury he left the defences in disrepair,[11] so his work may well have been domestic. At Warwick late fifteenth-century work includes the Bear and Clarence towers, angle turrets of a projected great tower, and perhaps also the remodelling of the south-west range and the Spy tower. These works are traditionally credited to Richard III,[12] which is unlikely: he never held the castle, which belonged to his nephew Warwick between 1478 and 1499. Warwick himself never had seisin, so Clarence is the likely builder: his 'nywe werk and byldyng within the Castell of Warwyk' cost at least the £178 that he borrowed from the local grazier Benet Lee.[13] If Clarence was indeed responsible, he was converting the castle into a princely residence of the most modern type. Other work projected but not undertaken, according to Rous, included the enclosure of the barn and stable to make an outer ward.[14]

In the West Midlands Clarence was heir to the long traditions of the Beauchamps and Despensers, ancestors of his wife: he was patron of their religious foundations, heir to their lands, to their retainers and to their ambitions. He successfully fulfilled this role, so that both the Tewkesbury chronicler and John Rous referred to him in terms similar to those applied to earlier lords.[15] Much of this was a conscious and deliberate achievement. Rous tells of his intention to carry out the will of his father-in-law, Warwick the kingmaker, regrettably now lost: one such provision, the conversion of Rous's chantry at Guyscliff into a hospital for impoverished gentlefolk, was never implemented. Clarence did arrange the consecration of the Beauchamp chapel at Warwick College, erected under the will of Earl Richard Beauchamp (d. 1439) as his own burial place. Clarence was good lord to the college, arbitrating its disputes with Worcester cathedral chapter and with its own steward.[16] At Tewkesbury, where he built his tomb among those of earlier generations of Despensers, he was on friendly terms with the abbot and gave land to the abbey.[17] He also increased the endowment of Elmley Castle College, another Beauchamp foundation. Rous claims that he secured two fairs for the borough of Warwick: he also claims that Clarence obtained other privileges from the king, which were thwarted by the chancellor. Also planned, but left unfinished, were a new deer park in Temple fields and the improvement of the hollow road as a way into Warwick. It is easy to point out how few projects reached fruition, but Clarence had only seven years as lord before 'froward fortune malyned soor a geyn hym and leyd al a part'. Other earls, with more time at their disposal, also left much unfinished.

All magnates had to win and retain the loyalty of their retainers. One indicator, unfortunately difficult to measure, is the extent to which the retainers relied on their lord's good lordship and in particular his arbitration. As arbiter Clarence combined a competent knowledge of the law with a genuine desire for peace and produced realistic solutions that seem to have lasted. In spite of this only four such judgements survive.[18] Others involving his retainers were made by other arbiters. It seems that he was less sought after as arbiter than, for example, his brother Gloucester. Some magnates, again including Gloucester, were frequently mentioned in retainers's wills, but Clarence occurs only once.[19] Does this mean that he failed to generate the confidence inspired by the most successful lords? In 1477-8 friends and members of his household, supposedly those tied most closely to him, were among the deserters from his service: perhaps an indication that loyalties and affection toward him were limited. On the other hand some stayed with him throughout the vicissitudes of his stormy career. With at least some retainers Clarence formed strong emotional bonds: witness his extravagant reaction on Burdet's execution or the violent revenge intended for Tocotes. As good lord he sometimes backed retainers to the hilt, beyond their deserts. Clearly he was a lord whose support was worth having, but whose wrath was to be avoided.

So far we have been surveying Clarence's public life, national and local: what of his family relations and private life? We know that he was considered handsome,[20] like other members of the house of York, but this does not seem to have led him into the sexual irregularities of his brothers and sisters: no bastards are known. In spite of his violent quarrels with his brothers, a residual loyalty to the house of York is suggested by their reconciliation in 1471 and by his presence at his father's re-interment in 1476: there is no evidence, however, that he returned the interest and affection shown by his mother and sister Margaret in 1477-8. Relations with his wife appear good and he showed interest in his children, although interest of a dynastic kind. We have already seen the apparently genuine feeling that he had for his Beauchamp, Despenser and Neville predecessors.

Rous says that Clarence was a great almsgiver.[21] A generous patron of religious houses, he was considered unusually pious by Salisbury cathedral chapter:

> 'Thanks be to God, who has given such a benevolent and devout prince into the tutelage of the church'.[22]

Adequately and conventionally educated, Clarence seems to have lacked literary interests. None of his books survive, even among the collection of his brother Edward, and his patronage of Caxton may have been purely formal.[23] He was not a competitive jouster like the Wydevilles, but was probably an enthusiastic hunter: apart from his projected deer-park at Warwick, he took an unusually strong line towards poachers, particularly at Tutbury but also elsewhere.[24] Like other magnates, he had his trumpeters, his mimes and his bearward, and he possessed a lively sense of humour.

If studied as a whole, Clarence's career proves to consist of a few bursts of sustained activity divided by years of apparent idleness. Does this tell us anything of Clarence himself? It is true that the pattern results wholly from defects in the sources: local evidence is so inadequate that Clarence can only be studied where he impinged on national politics. On the other hand, since local evidence was created by local activity, its absence may reflect inactivity. Because Clarence made less impression on the cities of Coventry and Exeter than Gloucester made on York, the records of Coventry and Exeter tell us significantly less about him. The itinerary that can be compiled from his estate records and deeds is much sketchier than that of the fourth Earl of Northumberland derived from similar sources. Never, throughout all his adult life, did Clarence officiate at the quarter sessions of any of the counties where he was on the commission of the peace. So well does this agree with the general impression of inactivity at court that it is reasonable to question Rous's portrait: was Clarence a magnate with plans that he carried out or should one stress what he left unfinished or unstarted? The conclusion most consistent with this negative evidence is that Clarence was indolent, seldom moved to action and only then when his vital interests were at stake: a figure surprisingly like the Edward IV sketched by Commines.[25]

So Clarence emerges as a conventional magnate, a mixture of virtues and vices, but temperamentally unsuited for the role in politics otherwise assigned by his royal blood, political power and personal ambition. But was he of more than transient significance? His short-term importance, as leading actor in all the crises of his adult life, is obvious enough. His long-term significance is harder to measure, especially in a positive way, since his career was a failure. Although deposed in 1470, Edward returned in 1471 sufficiently strong to be independent of Clarence's support. The duke died in disgrace in 1478. He was not identified with any political programme and left no political heirs.

Yet if his career is viewed in a negative light — what would have happened without him — his importance is clear. The Wars of the Roses might well have ended in 1461, at Edward IV's accession: by themselves the Lancastrians were too weak to restore Henry VI; Warwick alone was probably incapable of deposing Edward and there would have been no point without an alternative candidate. Certainly Clarence's behaviour in 1470-1, which placed Henry VI and his son in Edward's hands, resulted in the permanent extinction of the house of Lancaster. Clarence's death also had a negative importance. Had he been living in 1483, he — not his brother Richard — would have been senior uncle to Edward IV's son Edward V: Richard could not have usurped the throne and surely neither could Clarence, who was extremely unpopular and lacked support among the magnates. Edward V would have continued to reign and there would have been no Richard III. Without a Richard III to unite opposition behind the otherwise obscure Henry Tudor, there would have been no Tudor sovereigns. Had Clarence survived, history would have followed a different course.

Appendix I

Clarence's Death — The Malmsey Wine Story

Clarence is best known for the manner of his death — by drowning in a butt of malmsey wine. Malmsey was the sweet wine of Crete, since produced in the Canary Isles and renamed Madeira. There have been several variations in the story — such as Clarence's murder by agents of Gloucester, the future Richard III, in Shakespeare's play and Clarence's suicide in Sellar and Yeatman's *1066 and All That*[1] — but all lack foundation. It must be remembered that Clarence had been condemned to death for treason by due process of law; that he had been sentenced to death, drawing and quartering, a sentence that was commuted to mere execution; and that his death on 18 February 1478 was in pursuance of this sentence. Most condemned noblemen were beheaded: execution by drowning is otherwise unheard of and probably without precedent.

The story was current soon after his death and appears in most contemporary histories. As early as 1483 — only five years after the event — the story was recounted by Dominic Mancini, an Italian visitor to England, who moved in elevated circles. He had no doubt that

> 'The mode of execution preferred in this case was, that he should die by being plunged in a jar of sweet wine'.[2]

Then or soon after the story was known elsewhere in Europe, certainly in Naples, France and Burgundy, and was repeated by Jean de Roye,Philippe de Commines, Jean de' Molinet, Olivier de la Marche and a Neapolitan diarist.[3] The most circumstantial account is that of Roye, who records that the barrel was set on end, that Clarence was immersed head first while still alive, and that after extraction his corpse was beheaded.[4] The tale occurs in the London

Above: Duke and Duchess of Clarence with black bull of Clarence and bear of Warwick. A modern drawing from the stylised figures of the Rows Roll, *c.*1484.

Left: Funerary effigies of the Duke and Duchess of Clarence at Tewkesbury Abbey. Stylised figures, 1477-85.

chronicles of the 1490s, but must have been circulating in England earlier: it was certainly known to the Croyland chronicler in the mid 1480s[5] as well as to Mancini in 1483. It is frequently repeated by later writers, such as Polydore Vergil, Sir Thomas More, Edward Hall, John Stow and William Shakespeare.[6] Clarence's daughter Margaret, Countess of Salisbury was painted wearing a bracelet from which a miniature barrel hung[7] — a sign that she knew the story, not necessarily that she believed it, still less that she possessed first hand information: she was only four years old at her father's death! While common knowledge, the tale was not accepted without question: the Croyland chronicler avoided committing himself, merely recording that the 'execution, whatever its nature may have been, took place . . . in the Tower of London'; the version in the *Great Chronicle of London* is qualified by the phrase 'as the Fame Ran', that of Vergil by 'as they say'.[8] Such doubts are not surprising — it was, after all, a highly improbable story — but the chronicles deserve respect, since apparently nobody denied the story or suggested an alternative cause of death, even though the story was current when some of those directly involved were still living.

Having said that, it is clear that none of the writers were eyewitnesses: the Croyland chronicler, already an influential public servant, was best placed to know the truth, but obviously did not; Mancini may have known, but his history shows no sign of detailed knowledge; the most circumstantial account is by Roye, whom we have no reason to suppose possessed special information; and other accounts are late and probably derivative. There was no official statement. No supporting records have been found — regarding the disposal of spoilt malmsey at the Tower, for example. Barring unforeseen discoveries, the only remaining avenue of inquiry yet unexploited is by examination of the body, but this is also fraught with difficulty.

Clarence was buried with his duchess at Tewkesbury Abbey,[9] probably sharing her vault behind the high altar. This vault, 9 ft. long by 8 ft. wide and 4 ft. 6 in. tall, was lined with armorial tiles, one commemorating Richard III as king, and was reached by a flight of steps formerly covered by a stone slab bearing brasses,[10] presumably of the duke and duchess; their monument stood on the north side of the choir. The vault itself was appropriated by a family of Tewkesbury burghers, called Hawlings, probably in time for the death of Samuel Hawlings (d. 1709); his wife was added in 1729 and

Left: Reputedly Clarence's daughter Margaret, Countess of Salisbury. Note the barrel hanging from her right wrist. Painted *c.* 1530.

Below: Bones at Tewkesbury Abbey said to be those of the Duke and Duchess of Clarence.

their son John in 1753. The vault was rediscovered in 1787 and again in 1826, when it was opened and found to contain — apart from the Hawlings remains — two skulls and other bones of a man and a woman:

> 'but there was nothing by which these relics could be identified as belonging to the unfortunate Duke and Duchess of Clarence'.[11]

In 1829 the Hawlings family were moved elsewhere and the other bones were placed in a stone coffin. This coffin was found to be full of water in 1876 — the result of a flood in 1852 — and the bones were removed then or soon afterwards.[12]

From this brief resumé it seems clear that the vault behind the altar was the Clarence tomb, but it is uncertain whether it remained intact until 1709, whether it was robbed (as suggested in 1826), or whether others before Samuel Hawlings appropriated it to their use. One cannot be sure whether the bones belong to Clarence and his duchess. There is no record of any examination in 1826 or later to establish the cause of death and the bones may have deteriorated during their subsequent immersion. Should such an examination be made now, it might not be conclusive, particularly in view of the doubtful identity of the remains: if the corpse was found to have been decapitated, it might not be that of Clarence but of a victim of the battle of Tewkesbury buried in the abbey only seven years earlier; if no wounds were found, it might belong to anyone. What effect would drowning in malmsey wine have on a person's skeleton?

It is likely, however, that so obvious a peculiarity as a broken or severed neck would have been noticed in 1826 or 1876. The absence of any such observation suggests that the male corpse was not beheaded or hanged. If the body is indeed that of Clarence, this indicates that he died by some other means — such as drowning in malmsey wine. To the question why such an extraordinary method should have been adopted — was it Clarence's own choice? — there is no evidence on which an answer can be based.

Appendix II

Clarence's Estates

This appendix lists:

(a) Clarence's lands in 1467, 1473 and 1478.

(b) Clarence's feefarms and annuities in 1467, 1473 and 1478.

(c) Gloucester's share of the Warwick inheritance in 1474.

It is based on Hicks, 'Clarence', ch.5 and 6, tables X, XI, XII and XVI, and sources there cited.

All lands are manors of lordships unless distinguished by the following abbreviations: b.= borough; h.= hundred; m.= manor; p.= park; s.= soke.

The column headed 'Estates' refers to the estates to which property belonged before its acquisition by Clarence. The abbreviations used are:

B = Butler (Wiltshire); C = Courtenay (Devon); Cr. = Crown; G = Gournay; L = Duchy of Lancaster; N = Nuthill; P = Percy; R = Richmond; Ro. = Roos; T = Tailbois; W = Warwick Inheritance.

(a) Clarence's lands.

	Estates	1467.	1473.	1478.
BERKSHIRE.				
Crookham	W			x
BUCKINGHAMSHIRE.				
Little Linford	B		x	x
Newport Pagnell	B		x	x
Tickford p.	B		x	x
CAMBRIDGESHIRE.				
Iselham	P	x		
⅓ Bassingbourne	R		x	x
⅓ Arningford h.	R		x	x
⅓ Stow h.	R		x	x
⅓ Chiplow h.	R		x	x

⅓ Papworth h.	R		x	x
⅓ Newstoke h.	R		x	x
⅓ Chesterton h.	R		x	x
⅓ Whethley h.	R		x	x
CORNWALL.				
Sheviock	C	x	x	x
West Anthony	C	x	x	x
Trelowia	C	x	x	x
Portloo	C	x	x	x
Porpighan	C	x	x	x
Crofthole	C	x	x	x
Northill	C	x	x	x
Landrian	C	x	x	x
Lanihorne	C	x	x	x
Trelugon	C	x	x	x
½ Tregamure	C		x	x
½ Treverbyn	C		x	x
Oldawitta	B	x	x	x
Penpoll	B		x	x
Elerky	B			x
DERBYSHIRE.				
Bolsover	Cr.	x	x	
Horston	Cr.	x	x	
Beskwood p.	Cr.	x	x	
Duffield	L	x	x	
Belper	L	x	x	
Holbrook	L	x	x	
Alderwasley	L	x	x	
Southwood	L	x	x	
Highedge	L	x	x	
Gresley h.	L	x	x	
Idridgehey	L	x	x	
Holland	L	x	x	
Bigging	L	x	x	
Bonsall	L	x	x	
Iretonwood	L	x	x	
Brassington	L	x	x	
Matlock	L	x	x	
Spoundon	L	x	x	
Scropton	L	x	x	
Appletree h.	L	x	x	
Perimplementum	L	x	x	
Hartington	L	x	x	
Melbourne	L	x	x	
New liberty	L	x	x	
High Peak	L	x	x	
Winslands	L	x	x	

Peak liberty	L	x	x	
Ashbourne b.	L	x	x	
Wirksworth	L	x	x	
Wirksworth socage	L	x	x	
Risley h.	L	x	x	
DEVON.				
Aylesbeare	C	x	x	x
Whimple	C	x	x	x
Norton Dawney	C	x	x	x
Okehampton m.b.h.	C		x	x
Plympton m.b.h.	C		x	x
Tiverton m.b.h.	C		x	x
Chawleigh b.	C		x	x
Colcombe	C		x	x
Coliton	C		x	x
Colyford	C		x	x
Columpton	C		x	x
Musbury	C		x	x
Whitford	C		x	x
Exiland	C		x	x
Topsham	C		x	x
Fareway	C		x	x
Sampford Courtenay	C		x	x
East Budleigh h.	C		x	x
West Budleigh h.	C		x	x
Hayridge h.	C		x	x
Exe fishery	C		x	x
Torbrian	B	x	x	x
Slapton	B	x	x	x
Daundy	B	x	x	x
Northiam	B	x	x	x
Clifton Dartmouth	B	x	x	x
Lundy Isle	B	x	x	x
South Zeal b.	W			x
South Tawton	W			x
Stokenham	W			x
Yealmpton	W			x
Clyst St. Mary	W			x
DORSET.				
Puncknowle	B	x	x	x
Toller Porcorum	B	x	x	x
Haselbury	B	x	x	x
Clevecombe	B	x	x	x
Valet	B	x	x	x
Wraxall	B	x	x	x
Chilfrome	B	x	x	x
Nether Kentcombe	B	x	x	x

Mapperton	B	x	x	x
Swyre	B	x	x	x
Rampisham	B		x	x
Iwarne Courtenay	C	x	x	x
Ebberton	C	x	x	x
Ryme	G	x		
Corfe		x	x	x
Canford	W			x
Poole	W			x
Cambourne	W			x
Newton Montagu	W			x
ESSEX.				
Clavering	W			x
North Weald	W			x
Catmer Hall	W			x
Bretts in West Ham	W			x
GLOUCESTERSHIRE.				
Tewkesbury m.b.	W			x
Whittington	W			x
Tredington	W			x
Pamington	W			x
Fiddington	W			x
Northway	W			x
Mythe	W			x
Stoke Orchard	W			x
Kemerton	W			x
Chedworth	W			x
Sodbury	W			x
Lydney	W			x
Barton by Bristol m.h.	W			x
Earlscourt of the hon. of Gloucester	W			x
HAMPSHIRE.				
Christchurch m.b.h.	W			x
Ringwood m.h.	W			x
Hunton	W			x
Warblington	W			x
Thorley (I.O.W.)	W			x
Wellow (I.O.W.)	W			x
Swainstown (I.O.W.)	W			x
Brightstone (I.O.W.)	W			x
HEREFORDSHIRE.				
Fownhope	W			x
HERTFORDSHIRE.				
Cheshunt		x	x	x
Flamstead	W			x
Ashridge h.	W			x

KENT.				
Milton m.h.	B	x	x	x
Marden m.h.	B	x	x	x
Milton & Marden liberty	B	x	x	x
Queenborough	Cr.		x	x
Hendon	W			x
Dartford	W			x
Wilmington	W			x
LEICESTERSHIRE.				
Foston	P	x		
Castle Donington	L	x	x	
LINCOLNSHIRE.				
Boston b.	R[1]	x	x	x
Frampton m.s.	R	x	x	x
Kirton m.s.	R	x	x	x
Gayton m.s.	R	x	x	x
Skirbeck m.s.	R	x	x	x
Mumby s.	R	x	x	x
Washingborough	R	x	x	x
Leadenham & Fulbeck	R	x	x	x
Calceby	P	x		
Burwell	P	x		
South Kyme	T	x		
Freston	Ro.		x	x
Goddesfeld in Freston	Ro.		x	x
Roos part of Boston	Ro.		x	x
Somerton castle			x	x
LONDON.				
Le Erber & other mess.	W			x
NORFOLK.				
Swaffham m. & liberty	R	x	x	x
NORTHAMPTONSHIRE.				
More End	B		x	x
Potterspury	W			x
Yelvertoft	W			x
Easton Neston	W			x
Collyweston	W			x
NOTTINGHAMSHIRE.				
Mansfield	Cr.	x	x	
Mansfield Woodhouse	Cr.	x	x	
Clipstone	Cr.	x	x	
Linby	Cr.	x	x	
Sutton	Cr.	x	x	
Plumtree h.	L	x	x	
Ollerton h.	L	x	x	
OXFORDSHIRE.				
Shipton-u.-Wychwood	W			x
Chadlington h.	W			x

Caversham	W			x
Burford m.b.	W			x
RUTLAND.				
Uppingham	W			x
Preston	W			x
Essendine	W			x
Shillingthorpe	W			x
SOMERSET.				
Brean	B	x	x	x
Exton	B	x	x	x
Charlton Mackrell	B	x	x	x
Stoke St. Michael	B	x	x	x
Kingsdon	B	x	x	x
Batheaston	B	x	x	x
Shockerwick	B	x	x	x
Pensford	B	x	x	x
Horsey	B	x	x	x
Huntspill Mareys	B	x	x	x
Stoke-u.-Hamdon	G	x		
Curry Mallet	G	x		
Melton Fauconberg	G	x		
Shepton Mallet	G	x		
Stratton-on-the-Foss	G	x		
Englishcombe	G	x		
Walton	G	x		
Midsummer Norton	G	x		
Widcombe	G	x		
Laverton	G	x		
Farrington Gurney	G	x		
Crewkerne	C		x	x
Misterton	C		x	x
Yarlington	W			x
Shepton Montagu	W			x
Charlton Camville	W			x
Henstridge	W			x
Donyatt	W			x
Dunpole	W			x
Downhead	W			x
Somerton	W			x
STAFFORDSHIRE.				
Tutbury	L	x	x	
Marchington	L	x	x	
Uttoxeter b.	L	x	x	
Rolston	L	x	x	
Barton	L	x	x	
Agarsley	L	x	x	
Agard & Rodman hon. cts.	L	x	x	
New liberty	L	x	x	

Newcastle-u.-Lyme b.	L	x	x	
Pattingham	W			x
Perry Bar	W			x
Walsall b.m.	W			x
SUFFOLK.				
Cratfield	P	x		
Westley		x	x	x
SURREY.				
Witley	B	x	x	x
Worplesdon	B	x	x	x
SUSSEX.				
Ashurst	B	x	x	x
WARWICKSHIRE.				
Warwick b.m.	W			x
Wedgenock p.	W			x
Moreton Morrell	W			x
Lighthorne	W			x
Berkswell	W			x
Brailes	W			x
Tonworth	W			x
Sutton Coldfield	W			x
Claverdon	W			x
Winterton	W			x
Erdington	W			x
WILTSHIRE.				
Wardour castle	B	x	x	x
Ludgershall b.	R	x	x	x
Amesbury m.h.	W			x
Winterbourne Earls m.h.	W			x
Alderbury h.	W			x
Earl Stoke	W			x
Cherhill	W			x
Sherston	W			x
Broadtown	W			x
Wilton b.	W			x
WORCESTERSHIRE.				
Elmley Castle	W			x
Elmley Lovett	W			x
Yardley	W			x
Salwarpe	W			x
Hullplace	W			x
Hadzor	W			x
Abberley	W			x
Comberton Parva	W			x
Croom Simonds	W			x
Shrawley	W			x
Rock & Snead	W			x
Fickenappletree	W			x

Pury Court	W			x
Hanley Castle	W			x
Redmarley D'Abitot	W			x
Bushley	W			x
Wyre Piddle	W			x
Upton-on-Severn	W			x
Droitwich saltpits	W			x
Worcester tenements	W			x
Worcester shrievalty	W			x
YORKSHIRE.				
Richmond Castle	R	x	x	x
Nuthill	N	x	x	
Riston	N	x	x	
Stewton	N	x	x	
Linton	P	x		
Leathley	P	x		
Pocklington	P	x		
Kirkleavington	P	x		
Tadcaster	P	x		
Scorborough	P	x		
Nafferton	P	x		
Thurstanby	P	x		
Wandesford	P	x		
Seamer	P	x		
Healaugh	P	x		
Hull messuages	P	x		
York messuages	P	x		
⅓ Roos	Ro.		x	x
Harum	Ro.		x	x

(b) Clarence's feefarm and annuities.

	Estates.	1467.	1473.	1478.
DORSET.				
Puddletown £20	W			x
Lulworth £20	W			x
MIDDLESEX.				
Westminster Exchequer £40		x	x	x
NOTTINGHAMSHIRE.				
£110 2*s*. altogether	Cr.	x		
SOMERSET.				
Axbridge, Cheddar & Congresbury £54	W			x
WARWICKSHIRE.				
Coventry £138 6*s*. 8*d*.	Cr.	x		
£20 county	W			x
WILTSHIRE.				
Bedwin & Wexcombe £31 10*s*.		x	x	
County £20	W			x

YORKSHIRE.				
York £9 6*s*. 2½*d*.	Ro.	x		
York £26 13*s*. 4*d*.	Ro.		x	x

(c) Gloucester's share of the Warwick inheritance, 1474.

BERKSHIRE.
- Little Marlow
- Stanford-in-the-Vale
- Speenhamland[2]

BUCKINGHAMSHIRE.
- Olney
- Quarrendon
- Buckland
- Singleborough
- Aston Clinton
- Dunbridge
- Montjoy

BUCKINGHAMSHIRE.
- Aylesbury feefarm £60
- Hanslope & chamberlainship of the exchequer

CAMBRIDGESHIRE.
- Kirtling

CORNWALL.
- Carnanton
- Helston Thony
- Blisland

DERBYSHIRE.
- Scarsdale[3]

COUNTY DURHAM.
- Barnard Castle
- Gainsford

HAMPSHIRE.
- Ashley[2]
- Mapledurwell[2]
- Basingstoke feefarm £30
- Andover feefarm

HEREFORDSHIRE.
- Snodhill

HERTFORDSHIRE.
- Bushey
- Ware

HUNTINGDONSHIRE.
- £40 feefarm St. Ives

LINCOLNSHIRE.
- Market Deeping) misc.
- Barhalme) lands
- Stow

NORTHAMPTONSHIRE.
- Buckby
- Moulton
- Cosgrove

NORFOLK.
- Haverhill

NOTTINGHAMSHIRE.
- Perlethorpe

SUFFOLK.
- Blakeshall in Witnesham
- Burwash

SUSSEX.
- Rotherfield[2]

YORKSHIRE.
- Kimberworth
- Bawtry
- Hotham
- Cropton
- Cottingham[3]
- Falsgrave[3]
- Scarborough[3]
- Middleham
- Sheriff Hutton
- East Lilling
- Elvington
- Skirpenbeck
- Raskelf
- Hook
- Scoreby
- Rise in Holderness
- Wilberfoss
- Sutton-upon-Derwent
- Stamford Bridge
- Stourton
- Humberton
- Sutton in the Forest
- Carlton in Coverdale
- Thornthorpe
- Westwitton
- Wood Hill
- Kettlewell
- Newbiggin
- Thoralby
- Burton
- Burton Carlton
- Hope
- Westhorpe
- Forcett
- Sowerby
- Scotby
- Bainbridge
- Moulton
- Arkengarthdale
- New Forest
- Bowes
- Crakehall
- Aysgarth
- Brainthwaite
- Deighton

WALES.
- Abergavenny
- Glamorgan
- Pains Castle
- Elfael[4]
- Ogmore[4]
- Welsh Bicknor

Appendix III

Parliamentary Affinities

This appendix contains the following three tables:

(1) King's Servants in the Parliament of 1478.
(2) Magnate Connections at the Parliament of 1478.
(3) Clarence's Retainers at the Parliaments of 1467-8 and 1472-5.

In each case constituencies are on the left, their M.P.s on the right. Table 2 is subdivided into the connections of individual magnates or noble families; in table 3 Clarence's retainers at the two parliaments are arranged in columns.

(1) King's Servants in the Parliament of 1478.

Constituency	M.P.
Berkshire	Humphrey Talbot
Reading	Thomas Besteney
Wallingford	Thomas Vincent
Windsor	Thomas Joys
	William Evington
Buckinghamshire	Thomas Fowler
Wycombe	Thomas Wellsbourne
Cambridgeshire	Sir Thomas Grey
	Sir William Allington
Cornwall	Sir Thomas Vaughan
Bodmin	John Fyneux
Helston	John Bamme
Liskeard	Ralph Sheldon
Lostwithiel	Thomas Kebell
Cumberland	Sir William Parre
	Sir James Moresby
Devon	John Courtenay
Dartmouth	Thomas Gale
	Thomas Greystoke

Plymouth	Avery Cornburgh
	Richard Page
Plympton	John Leigh
Essex	Sir Thomas Montgomery
	Thomas Tyrell
Herefordshire	Sir Richard Croft
Leominster	Thomas Croft
Hertfordshire	John Sturgeon
	Sir John Say
Kent	Sir John Fogge
Lancashire	Sir George Stanley
Leicester (Leics.)	Piers Curteys
Lincolnshire	Sir Thomas Burgh
Lincoln	Thomas FitzWilliam
Middlesex	John Elrington
Northamptonshire	John Hulcote
	Robert Pemberton
Bramber (Suss.)	Christopher Furness
Rutland	Richard Sydale
Shropshire	Sir William Yonge
Somerset	Sir Giles Daubeney
Bridgewater	William Clerk
Southampton	William Berkeley
Portsmouth	Thomas Uvedale
Newcastle (Staffs.)	William Yonge, jnr.
Surrey	John Wood
Gatton	Ralph Wolseley
Guildford	Thomas Stoughton
Coventry	Henry Boteler
Warwick	Degory Haynes
Appleby (Westmor.)	Charles Nowell
	Piers Wrayton
Wiltshire	John Cheyne
Chippenham	Roger Hopton
Hindon	John Waller
Ludgershall	William Slefeld
Worcestershire	John Acton
Yorkshire	Sir John Pilkington

(2) Magnate Connections at the Parliament of 1478.

(a) **Wydeville.**[2]

Bedfordshire	John Rotherham
Cambridgeshire	Sir Thomas Grey
	Sir William Allington
Cornwall	Sir Thomas Vaughan
Launceston	John Fogge, jnr.
Truro	Robert Courte

Essex	Sir Thomas Montgomery
Gloucestershire	John Twynho, snr.
Herefordshire	Sir Richard Croft
Hertfordshire	Sir John Say
Kent	Sir John Fogge
Canterbury	Richard Haute
Lincolnshire	Sir Thomas Burgh
Stamford	Richard Forster
Great Yarmouth (Norf.)	John Russh
	Sir John Paston
Northamptonshire	John Hulcote
	Robert Pemberton
Somerset	Giles Daubeney
Surrey	John Wood
Southwark	Nicholas Gaynesford
Sussex	John Dudley
	John Fiennes
East Grinstead	Richard Alfrey
Horsham	Thomas Stidolf

(b) **Mowbray.**[3]

Berkshire	Humphrey Talbot
Norfolk	Thomas Howard
	Lord FitzWalter
Suffolk	John Broughton
	Sir John Wingfield
Ipswich	John Timperley
	James Hobart
Appleby (Westmor.)	Charles Nowell
East Grinstead (Suss.)	Richard Leukenor
Horsham	Thomas Hoo
Reigate (Surr.)	Richard Skinner
Southwark	Nicholas Gaynesford

(c) **Duke of Buckingham.**[4]

Essex	Sir Thomas Montgomery
Gloucestershire	John Twynho, snr.
	Thomas Cokesey
Newcastle (Staffs.)	Reginald Bray
Bletchingley (Surr.)	Richard Harper
	Sir William Knyvet
Bedwin (Wilts.)	William Paston
Horsham (Suss.)	Thomas Stidolf

(d) **Duke of Gloucester.** [5]

Cornwall	Sir James Tyrell
	Thomas Tresawell

Cumberland	Sir William Parre
Carlisle	Edward Redmayn
Westmorland	William Redmayn
Dorchester (Dors.)	Sir Ralph Ashton
Yorkshire	Sir John Pilkington

(e) **Earl of Northumberland.**[6]

Northumberland	Ralph Hothom
	Robert Collingwood
Newcastle-upon-Tyne	John Carlisle
Reigate (Surr.)	Thomas Leukenor
Sussex	John Dudley
Yorkshire	Sir Robert Constable
Hull	William Eland
Scarborough	Edmund Thwaites

(f) **Lord Hastings.**[7]

Derbyshire	Henry Vernon
	Sir John Gresley
Lostwithiel (Corn.)	Thomas Powtrell
Leicestershire	William Trussell
	William Motton
Leicester	John Wyggeston
Stafford (Staffs.)	Thomas Gresley
Warwickshire	Sir Simon Mountford
Downton (Wilts.)	Thomas Danvers
Westbury	Robert Staunton

(3) Clarence's Retainers at the Parliaments of 1467-8 and 1472-5. [8]

Constituency	1467-8	1472-5
Bedford	John Boston[9]	John Boston
Derbyshire	William Blount	Nicholas Langford[10]
	Sir William Vernon	
Derby		Roger Wilkinson[11]
Devon		Sir Philip Courtenay
Dartmouth		Miles Metcalf[12]
Plympton		John Twynho, jnr.
Dorset		Sir Nicholas Latimer
Dorchester	John Dyve[13]	
Melcombe		William Knyvet
Shaftesbury		John Latimer[14]
Essex	Walter Writtle	Walter Writtle
Gloucestershire		Thomas Limerick
Herefordshire		Thomas Brugges[15]
Kent		Sir Henry Ferrers

Leicestershire	Robert Staunton	
Lincolnshire	Thomas Burgh[16]	
Norfolk	William Knyvet	
Nottinghamshire		Sir Henry Pierpoint[17]
Staffordshire	Sir John Stanley[18]	Sir John Stanley
	John Delves[19]	Sir Edmund Dudley[29]
Newcastle-under-Lyme	James Norreys[21]	William Paston[22]
	Robert Hill	
Stafford		Robert Hill
Guildford (Surr.)		Sir George Browne
Warwickshire		John Hugford
Warwick		Edmund Bowdon[23]
Wiltshire	Sir Roger Tocotes	Sir Roger Tocotes
Cricklade	Edward Hungerford	
Ludgershall	Sir Arthur Ormesby[24]	Robert Sheffield[25]
		Richard Kingsmill[26]
Wootton Basset		John Throckmorton
Worcestershire		Richard Hyde[27]
		Thomas Lygon[28]

Abbreviations

Anstis, *GR*	J. Anstis, *Register of the Most Noble Order of the Garter* (2 vols. 1724)
AO	Archives Office
Arrivall	*Historie of the Arrivall of King Edward IV and the Finall Recouerye of his kingdomes* (Camden Society i, 1838)
Basin, *Louis XI*	T. Basin, *Histoire de Louis XI*, ed. C. Samaran, 3 vols (Les Classiques de L'histoire de France au moyen âge 26, 29, 30, 1963-72)
BIHR	*Bulletin of the Institute of Historical Research*
BL	British Library
Borthwick IHR	Borthwick Institute of Historical Research
Bristol GRB	*Great Red Book of Bristol*, ed. E.W. W. Veale, i, ii (Bristol Record Society viii, xvi, 1938, 1951)
Bristol LRB	*Little Red Book of Bristol*, ed. F.B. Bickley (2 vols. 1900)
BRL	Birmingham Reference Library
CAB	Chapter Act Book
C&P	J. Calmette and G. Périnelle, *Louis XI et l'Angleterre 1461-83* (Societé de l'Ecole des Chartes, Memoires et Documents, xi, 1930)

CC	'Historiae Croylandensis Continuatio', *Rerum Anglicarum Scriptorum Veterum*, i, ed. W. Fulman (1684)
CCR	*Calendar of Close Rolls*
CFR	*Calendar of Fine Rolls*
Chastellain, *Oeuvres*	G. Chastellain, *Oeuvres*, v, ed. Kervyn de Lettenhove (1864)
CIPM	*Calendarium Inquisitionum post mortem sive Escaetarum*, iv (Record Commission, 1828)
CJS	*Chronicle of John Stone*, ed. W.G. Searle (Cambridge Antiquarian Society, octavo series, xxiv, 1902)
CL	Cathedral Library
CLB	*Coventry Leet Book or Mayors Register*, ed. M.D. Harris (Early English Text Society Original Series 134-5, 138, 146, 1907-13)
CO	*Collection of Ordinances and Regulations for the Government of the Royal Household* (Society of Antiquaries, 1790)
Coles, 'Middleham'	G.M. Coles, 'The Lordship of Middleham, especially in Yorkist and early Tudor times (unpublished Liverpool University M.A. thesis, 1961)
Commines, *Mémoires*	P. de Commines, *Mémoires*, ed. J. Calmette and G. Durville, 3 vols (Les Classiques de l'histoire de France au moyen âge 3,5,6, 1923-5)
CPR	*Calendar of Patent Rolls*
CRO	County Record Office
CS	Camden Society
CSPM	*Calendar of State Papers and Manuscripts existing in the Archives and Collections of Milan*, i, ed A.B. Hinds (1902)

Devon, *Issues*	*Issues of the Exchequer*, ed. F. Devon (1837)
DRO	Diocesan Record Office
Duclos, *Louis XI*	C.P. Duclos, *L'histoire de Louis XI* (3 vols. 1745)
Dunham, *Hastings*	W.H. Dunham, *Lord Hastings' Indentured Retainers 1461-83* (Transactions of the Connecticut Academy of Arts and Sciences, xxix, 1955)
EH	*Excerpta Historica*, ed. S. Bentley (1831)
EHD	*English Historical Documents*, iv, ed. A.R. Myers (1969)
EHR	*English Historical Review*
Ellis, *Letters*	*Original Letters illustrative of English History*, ed H. Ellis, 4 series (1827-40)
Emden, *BRCU*	A.B. Emden, *Biographical Register of the University of Cambridge to AD 1500* (1963)
Emden, *BROU*	A.B.Emden, *Biographical Register of the University of Oxford to AD 1500* (3 vols. 1957-9)
FC	R Fabyan, *New Chronicles of England and France*, ed. H Ellis (1811)
15th-cent. Engl.	*Fifteenth-century England, 1399-1509: Studies in politics and society*, ed. S.B. Chrimes, C.D. Ross and R.A.Griffiths (1972)
Fortescue Family	T. Fortescue, *Family of Fortescue* (1880)
Fortescue, *Governance*	J. Fortescue, *Governance of England* ed. C. Plummer (1885)
Gairdner, *Richard III*	J.Gairdner, *Life and Reign of Richard the Third* (1898)
GC	*Great Chronicle of London*, ed. A.H. Thomas and I.D. Thornley (1938)

GEC	G.E. Cokayne, *Complete Peerage of England, Scotland, Ireland, Great Britain and the United Kingdom*, ed. H.V. Gibbs and others (12 vols. 1910-59)
Gregory's Chron.	*Historical Collections of a Citizen of London in the Fifteenth Century*, ed. J. Gairdner (Camden Society, new series xviii, 1876)
Hanserecesse	*Hanserecesse von 1431-76*, ed. G. von der Ropp, Abteil II, Bänder vi, vii
HBC	*Handbook of British Chronology*, ed. F.M. Powicke and E.B. Fryde (1961)
HC	*Hall's Chronicle*, ed. H. Ellis (1809)
Hicks, *BIHR*	M.A. Hicks, 'Descent, Partition and Extinction: The "Warwick Inheritance"', *Bulletin of the Institute of Historical Research* lii (1979)
Hicks, 'Clarence'	M.A. Hicks, 'The Career of George Plantagenet, Duke of Clarence 1449-1478' (unpublished Oxford D. Phil. thesis, 1974)
Hicks, *NH*	M.A. Hicks, 'Dynastic Change and Northern Society: The Career of the Fourth Earl of Northumberland 1470-89', *Northern History* xiv (1978)
Hicks, 'Northumberland'	M.A. Hicks, 'The Career of Henry Percy, Fourth Earl of Northumberland, with special reference to his retinue' (unpublished Southampton University M.A. thesis, 1971)
Hicks, *PPP*	M.A. Hicks, 'The Changing Role of the Wydevilles in Yorkist Politics to 1483', *Patronage, Pedigree and Power in Late Medieval England*, ed. C.D. Ross (1979)

HMC	Historic Manuscripts Commission
HP	J.C. Wedgwood, *History of Parliament, 1439-1509* (2 vols. 1936-8)
IC	*Ingulph's Chronicle of the Abbey of Croyland*, ed. H.T. Riley (Bohn's Antiquarian Library, 1854)
Illustrations	'The Narrative of the Marriage of Richard, Duke of York, with Anne of Norfolk, the Matrimonial Feast and the Grand Justing', *Illustrations of Ancient State and Chivalry*, ed. W.H. Black (Roxburghe Club, 1840)
Kendall, *Richard III*	P.M. Kendall, *Richard III* (1955)
Kingsford, *EHL*	C.L.Kingsford, *English Historical Literature in the Fifteenth Century* (1913)
Kingsford, *London Chrons.*	C.L.Kingsford, *Chronicles of London* (1905)
Lander, *Crown and Nobility*	J.R. Lander, *Crown and Nobility 1450 -1509* (1976)
LS	*List of Sheriffs* (Public Record Office, Lists and Indexes, ix)
Mancini	D. Mancini, *Usurpation of Richard III*, ed. C.A.J. Armstrong (2nd edn. 1969)
More, *Richard III*	T. More, *History of Richard III*, ed. R.S. Sylvester (Yale Edition of the Complete Works of St. Thomas More, ii, 1963)
Morgan, *TRHS*	D.A.L. Morgan, 'The King's Affinity in the Polity of Yorkist England', *Transactions of the Royal Historical Society*, 5th series xxiii (1973)
Myers, *BJRL*	A.R. Myers, 'The Household of Elizabeth Woodville, 1466-7', *Bulletin of the John Rylands Library* 1 (1967-8)
Myers, *Household*	A.R. Myers, *The Household of Edward IV* (1959)

NMS	*Nottingham Medieval Studies*
ns	*new series*
Paston L&P	*Paston Letters and Papers of the Fifteenth Century*, ed. N. Davis (2 vols. 1973-6)
Plumpton Corr.	*Plumpton Correspondence*, ed. T. Stapleton (Camden Society iv, 1839)
PPP	*Patronage, Pedigree and Power in Late Medieval England*, ed. C.D. Ross (1979)
Pugh, *GCH*	*County History of Glamorgan*, iii, ed. T.B. Pugh (1971)
Rawcliffe, *Staffords*	C. Rawcliffe, *The Staffords, Earls of Stafford and Dukes of Buckingham 1394-1521* (1978)
Reg.	Register
Reg. Bourgchier	*Registrum Thome Bourgchier 1454-1486*, ed. F.R.H. Du Boulay, 2 vols. (Canterbury and York Society, 1955-6)
RGS	*Register of the Gild of Holy Cross, the Blessed Mary and St. John the Baptist of Stratford-on-Avon*, ed. J.H. Bloom (1907)
RO	Record Office
Ross, *Edward IV*	C.D. Ross, *Edward IV* (1974)
Rot. Scot.	*Rotuli Scotiae*, 2 vols. (Record Commission, 1819)
Rows Roll	*Rows Roll*, ed. W.H. Courthope (1845)
Roye, *Journal*	J. de Roye, *Journal*, ed. B.de Mandrot, 2 vols. (Société de l'histoire de France 1894, 1896)
RP	*Rotuli Parliamentorum*, v, vi (Record Commission)
RS	Rolls Series

Scofield, *Edward IV*	C.L. Scofield, *Life and Reign of Edward the Fourth* (2 vols. 1923)
SGA	*Stratford-on-Avon Corporation Records: The Gild Accounts (1912)*
Smith, *Coronation*	*The Coronation of Queen Elizabeth Wydeville, Queen Consort of Edward IV, on May 26th, 1465 (1935)*
Somerville	R. Somerville, *History of the Duchy of Lancaster*, i (1953)
SS	Surtees Society
Stonor L&P	*Stonor Letters and Papers of the Fifteenth Century 1290-1483*, ed. C.L. Kingsford (Camden Society, 3rd series. xxxix, xxx, 1919)
Tewkesbury chron.	Bodl. MS. Top Glouc d.2, Chronica de fundatoribus et fundatione ecclesiae de Theokesburie
TRHS	*Transactions of the Royal Historical Society*
Tudor-Craig, *Richard III*	*Richard III*, ed. P. Tudor-Craig (National Portrait Gallery Catalogue, 1973)
TV	*Testamenta Vetusta*, ed. N.H. Nicolas (2 vols. 1826)
UL	University Library
Vaesen, *Lettres*	*Lettres de Louis XI*, ed. J. Vaesen and E. Charavay, 12 vols. (Societé de l'histoire de France 1883-1909), iv
Vergil	*Three Books of Polydore Vergil's English History*, ed. H. Ellis (Camden Society xxix, 1844)
WAM	Westminster Abbey Muniments

Waurin, *Croniques*	J.de Waurin, *Recueil des Croniques et Anchiennes Istories de la Grant Bretaigne*, ed. W. and E.L.C.P. Hardy, v (Rolls Series, 1891)
WC	J. Warkworth, *Chronicle of the First Thirteen Years of the Reign of King Edward the Fourth*, ed. J.O. Halliwell (Camden Society vi, 1839)
Wolffe, *Royal Demesne*	B.P. Wolffe, *Royal Demesne in English History* (1971)
Worcester, *Annales*	'Annales Rerum Anglicarum', *Letters and Papers illustrative of the Wars of the English in France*, ed. J. Stevenson, ii. ii (Rolls Series, 1864)
Worcestre, *Itineraries*	W. Worcestre, *Itineraries*, ed. J.H. Harvey (1969)

Notes to Chapter I

1. For the above, see *GEC passim*.
2. McFarlane, *Nobility*, 177n, 178, 199; Rawcliffe, *Staffords*, 110. The dower of Eleanor, Countess of Northumberland as Lady Despenser should be subtracted from Warwick's income.
3. Pugh, *15th-cent.Engl.*106.
4. Ibid.118n; McFarlane, *Nobility*, 98; review by C.D.Ross in *Welsh History Review*, iii(1966-7), 302.
5. Scofield, *Edward IV*, i.9-11.
6. *Marcher Lordships of South Wales 1415-1536*, ed.T.B.Pugh(1963), 177-9; Ross, *Welsh History Review*, iii.299-302. For the next phrase, see *CPR 1461-7*, 107.
7. Gairdner, *Richard III*, 5.
8. Worcester, *Annales*, 765; *Annals of the Kingdom of Ireland of the Four Masters*, ed.J.O'Donavan(1848), i.965.
9. C.A.J.Armstrong, 'Politics and the Battle of St. Albans, 1455', *BIHR* xxxiii (1960), 1-72; Scofield, *Edward IV*, i.32-7.
10. *Registrum Abbathiae Johannis Whethamstede*,i, ed.H.T.Riley (RS 1872), 345; *FC* 635.
11. *Gregory's Chron*. 206-7; Scofield, *Edward IV*, i.37.
12. *Gregory's Chron*. 208; Worcester, *Annales*, 774; Scofield, *Edward IV*, i.88-9, 101-2.
13. Scofield, *Edward IV*, i.103-6.
14. C 81/1486/85(my trans.).
15. *English Chronicle of the Reigns of Richard II, Henry IV, Henry V and Henry VI*, ed.J.S.Davies(CSlxiv,1856), 109-10; *CSPM* 67; *GC* 195.
16. *CSPM* 67.
17. *CSPM* 72-3; *HC* 253; Scofield, *Edward IV*, i.178; Waurin, *Croniques*, 357-8.
18. Waurin, *Croniques*, 357.
19. Scofield, *Edward IV*, i.178; for what follows, see *Munimenta Civitatis Oxonie*, ed.H.E.Salter(Oxford Hist.Soc.lxxi, 1917), 222; C.A.J.Armstrong, 'The Inauguration Ceremonies of the Yorkist Kings', *TRHS* 4th ser. xxx(1948), 68n.
20. E 404/72/1/14.
21. Scofield, *Edward IV*, i.182-4.
22. E 404/71/1/14.
23. Scofield, *Edward IV*, i.216.
24. E 404/72/1/59.
25. E 405/40 m.6; E 404/72/3/47.
26. E 13/149mm.63, 77,/151 m.2d.
27. E 405/40 m.6; E 403/829 mm. 1-2, /835 mm. 3,4, /837 mm. 3,4, /838 mm. 3,6;E 13/151 mm.34d, 54.
28. Myers, *Household*, 290.
29. E 361/6 m.53d. The following two paras. are based on E 361/6mm. 53d, 54.
30. E 403/825 m.2.
31. *CPR 1461-7*, 52.
32. Myers, *Household*, 126-7.
33. E 159/240, brevia Hill.3 Edw.IV m.1.

34. *CPR 1461-7*, 270; C 81/793/1166 (my trans.).
35. But there is such a letter for Gloucester, Salisbury DRO Reg.Beauchamp, i,f.97-v.
36. DL 43/15/15 m.17.
37. *CPR 1461-7*, 213; DL 29/639/10376 m.7d; C.S.Perceval, 'Documents of Sir John Lawson, Baronet', *Archaeologia* xlvii (1882), 189.
38. DL 43/15/15 m.17.
39. E 361/6 m.56d; Salisbury DRO CAB 12 p.82; *CO* 98-9.
40. *CO* 131-3.
41. DL 37/31/36. For what follows see Dunham, *Hastings*, 133.
42. *CJS* 88.
43. Ibid. For what follows, see *CPR 1467-77*, 295-6.
44. Devon, *Issues*, 490. For what follows, see Warwick CRO CR 26/4 f.69; *SGA* 39; Tudor-Craig, *Richard III*, 63-4.
45. Anstis, *GR* ii.176-7; Smith, *Coronation*, 14; Salisbury DRO CAB 12 p. 82; KB 9/314/87-d.
46. PSO 1/64/41.
47. *Plumpton Corr.* 17; see below pp. 176, 184.
48. Waurin, *Croniques*, 455-6.
49. *Gregory's Chron.* 226-7.
50. Scofield, *Edward IV*, i.354; Waurin, *Croniques*, 455; *Mancini*, 60-1; *Vergil*, 117. The following paragraph is based on Lander, *Crown and Nobility*, 104-110.
51. *GEC* v.358-60; xi.507.
52. Commines, *Mémoires*, 111. For the next sentences, see Waurin, *Croniques*, 455. This para. is based on Hicks, *PPP* 60-4.
53. Smith, *Coronation*, 28-32; *Essex Feet of Fines*, iv. 58.
54. Ross, *Edward IV*, 95; for what follows, see J.E.Doyle, *Official Baronage of England*, iii(1886), 141; *GEC* xi.20n.
55. *Mancini*, 63.
56. *CPR 1461-7*, 327.
57. Ibid. 327-9, 331, 362, 366, 454-5; E 159/248, rec. Hill. 11 Edw. IV m.9; Worcester, *Annales*, 783; Smith, *Coronation*, 14.
58. Pugh, *GCH* 198.
59. Ellis, *Letters*, ii.i.124-6; BRL box 22, print 29, negative 26731; Pugh, *15th-cent.Engl.* 92.
60. *GEC* vii.373; *CPR 1461-7*, 104; *1467-77*, 456.
61. Worcester, *Annales*, 783.
62. Pugh, *15th-cent.Engl.*91.
63. Myers,*BJRL* 1.217; DL 29/735/12056 m.1.
64. *CPR 1461-7*, 298; Scofield, *Edward IV*,i.397. The paragraph is based on Hicks, *PPP* 67-9.
65. Myers, *BJRL* 1.450, 451; E 404/74/1/100.
66. KB 9/310/4; KB 9/317/28, /34; *Stonor L&P* i.103.
67. BL MS.Egerton 2822 m.2d.
68. *GEC* ii.389; *CPR 1467-77*, 34; PSO 1/29/1510.
69. Hicks, 'Northumberland', 8.

70. Pugh, *15th-cent.Engl.*93.
71. E 28/89/23, /24, /37; *HBC* 103.
72. C 49/56-65, *passim*; E 28/89/21, /23, /24, /37, /40, /41; *HBC* 85, 92,103; Myers, *Household*, 286-8; HMC *5th Rep*. 544.
73. Smith, *Coronation*; C81/803/1682-3; Worcester, *Annales*, 783-4.
74. Scofield, *Edward IV*, i.397-8.
75. Ibid.i.437; Worcester, *Annales*, 788; *CPR 1467-77*, 19, 41; C 81/824/2723; C 81/815/2287; Myers, *Household*, 286.
76. *CPR 1461-7, 22-3; 1467-77*, 17-18; for the next sentence see M.A.Hicks, 'The case of Sir Thomas Cook, 1468', *EHR* xciii (1978), 82-96.
77. *WC* 6.
78. E 405/50 m.5.
79. Worcester, *Annales*, 786; *CPR 1467-77*, 25, 49, 51; *GEC* vi.140-1; viii.58; E 101/412/2 p.13; Hicks, 'Northumberland', 6, 8.
80. *CC* 551. For the next phrase, see Pugh, *15th-cent.Engl.* 92.
81. *WC* 10; see below pp. 84-5.
82. Pugh, *GCH* 198.
83. *TV* i.305.
84. Worcester, *Annales*, 786.
85. J.Smyth, *Lives of the Berkeleys*, ed.J.Maclean(1883), 109-11; A.J.Pollard, 'The family of Talbot, Lords Talbot and Earls of Shrewsbury in the 15th Century' (unpub. Bristol Univ.Ph.D.thesis, 1968), 51-61; Hicks, 'Clarence', 303-7, 317-24.
86. C 149/226/6; CP 25(1)/294/74/37; *Essex Feet of Fines*, iv. 61,62.
87. HMC 78 *Hastings*,i.301-2.
88. E.g. C 49/56/35,/51.
89. Hicks, *PPP* 69.
90. Worcester, *Annales*, 785.
91. Scofield, *Edward IV*, i. 416; for the next clause, see E 403/835 m.4.
92. This para. is based on Hicks, *BIHR* 117.
93. *CC* 551; Basin, *Louis XI*, i.294-5.
94. *CSPM* 121.
95. *Foedera*, xi.565; Scofield, *Edward IV*, i.405; R.Vaughan, *Charles the Bold* (1973),45.
96. *EH* 176-212; *CCR 1461-8*, 456-7; Worcester, *Annales*, 786.
97. Worcester, *Annales*, 788-9.
98. *EH* 204,210; *CCR 1461-8*, 456.
99. Vaughan, *Charles the Bold*,44; Waurin,*Croniques*, 544-6.
100. E 101/71/5/948; Scofield,*Edward IV*,i.437-9; E 403/839 m.12.
101. Hicks, 'Clarence', 277-8.
102. Ibid.356-7.
103. *RP* v.572, 578-9; *CO* 105.
104. Waurin, *Croniques*, 458-9.
105. G.I.Keir, 'The Ecclesiastical Career of George Neville 1432-76'(unpub. Oxford B.Litt.thesis, 1970), 209-10, 213, 218-9; Worcester, *Annales*, 788, 789.
106. Scofield, *Edward IV*, i.495n; *C&P* 120n; PRO 31/9/62/530. Dugdale may have seen the original dispensation: Bodl. MS. Dugdale 15 p.75.

107. *GC* 206.
108. Worcester, *Annales*, 788; KB 29/99 m.31; KB 9/319, /320.
109. *Foedera*, xi.641-2; *Paston L&P* ii.397. The next paragraph is based on *CJS* 109-11.
110. Kent AO Sa/FAt6 m.4.
111. *CLB* 341-2.
112. *Reg.Bourgchier*, 35-6.
113. *CO* 98. The next four paragraphs are based on *WC* 46-51.
114. Hicks,*PPP* 72-3.
115. The Canterbury contingent was led by Nicholas Faunt, brewer and merchant, Kent AO Sa/At6 m.4; Canterbury CL F/Az f.137v; KB 27/836 m.61d; W.Boys, *Collections for a History of Sandwich* (1792), 676; HMC *5th Rep.*525, 545; *Calendar of the Black and White Books of the Cinque Ports*, ed.F. Hull(1966), 55.
116. *CPR 1467-77*, 214-16; Bodl.MS.Dugdale 18 f.41; A.J.Pollard, 'The Richmondshire Community of Gentry during the Wars of the Roses', *PPP* 40-2.
117. *GC* 209; *WC* 7; *GEC* vii.481, iv.480n; Coles,'Middleham', appx.B p.12; Worcestre, *Itineraries*, 340.
118. This paragraph is based on KB 27/836 m.61d.
119. Worcs.RO 989/112 m.2, /113 m.2; G.Wrottesley,'Extracts from the Plea Rolls', *Collections for a History of Staffordshire*, ns iv(1901), 175n; *CPR 1467-77*, 290.
120. Scofield, *Edward IV*, i.495-6.
121. KB 27/843 m.9,/848 m.8d.
122. *WC* 7; *CC* 543, 551; Waurin, *Croniques*, 585-6; Scofield, *Edward IV*, i.497n.
123. KB 27/836 m.6; *C&P* 306-7.
124. *CPR 1461-7*, 190; C 81/827/2875; C 81/830/3033; *CC* 543.
125. *Paston L&P* i.403.
126. C 81/1381/31; C 81/1547/8.
127. This paragraph is based on *Paston L&P* i.340, 345, 403-4, 407-8, 543-6; ii.577-80; Worcestre, *Itineraries*, 186-9.
128. *CC* 552; C 81/1547/8. For the rest of the paragraph, see C 81/827/2884; *Paston L&P* i.406; Kent AO NR/FAc4 f.16.
129. *CC* 552.

Notes to Chapter II

1. *CC* 552.
2. *Paston L&P* i.409.
3. Ibid.i.409-10; *CPR 1467-77*, 194-6.
4. *IC* 458-9; *CC* 552. For the next sentence, see Scofield, *Edward IV*, i.505; PSO 1/33/1722; E 404/74/2/67; *CPR 1467-77*, 191.
5. The Dukes of Gloucester, Norfolk and Suffolk, the Earls of Arundel, Kent, Essex and Northumberland, Lords Dynham, Ferrers of Chartley, Hastings, Howard, Dacre of the South and Mountjoy, Cardinal Bourchier, the Bishops of Bath, Lincoln, London, Salisbury and Ely, *Paston L&P* i.409-10; *CCR 1468-76*, nos.403-4; WAM 12184 f.22v; Cambridge UL G/I/5 ff.77v-78; Guildhall MS.9531/7 ff.119-20v; Lincs.AO Reg.20 f.99v; Salisbury DRO Reg. Beauchamp, i, f.149-v. Four bishops who made loans, Rochester, Carlisle, Durham and Exeter, may also have attended, E 404/74/2/108.
6. *Vergil*, 126.
7. *CC* 552; *CCR 1468-76*, no. 407.
8. C 81/830/3025; *CRL* 14.
9. *CPR 1467-77*, 178; *CCR 1468-76*, nos. 198, 408; DL 37/38/22; E 404/73/2/56, /65, /76; PSO 1/33/1726A. For the next sentence, see C 81/1547/8; Kendall, *Richard III*, 78-9.
10. PSO 1/33/1705, /1716, /1759; C 81/828/2914; DL 37/38/18; *CPR 1467-77*, 179, 185; Kendall, *Richard III*, 78-9.
11. C 81/828/2930 (executed 25 May 1470). For the next sentence, see WAM 5472 f.42v.
12. *CPR 1467-77*, 175; C 81/828/2911; PSO 1/33/1714.
13. WAM 5472 ff.8v, 38, 41v sqq. There is no entry on the chancery rolls.
14. The charter was warranted by writ of 4 January, but the grant was probably decided in November, C 81/829/2975.
15. C 81/829/2905; *CPR 1467-77*, 175. For the rest of the paragraph, see WAM 5472 ff.43, 45; *Paston L&P* i.409.
16. *CPR 1467-77*, 175; C 81/828/2948; PSO 1/33/1707.
17. E 404/74/2/67; PSO 1/33/1722; Hicks, 'Clarence', 355-7; National Register of Archives List, Derbys. RO Gell MSS. Muniments of Title 105.
18. *CPR 1467-77*, 185, 209; C 53/195/4; C 81/828/2923; C 81/830/3013, /3017; *GEC* vii. 481.
19. *CPR 1467-77*, 182; C 81/828/2926; Emden, *BROU* ii.809.
20. *CCR 1468-76*, nos. 403-4; Hicks, 'Northumberland', 11-12.
21. J.M.W. Bean, *Estates of the Percy Family 1416-1537* (1958), 109.
22. *CPR 1467-77*, 189; C 81/830/3022.
23. Exeter City AO Grigson MSS. CR292 m.3; C 140/32/10/2; *CPR 1467-77*, 174.
24. *Paston L&P* ii.433; Bean, *Estates*, 109; C 53/195/1; C 81/1501/47.
25. C 81/829/2976.
26. Hicks, 'Clarence', 57, 301; Hicks, *BIHR* 117; Coles, 'Middleham', table V.
27. Trans. from Worcester, *Annales*, 786.
28. *CRL* 6-7.
29. *CPR 1467-77*, 183; C 81/829/2982; *RP* vi.43-4; *GEC* iv.8-9, 18-19. For the next sentence, see Myers, *BJRL* 1.466; Emden, *BRCU* 560.

30. E 315/49/157; *Rot. Scot.* ii. 407-8; for what follows, see *Rot. Scot.* ii. 422, 428.
31. Bodl. MS. Dugdale 18 f.41.
32. *WC* 4, 10-11.
33. *CRL* 14-15.
34. *CRL* 5-18; Waurin, *Croniques*, 587-602; *WC* 8-9. These, and the confession of Sir Robert Welles in *EH* 282-4, are the source of the following eighteen paragraphs.
35. C. Oman, *Warwick the Kingmaker* (1891), 196.
36. *Paston L&P* i. 415; ii. 432; *Foedera*, xi. 652-3; *Vergil*, 127-8; *CC* 553; *WC* 8-9.
37. *CPR 1467-77*, 218; Lichfield Joint RO B/A/12 ff.45v, 47; Lincoln AO Reg. 20 f.144; Emden, *BRCU* 39.
38. *CPR 1467-77*, 218, 212; *LS* 158.
39. *WC* 8.
40. R.L. Storey, 'Lincolnshire and the Wars of the Roses', *NMS* xiv (1970), 71-2.
41. C 67/47 m.8.
42. Scofield, *Edward IV*, i.509n.
43. *WC* 8.
44. C 67/47 m.8; for Yerburgh, see DL 29/639/10376 m.9; CP 40/846 m.290.
45. *GC* 209.
46. C 81/830/3025; C 81/1501/27.
47. Scofield, *Edward IV*, i. 510; *Paston L&P* i.415.
48. *GC* 209-10.
49. *GC* 210.
50. Ibid.
51. *CPR 1467-77*, 218; *Foedera*, xi. 652-3; see also Scofield, *Edward IV*, i. 512. For an analysis of the commissioners, see Hicks, 'Clarence', 71.
52. E.g. *Vergil*, 127.
53. *CCR 1468-76*, nos. 528, 534.
54. *Paston L&P* ii. 432-3.
55. Ibid. ii. 432; Waurin, *Croniques*, 602. For Shrewsbury's part, see *CSPM* 137; C 81/837/3068; C 67/47 m.2.
56. R.R. Rickart, *The Maire of Bristowe is Kalendar*, ed. L. Toulmin-Smith (CS ns v, 1872), 44; Roye, *Journal*, i. 245.
57. *CPR 1467-77*, 174, 176, 189, 217.
58. Based on J. Hoker, *Description of the city of Excester*, ed. W.J. Harty, J.W. Schopp and H. Tapley Soper (Devon and Cornwall RS, 1919), ii. 51-5. In Hooker's time the relevant receiver's account survived. This is the source of the next two paragraphs.
59. *CRL* 8.
60. Hoker, *Excester*, ii. 53.
61. *CPR 1467-77*, 218: the source of this and the next two paragraphs.
62. Ibid. 208, 210, 218.
63. *Foedera*, xi. 651-2; *GC* 210; H.A. Napier, *Historical Notes of the Parishes of Swyncombe and Ewelme* (1858), 131. For what follows, see *CPR 1467-77*, 205.
64. *CPR 1467-77*, 219. For the next clause, see PSO 1/34/1777.
65. Hoker, *Excester*, ii. 54-5. For the next sentence, see *CPR 1467-77*, 217; Scofield, *Edward IV*, i. 519.

66. *CPR 1467-77*, 205; *CCR 1468-76*, no. 536.
67. Scofield, *Edward IV*, i. 519-20.
68. *C&P* 110; Chastellain, *Oeuvres*, 449-53; *Mémoires de Messire Philippe de Comines*, ed. Lenglet de Fresnoy (1747), iii. 120-4; BN French MS. 6977 ff.91 sqq.
69. Chastellain, *Oeuvres*, 493.
70. *CSPM* 136.
71. Commines, *Mémoires* (1747 edn.), iii. 124-5.
72. Vaesen, *Lettres*, iv. 110-14; BN French MSS. 6977 f.26v; 20485 f.101; 20489 f.88; 20490 f.91.
73. *CSPM* 136. For the rest of the paragraph, see Duclos, *Louis XI* (1745), iii. 349-50, 353-5; Vaesen, *Lettres*, iv. 122, 131; BN French MS. 20489 f.88.
74. BN French MSS. 6602 f.4; 20486 f.6; 20487 ff.18-19; 20489 ff.5,23; 20491 f.17.
75. Duclos, *Louis XI*, iii. 353; Vaesen, *Lettres*, iv. 121-2.
76. Miss Scofield's phrase, *Edward IV*, i. 520.
77. *Fortescue Family*, 80-2. The original, BN French MS.6974 f.27-v is dated 1470 in a later hand. Only the copy, BN French MS.6975 ff.108-10, is dated 1468, again in a later hand. Internal evidence indicates that 1470 is correct.
78. Commines, *Mémoires* (1747 edn.), iii. 124-5.
79. *CSPM* 139-40.
80. Ibid. 140.
81. Ellis, *Letters*, ii. i. 132-4. The next two paragraphs are based on ibid.; *CSPM* 140-1.
82. Duclos, *Louis XI*, iii. 356.
83. Ellis's text is from BL MS. Harley 543, itself based on BL Add. MS. 48031.
84. The following quotation is my translation of *Fortescue Family*, 81.
85. *CSPM* 117.
86. *Hanserecesse*, ii. vi. 277-8.
87. Ellis, *Letters*, ii. i. 134.
88. *CSPM* 142.
89. Ibid.
90. BN French MS. 6758 ff.57v, 61 (my trans.).
91. *CSPM* 140.
92. Ibid.; Basin, *Louis XI*, ii. 24-9.
93. Commines, *Mémoires*, ii. 199.
94. *Foedera*, xi. 700-5. For the next sentence, see Ellis, *Letters*, ii. i. 134.
95. *WC* 10.
96. *Fortescue Family*, 81-2; *CSPM* 140; Basin, *Louis XI*, ii. 24-7; Waurin, *Croniques*, 608-10.
97. Fortescue, *Governance*, 349-53.
98. Ellis, *Letters*, ii. i. 135-7; *GC* 211.
99. Scofield, *Edward IV*, i. 538-9.
100. Morgan, *TRHS* 10.
101. *GC* 211; Morgan *TRHS* 11; *Hanserecesse*, ii. vii. 416.
102. *EHD* 306-7; Kingsford, *Chrons. London*, 182; *GC* 211; *FC* 659; *WC* 11.
103. *WC* 11-12.
104. Ellis, *Letters*, ii. i. 134; *HC* 286; see below p. 96.

105. C 81/1626/82-3; *CFR 1461-71*, 289.
106. Ibid.
107. My trans. of *Foedera*, xi. 700.
108. My trans. of ibid. xi. 701. This paragraph is based on ibid. xi. 700-1.
109. *CFR 1461-71*, 291.
110. *CPR 1461-7*, 91, 115-6, 141, 151, 185, 186, 432. For the next sentence, see ibid. *1461-7*, 486; *1467-77*, 22, 24, 176, 480.
111. Hicks, *BIHR* 117.
112. *CPR 1467-77*, 236, 243; *CFR 1461-71*, 283-4.
113. *Paston L&P* i. 564; *Rot. Scot.* ii. 422, 425.
114. *Arrivall*, 3-5.
115. The Dukes of Clarence, Exeter and Somerset, Marquis Montagu, the Earls of Devon, Dorset, Oxford, Pembroke, Shrewsbury and Warwick, Viscount Beaumont, Lords Stanley, FitzHugh, Scrope of Bolton, Wenlock and Sudeley, and the Prior of St. John, although not all were in England when the parliament opened, *HP* ii. 378-82, esp. 379n, 380n. For what follows, see ibid.
116. *HBC* 85, 93, 103; Lincs. AO Reg. 20 f.321.
117. *CPR 1467-77*, 227. For the next sentence, see Scofield, *Edward IV*, i. 542n; Nottingham UL MiC5b; Morgan, *TRHS* 7.
118. Fortescue, *Governance*, 348-53: the source of the next two paragraphs.
119. This paragraph is based on C 66/491.
120. Exeter City AO rec. acct. 10-11 Edw. IV m.2. For the next sentence, see *EHD* 306-7.
121. BL Add. MS. 48031 f.146; HMC 12 *Rutland*, i.4.
122. *Vergil*, 134.
123. C 66/491 m.8d; *CPR 1467-77*, 252.
124. E 404/71/6/15, /16, /19-27.
125. *EHD* 306; C 66/491 mm.8d, 13d; C 81/780/11035,/11044,/11065; E 404/71/6/10,/21,/27. For the ensuing quotation, see C 81/780/11029.
126. C 81/780/11035; *Bristol GRB* ii. 136-7.
127. C 81/780/11045.
128. Exeter City AO rec. acct. 10-11 Edw. IV m.2; Kent AO NR/FAc4 ff.23, 23v, 30; Kent AO Sa/Ac1 f.199v; *Paston L&P* i. 564.
129. E 159/247, brevia Hill. 49 Hen. VI m.3d; *C&P* 324.
130. E.g. Somerset, Exeter and Ormond, see below.
131. *EHD* 306; *Bristol GRB* ii. 136-7; C 81/780/11033, /11035; Kent AO NR/FAc4 ff. 23-v, 30-v; BL Add. MS. 48031 f.43. For what follows, see Kingsford, *London Chrons*. 183; Lincs. AO Reg. 20 f.321.
132. *LS* 36, 38; Ellis, *Letters*, ii. i. 139-40; Exeter City AO rec. acct. 10-11 Edw. IV m.2; Salisbury DRO CAB 13 p.45; Lincs. AO Reg. 20 f.321.
133. *CPR 1467-77*, 234, 243; *CCR 1468-76*, no. 624; C 81/1297/11.
134. *Foedera*, xi. 700. This paragraph is based on ibid. xi. 700-5; C 81/781/11110.
135. *CPR 1461-7*, 226; *1467-77*, 243-4; *CCR 1468-76*, no. 580.
136. *Foedera*, xi. 701; see appendix III.
137. PROB 11/6 (Wattys) f.34-v; WAM 12183 ff.19 sqq.
138. *CPR 1461-7*, 281-2.
139. WAM 12183 ff.14v, 15 sqq.

140. Ibid. f. 19-v. Stafford was still corresponding with Somerset on 28 March, ibid. ff.39v, 40v.
141. *Foedera*, xi. 704; C 81/781/11110.
142. Griffiths, *PPP* 17-36.
143. *Vergil*, 135.
144. Pugh, *15th-cent. Engl.* 118n; R.L. Storey, *End of the House of Lancaster* (1966), 144, 145n.
145. *HC* 286; *WC* 10; *RP* vi. 194; but see below pp.159sqq.
146. *Arrivall*, 10.
147. Ibid.
148. Ibid.; *CC* 554.
149. *CPR 1461-7*, 186, 189; *CFR 1461-71*, 291.
150. R.S. Thomas, 'Career, Estates and "Connection" of Jasper Tudor, Earl of Pembroke and Duke of Bedford (d. 1495)' (unpub. Wales Univ. Ph. D. thesis, 1971), 325; *CFR 1461-71*, 40, 293. But Warwick was granted the custody of the lordship of Newport and a half-share of Pembroke's custody of Cantref Selyf, *CFR 1461-71*, 293, 295.
151. *CPR 1467-77*, 239; *CFR 1461-71*, 289, 291; *Rot. Scot.* ii. 425; Exeter City AO Grigson MS.CR292 m.3. For what follows, see Chastellain, *Oeuvres*, 499-500; *Arrivall*, 9.
152. *CPR 1461-7*, 215, 217, 485.
153. *Arrivall*, 7; *WC* 14. Skipton was a Clifford lordship, *CPR 1461-7*, 115-6, 342, 474. For Parre, see *CRL* 15-16.
154. But see DL 29/59/1116; *CPR 1467-77*, 235, 245.
155. *CPR 1467-77*, 236, 243; *CFR 1461-71*, 293.
156. *CSPM* 154.
157. *Arrivall*, 23. For what follows, see ibid. 10; Commines, *Mémoires*, i.211-12.
158. My trans. of J. Bain, 'Notes on an Original Letter referring to Edward IV while in exile', *Genealogist* ns iii (1886), 65; see also *C&P* 321-3.
159. *Testamenta Eboracensia*, iii (SS xlv, 1864), 306.
160. PROB 11/6 (Wattys) ff.34-v, 40; /5 (Godyn) ff.255v-6v.
161. WAM 12183 ff.6, 19v, 32.
162. *CFR 1461-71*, 282.
163. *C&P* 130.
164. Scofield, *Edward IV*, i. 550-1.
165. Ibid. i. 563; *C&P* 323.
166. Scofield, *Edward IV*, i. 562.
167. *EHD* 307. Louis XI also attacked Burgundy, Scofield, *Edward IV*, i. 562.
168. The Canterbury M.P.s left respectively on 18 and 24 January, New Romney's M.P.s on 21 January, Canterbury CL F/A5 f.113v; Kent AO NR/FAc4 f.32.
169. *45th Report of the Deputy Keeper of the Public Records* (1884), 333 [henceforth cited as *DKR*]; *Foedera*, xi 683-92; *EHD* 307.
170. Kent AO NR/FAc4 f.32.
171. *Stonor L&P* i. 117; *Arrivall*, 12.
172. *CPR 1467-77*, 252.
173. She is not mentioned in Queen Margaret's entourage in late 1470, Roye, *Journal*, i. 249; Exeter City AO rec. acct. 10-11 Edw. IV m.2.

174. *C&P* 323.
175. Salisbury DRO CAB 13 p. 214.
176. HMC 12 *Rutland*, i. 2-3; CP 40/842 m.71d; C 81/1505/16.
177. HMC 12 *Rutland*, i.3-4.
178. Ibid. i. 2-3.
179. *Arrivall*, 6-7; Hicks, 'Northumberland', 19-22.
180. *Arrivall*, 8-9; Dunham, *Hastings*, 25.
181. *Arrivall*, 8; *Paston Letters 1422-1509*, ed. J. Gairdner (1904), v.94-6; S.A.A. Majendie, *Some Account of the Family of de Vere* (1904), 24. For what follows, see HMC 12 *Rutland*, i. 3-4; *Arrivall*, 11.
182. *Arrivall*, 12.
183. Ibid. 15-17; *Hanserecesse*, ii. vi. 416-17; *WC* 15, 17. For the next paragraph, see Ross, *Edward IV*, 167-8.
184. E.g. Sir Edward Grey, Sir Nicholas and Sir Robert Strelley, Sir Henry Lewis, John Rugge, William Berkeley, Thomas Stafford, John Otter, Richard Scrope, John Rufford, KB 9/41/38; *RP* vi. 144; *CPR 1467-77*, *passim*; C 81/1502/14, /17.
185. C 81/1502/17; *Plumpton Corr.* 25.
186. E.g. Thomas Tothoth, John Kirton, William Yerburgh, Thomas FitzWilliam the younger, Robert and Margaret Dymmock, *CPR 1461-7*, 71; *1467-77*, 285; SC 6/1118/2 mm.1-2; see above p. 67.
187. *Arrivall*, 22-31; Ross, *Edward IV*, 170-2.
188. J.A.F. Thomson, ' "The Arrivall of Edward IV": the development of the text', *Speculum* xlvi (1971), 88. Roger, Lord Camoys, associated with Hastings in 1465 and 1473, died shortly before 1 March 1477, HMC 78 *Hastings*, i. 273; BL Harl. MS. 3881 f.18; *CFR 1471-85*, no. 331.
189. Kingsford, *EHL* 375. For the Kent contingent, see *CJS* 116.
190. *Foedera*, xi. 714-15.

Notes to Chapter III

1. *Arrivall*, 10-12.
2. Lander, *Crown and Nobility*, 138, 139n.
3. *Bristol LRB* ii. 130-1; *Bristol GRB* iii. 95; *Arrivall*, 12.
4. Lander, *Crown and Nobility*, 136-7; *RP* vi. 27, 47-8, 69; Myers, *Household*, 287; Emden, *BRCU* 413.
5. *GEC passim*.
6. C 81/1310/1-2.
7. C 81/834/3241.
8. *CPR 1467-77*, 262, 344; C 81/1504/22.
9. See above.
10. KB 9/41/38; the next thirteen paragraphs are based on Hicks, *BIHR* 117-22.
11. *Paston L&P* i. 447.
12. *CC* 557.
13. C 81/1504/5, /7.
14. *CPR 1467-77*, 330, 335-6; Kingsford, *EHL* 382-3; *RP* vi.3; E 101/71/5/948; C 81/1504/14.
15. *Paston L&P* i. 464.
16. HMC *11th Rep*. vii. 95.
17. *CSPM* 178.
18. *Paston L&P* i. 468, 472.
19. Ibid. i. 469; Scofield, *Edward IV*, ii. 58-60; Kendall, *Richard III*, 110-12.
20. *Paston L&P* i. 344-5, 544, 636-8. For what follows, see ibid. i. 471.
21. Ibid. i. 468-9. For what follows, see ibid. i. 464.
22. Scofield, *Edward IV*, ii. 58.
23. *CSPM* 166, 176.
24. KB 9/41/37, /41; Scofield, *Edward IV*, ii. 28.
25. *CSPM* 166.
26. *Arrivall*, 12.
27. C 81/1507/2, /49.
28. Ibid. /49.
29. Scofield, *Edward IV*, ii. 87-8.
30. *CC* 557.
31. Hicks, *PPP* 76, 78.
32. SC 6/1123/3 m.9d. For the next sentence, see KB 9/334/85, /86; Scofield, *Edward IV*, ii. 54-5.
33. E 315/40/75.
34. KB 9/334/87.
35. Salop RO Bridgewater coll. box 87 min. accts. 13-15 Edw. IV rot. 5 m.ld; Scofield, *Edward IV*, ii. 60n.
36. Hicks, *NH* 83. For the next sentence, see Scofield, *Edward IV*, ii. 60; J.S. Roskell, 'William Allington of Bottisham, Speaker in the Parliaments of 1472-5 and 1478', *Proceedings of the Cambridge Antiquarian Society* lii (1959), 49.
37. KB 9/333/22; KB 9/334/85, /86, /87. For the next sentence, see *Paston L&P* i. 464.
38. Scofield, *Edward IV*, ii. 93; Kendall, *Richard III*, 113; Gairdner, *Richard III*, 30.
39. Lander, *Crown and Nobility*, 138, 139n; Wolffe, *Royal Demesne*, 154-5.

40. *RP* vi. 15-16, 25, 57, 60; C 81/1504/7, /22; C 81/1507/51. The following four paragraphs are based on Hicks, *BIHR* 122-3.
41. See appendix II.
42. Wolffe, *Royal Demesne*, 154-5, 160n; for the next phrase, see *RP* vi. 13; see above p. 97.
43. E 379/176; E 199/12/2 mm.2,3; *CPR 1467-77*, 457-8, 594; E 159/253, brevia East. 16 Edw. IV m.6-d.
44. SC 6/1089/4; DL 29/403/6467.
45. Cf. DL 37/43 mm.1-5; DL 29/403/6467; see also Hicks, 'Clarence', 348-60 and table XVIII.
46. DL 37/49/9.
47. *CPR 1467-77*, 428.
48. Hicks, 'Clarence', 281.
49. *CPR 1467-77*, 457-8, 530, 597; Tewkesbury chron. f.39; Hicks, 'Clarence', 278-9; E 159/252, brevia Trin. 15 Edw. IV m.9d.
50. *CPR 1467-77*, 335-6.
51. A.J. Otway-Ruthven, *History of Medieval Ireland* (1968), 396-7; *CPR 1467-77*, 458, 461, 468; C 81/849/3984, /3985, /3995, /3998; C 81/850/4003; E 101/71/5/947; E 404/75/4/39.
52. E 404/75/4/39; C 47/10/29; see also Scofield, *Edward IV*, ii. 110-12; Otway-Ruthven, *Medieval Ireland*, 395-6.
53. Hicks, *PPP* 75-82; Hicks, *NH* 83-9.
54. *CC* 561.

Notes to Chapter IV

1. *Rows Roll*, no. 58; Tewkesbury chron. ff.39v-40v. For Webb see Worcs. R O BA 2648/6 (ii) p. 426.
2. *RGS* 163.
3. *Rows Roll*, no. 58.
4. Ross, *15th-cent. Engl.* 52. For a general discussion of these issues, see Scofield, *Edward IV*, ii. 175; *C&P* 219-20.
5. *Paston L&P* i.498-9.
6. Scofield, *Edward IV*, ii. 136; Commines, *Memoires*, ii. 240.
7. Anstis, *GR* ii. 197; *Paston L&P* i. 498-9; Borthwick IHR Reg. Lawrence Bothe f.255; Lincoln AO Reg. 21 f.14v; Guildhall Library MS. 9531/7 ff.159v-60.
8. Scofield, *Edward IV*, ii. 175-8; *C&P* 221n, 222-5.
9. *CC* 561.
10. Scofield, *Edward IV*, ii. 185.
11. *CC* 561; *IC* 478.
12. Charles the Bold had an independent claim through John of Gaunt's second marriage, Scofield, *Edward IV*, ii. 24.
13. Ibid. ii. 191-2.
14. *RP* vi. 194.
15. *Letters of the Kings of England*, ed. J.O. Halliwell (1846), i.147.
16. *CC* 561; *IC* 478.
17. *CC* 561; *IC* 478.
18. *CC* 561; *IC* 478-80; *DKR* iii. 213-4, summarising KB 8/1/1-14. These are the basis of the next six paragraphs.
19. J. Stow, *Annales of England* (1600), 715-16.
20. Emden, *BROU* i. 197; iii. 1749.
21. DL 37/41/4; E 404/76/1/77.
22. PSO 1/44/2288.
23. E 405/56 m.4.
24. *CIPM* 387; *HP* i. 132-3; *Warwicks. Feet of Fines* iii (Dugdale Soc. xviii, 1943), nos. 2687-8; KB 9/344/18; KB 27/855 m.37d, /856 m. 5d, /862 m.47, /863 m.5. He attended a court at Alcester in 1462-3, Warwicks. CRO B. Alc/Blo. p.31.
25. Emden, *BROU* iii. 1749; BRL 168023 m.3.
26. *LS* 158; *Stratford-on-Avon Corporation Records. The Gild Accounts* (1912), 37; *CC* 561; *CPR 1467-77*, 346-7.
27. C 81/1512/51-2.
28. Anstis, *GR* ii. 200-1.
29. *CC* 561.
30. Emden, *BRCU* 776; Scofield, *Edward IV*, ii. 190; E 101/411/13, /15 f.12; E 101/412/2 f.32.
31. Scofield, *Edward IV*, ii. 188, 190.
32. *CC* 562; *IC* 479.
33. *DKR* iii. 214. The next two paragraphs are based on *DKR* iii. 214-5; *RP* vi. 173-5; *CPR 1476-85*, 72-3.
34. See also KB 9/347/28.
35. *LS* 158; E 159/261, brevia Trin. 2 Ric. III m.2.
36. KB 8/1/60; *RGS passim*; Bodl. MS. Dugdale 15 p.73.

37. Tewkesbury chron. f. 39v. For the date of Isabel's death, see also *Rows Roll*, no. 58; *DKR* iii. 215.
38. Lander, *Crown and Nobility*, 248.
39. Emden, *BROU* i. 137-8; *HP* i. 859; *GEC* xi. 301n; *CPR 1467-77*, 517-8, 530, 597; *CCR 1468-76*, nos. 952, 962; *Calendar of the Feet of Fines relating to the County of Huntingdon* (Cambs. Antiq. Soc. octavo ser. xxxvii, 1913), 111; C 49/56/18.
40. PROB 11/7 (Logge), f.105v; *CCR 1468-76*, nos. 541-2; *HP* i. 886-8; DL 29/638/10371 m.8d.
41. *CC* 561-2.
42. *CSPM* 230.
43. Scofield, *Edward IV*, ii. 204.
44. *CLB* 420-1.
45. *RP* vi. 193-5.
46. *CC* 562; *IC* 479-80.
47. *Christ Church Letters*,ed. J.B. Sheppard (CS ns xix, 1877), 36-7. For his tomb see the engravings in R. Atkyns, *Ancient and Present State of Gloucestershire* (1768),betw. pp. 380-1 [copy at Bodl. Libr.].
48. PSO 1/46/2375, /2399; PSO 1/47/2427A, /2442; PSO 1/49/2522A; E 28/91/84; E 403/848 m.11; E 159/258, brevia Mich. 21 Edw. IV m.1d; DL 29/638/10373 m.2-d; C 81/867/4885, /4886; *CPR 1476-85*, 115, 132, 135, 137; C 66/543 m. 10; BL Harl. MS. 433 f.110.
49. More, *Richard III*, 6.
50. *Vergil*, 168.
51. Ibid. 167.
52. My trans. of Roye, *Journal*, ii. 64.
53. *CC* 562.
54. *Illustrations*, 27-40. This is the source of the next three paragraphs.
55. BL Add. MS. 6113 f.72v; *Paston L&P* i.612.
56. BL Add. MS. 6113 ff.74-5.
57. Tudor-Craig, *Richard III*, 31.
58. *Mancini*, 62-3.
59. More, *Richard III*, 6.
60. *Mancini*, 62-3.
61. *Vergil*, 168.
62. Lords Strange and Berkeley, summoned to the previous parliament, were still alive; the Earl of Pembroke, Lords Ogle, Lovell and Welles, each summoned in 1483, were already of age. *HP* ii. 428-31; *GEC passim*. For what follows, see Hicks, 'Clarence', table VII; J.S. Roskell, 'The Problem of the Attendance of the Lords in Medieval English Parliaments', *BIHR* xxix (1956), 199.
63. *HP* ii. 433, 439, 443; *Illustrations*, 31, 34-40.
64. Ross, *Edward IV*, 318-22; R.J. Knecht, 'The Episcopate and the Wars of the Roses', *University of Birmingham Historical Journal*, vi(1957-8), 108-31, esp. 131. For what follows see *RP* vi. 167; Emden, *BROU*, *BRCU*, *passim*.
65. Ross,*Edward IV*, 185; DL 29/59/1117 mm.3-4; E 28/91/46, /49, /66.
66. Pugh, *15th-cent. Engl.* 116-17. For what follows, see ibid.;Lander, *Crown and Nobility*, 309-15; Myers, *Household*, 286-8; HMC *5th Rep.* 544; *Paston L&P* i.524.

67. *RP* vi.167.
68. Morgan, *TRHS* 18n.
69. *RP* vi.195; *CPR 1476-85*, 83; *CC* 562; E 405/65 m.2; DL 37/46/20.
70. DL 29/59/1117 mm.3-4; /1120 m.3, /1121 m.3; *GEC* iv. 9, 479-80.
71. *CPR 1467-77*, 283.
72. *GEC* ii.132-3; vi. 583; *RP* vi. 168-70.
73. *Mancini*, 62-3; More, *Richard III*, 6-8; Gairdner, *L&P Ric. III and Hen. VII*, i. 68.
74. Hicks, *BIHR* 124; *RP* vi. 170-1.
75. C 81/863/4658, /4665, /4669-71, /4687; for the enrolments, see *CPR 1476-85*, 67-8, 90.
76. Hicks, *BIHR* 124.
77. DL 37/46/15.
78. Tudor-Craig, *Richard III*, 31; *Illustrations*, 27-8; BL Add. MS. 6113 f.74v.
79. Hicks, *NH* 83 sqq; *Illustrations*, 33.
80. *GEC* xii. ii. 449; *RP* vi. 171-2; BL Add. MS. 6113 f.74v.
81. *GEC* iv. 381; CP 40/842 m.222; E 159/257, rec. East. 20 Edw. IV mm.20 (1)d, 20(2); CP 40/856 m.518.
82. *GEC* xii. ii. 447-8; ix. 337; Dunham, *Hastings*, 25, 133.
83. DL 29/641/10411 m.2d; *CPR 1476-85*, 97, 137; *Manners and Household Expenses in the Thirteenth and Fifteenth Centuries*, ed. B. Botfield (Roxburghe Club, 1841), 175, 299.
84. *CPR 1476-85*, 97; *RP* vi. 167; *Arrivall*, 26-7.
85. DL 29/639/10379; SC 6/1123/6 m.3d.
86. BL Add. MS. 6113 f.74v.
87. J.S. Roskell, *The Commons in the Parliament of 1422* (1954), 132, 135-6; M. McKisack, *Parliamentary Representation of the English Boroughs during the Middle Ages* (1932), 106-12.
88. Roskell, *Commons*, 136n; see above, appendix III.
89. *HP* ii. 433-46; i, *passim*; Myers, *Household*, 288-93.
90. See appendix III. The following nine paragraphs are based on *HP* i, ii, *passim*; appendix III; *LS passim*.
91. K.N. Houghton, 'Theory and Practice in Borough Elections to Parliament during the Later Fifteenth Century', *BIHR* xxxix (1966), 137n. 3; C 219/17/3/i/14-20. Wedgwood misread a Truro M.P. as 'Cinte'; he was 'Curte', ibid. /17.
92. E.W. Ives, 'Andrew Dymmock and the Papers of Antony, Earl Rivers, 1482-3', *BIHR* xli. 222-3, 227-8.
93. See below pp. 186-7 & appendix III.
94. DL 29/454/7312; SC 6/1123/3 m.8.
95. DL 29/454/7312 m.4; SC 8/344/1281. For what follows see DL 29/454/7312.
96. Ibid. m.4; Ives, *BIHR* xli. 222, 226-7.
97. Petworth House MAC 20 m.4; *GEC* iv. 9. They were also her officers, DL 37/46/18; DL 29/736/12059 m.6.
98. The indenture was tampered with, C 219/17/3/iii/115.
99. *Stonor L&P* i. 151, 154; ii. 14.
100. Richard Carlile, Thomas Burton and William Tanfield, who was a cadet of the Cransley family, of whom Robert was a Grey retainer, *Grey of Ruthin Valor*, ed. R.I. Jack (1965), 46, 75, 122-3, 125, 126.

101. *RP* vi. 193-4.
102. *RP* vi. 193-5; Lander, *Crown and Nobility*, 242-66. These are the source of the next five paragraphs.
103. E.g. *Bristol Charters 1378-1499*, ed. H.A. Cronne (Bristol Rec. Soc. xi, 1946), 138-42.
104. *WC* 12.
105. Bishop Grey was in prison during the Readeption parliament, *Hanserecesse*, ii. vi. 416.
106. *WC* 10.
107. Ellis, *Letters*, ii. i. 132-5.
108. *CPR 1467-77*, 241-2. For what follows, see also above p. 96.
109. Grey's register leaves his movements in doubt, Cambridge UL G/I/5.
110. *HC* 286, 326.
111. See above pp. 49-50.
112. *RP* vi. 141; M. Levine, 'Richard III — Usurper or Lawful King?', *Speculum* xxxiv (1959), 391-401.
113. *GC* 231-2; *Mancini*, 94-7; More, *Richard III*, 59-75. Vergil only mentions Edward's supposed bastardy, *Vergil*, 183-5.
114. *Mancini*, 60-3.
115. Levine, *Speculum* xxxiv. 392n.
116. Scofield, *Edward IV*, ii. 213.
117. Commines, *Mémoires*, ii. 232-3.
118. *Arrivall*, 10; C 81/1505/16; Tewkesbury chron. f.39.
119. *RP* vi. 167, 187; Emden, *BROU* iii. 1778.
120. *Stonor L&P* ii. 42; HMC *Various collections*, i. 215.
121. *Mancini*, 62-3.
122. Scofield, *Edward IV*, ii. 24.
123. *RP* vi. 173-5.
124. He was at Windsor from 4 March to 31 July 1477 and at Westminster from 7 November 1477 to 25 February 1478, Salisbury DRO Reg. Beauchamp, ii, ff.8-12v, 13v-15.
125. *CC* 561.
126. Tewkesbury chron. ff.37v, 39-40v; *CPR 1467-77*, 242, 346-7, 513, 530.
127. *CPR 1476-85*, 68, 71, 89; Emden, *BRCU* 576. Hugh and William were dismissed on Clarence's fall.
128. DL 43/15/15 m.17; PROB 11/5 (Godyn) f.209.
129. *CC* 562; *IC* 479.
130. *CC* 561; *IC* 478.
131. *Bristol GRB* iv. 92.
132. He executed it in person and received expenses, DL 29/724/11810 m.2, /11813 m.3.
133. *Vergil*, 167-8; *GC* 226; More, *Richard III*, 70.
134. Scofield, *Edward IV*, ii. 194.

Notes to Chapter V

1. *CPR 1461-7*, 197-9, 212-13, 340-1. The detailed evidence for this section is in Hicks, 'Clarence', ch.5. Clarence's lands in 1467, 1473 and 1478 are listed in appendix II.
2. See above p.32.
3. Tailbois's attainder was reversed in 1472, Tresham's in 1467, Nuthill's in 1478, *RP* v. 616-17; vi. 18-19, 175-6. None of these lands were held by Clarence at death.
4. Hicks, *BIHR* 116-28. For the Montagu earldom of Salisbury, see also M.A. Hicks, 'The Neville earldom of Salisbury 1429-71', *Wiltshire Archaeological Magazine* lxxii (1980) 141-7; for the other constituent inheritances, see also Hicks, 'Clarence', 292-4, 310-10.
5. *Ministers' Accounts of the Warwickshire Estates of the Duke of Clarence 1479-80*, ed. R.H. Hilton (Dugdale Soc. xxi, 1952), xvi-xix. The detailed references for this section are in Hicks, 'Clarence', chs. 5 and 6.
6. *Grey of Ruthin Valor*, ed. R.I. Jack (1965), 49n.
7. Hilton, loc. cit.
8. DL 29/640/10388 m.5.
9. DL 29/638/10371 mm.7, 8d, 12d; DL 29/644/10445 mm.1-d, 2; /10446 m.2; /10457 mm.1, 6; DL 29/645/10461 m.7d; East Sussex RO Aber 68 ff.27 sqq.
10. C 81/1639/33.
11. This section is based on Hicks, 'Clarence', 208-342 and tabulated accounts in appended portfolio.
12. *CO* 89-105.
13. E.g. R.A. Griffiths, 'Local Rivalries and National Politics: The Percies, the Nevilles and the Duke of Exeter, 1452-55', *Speculum* xliii (1968), 589-632. The argument is elaborated in Hicks, 'Clarence', chapter 7: I hope to discuss it fully elsewhere.
14. See above p. 106.
15. The following quotations are from HMC 12 *Rutland*, i. 2-3.
16. These aspects are explored in Hicks, 'Clarence', 341-85.
17. Discussed in ibid. 352-3.
18. Clarence wrote repeatedly to Vernon from 15 March, but without effect even by 10 May, after the battle of Tewkesbury, HMC 12 *Rutland*, i. 2-6.
19. *RP* vi. 194; KB 27/862, placita, rot. 12; Emden, *BRCU* 576-7. Unless otherwise stated, names of household servants are from E 28/91/84.
20. *Somerville*, i. 512; see above p. 20.
21. 'Catalogue of some medieval armorial seals in the Berkshire Record Office', *Berkshire Archaeological Journal* lv (1956-7), 39; *CPR 1467-77*, 513, 530; *1476-85*, 88; DL 29/640/10388 m.3d.
22. *CPR 1476-85*, 118; T.W.M. De Guerin, 'Notes on some old documents', *Transactions of the Guernsey Society of Natural Sciences and Local Research* vii (1914), 166-8; C 47/10/29; DL 29/403/6467 m.6; DL 29/645/10464 m.7d; E 159/255, brevia Hill. 18 Edw. IV m.8d; PSO 1/45/2336; Lincs. AO Reg. 20 f.144; Lichfield Joint RO Reg. Hales ff.45v, 47. In addition to such straightforward patronage, they benefited from his 'good lordship'.
23. *CO* 99-105.

24. *Foedera*, xi. 845; F.P. Barnard, *Edward IV's French Expedition of 1475. The leaders and their badges* (1925), lv; PSO 1/41/2116A.
25. E 101/72/2/1049; J. Prince, *Worthies of Devon* (1810), 373.
26. The next three paragraphs are based on appendix III.
27. This discussion has been influenced by an unpublished paper by Dr. R. Horrox delivered at a symposium at Swansea in 1979.
28. *CLB* 381; see above p. 111. For the next sentence, see H. Hatcher, 'Old and New Sarum', in R.C. Hoare, *History of Modern Wiltshire* (1840), vii, 180; Exeter City AO rec. acct. 11-12 Edw. IV m.2.
29. See appendix III.
30. *CCR 1468-76*, no. 962.

Notes to Chapter VI

1. W. Shakespeare, *Life and Death of King Richard III*, Act I, scene iv.
2. Wolffe, *Royal Demesne*, 156.
3. *RP* vi. 193-5.
4. *Political Poems and Songs*, ii, ed. T. Wright (RS 1861), 281.
5. *RP* vi. 193.
6. J.H. Ramsay, *Lancaster and York* (1892), ii. 419.
7. *IC* 470.
8. He sat on oyer and terminer commissions at Winchester in August 1466, at Derby in April and at London in July 1468 (KB 9/13; KB 9/319/49; KB 9/314/87), but apparently on no other occasion.
9. See above p. 182.
10. *Rows Roll*, no. 59.
11. DL 42/19 f.57.
12. See Tudor-Craig, *Richard III*, 7.
13. E 159/259, rec. East. 22 Edw. IV m.26-d.
14. *Rows Roll*, no. 59.
15. This para is based on Tewkesbury chron.; *Rows Roll*, no. 59, elaborated in Stratford-on-Avon, Shakespeare Birthplace Trust, DR 37/49 p. 138.
16. Worcs. RO BA2648/6 (iii) pp. 138-41; BRL 437204.
17. See above p. 166.
18. Hicks, 'Clarence', 385-94.
19. In that of Sir Arthur Ormesby, PROB 11/5 (Godyn) f.209.
20. Lander, *Crown and Nobility*, 242 & n.
21. *Rows Roll*, no. 59. In 1468 his almoner received a daily allowance of 12*d.*, *CO* 89-90.
22. Salisbury DRO CAB 13 p. 214.
23. Scofield, *Edward IV*, ii. 456.
24. *Rows Roll*, no. 59; see above p. 184; e.g. CP 40/856 m.518.
25. Paraphrased in Lander, *Crown and Nobility*, 161-2.

Notes to Appendix I

1. W. Shakespeare, *Life and Death of King Richard III*, Act I, scene iv; W.C. Sellar and R.J. Yeatman, *1066 and All That* (Penguin edn. 1960), 56.
2. *Mancini*, 62-63.
3. Ibid. 111 (notes to the above).
4. Roye, *Journal*, ii. 64.
5. See below.
6. *Vergil*, 167; More, *Richard III*, 7-8; *HC* 326; J. Stow, *Survey of London*, ed. C.L. Kingsford (1908), i. 58; Shakespeare, loc. cit.
7. Tudor-Craig, *Richard III*, 81-2.
8. *IC* 480; *GC* 226; *Vergil*, 167.
9. *GC* 226; see also above pp. 128, 142.
10. 'Vault in Tewkesbury Abbey Church', *Gentlemen's Magazine* xcvi. i. (1826), 628-9; 'Proceedings at the Annual Summer Meeting at Tewkesbury', *Transactions of the Bristol and Gloucestershire Archaeological Society* xxv (1902), 44.
11. *Gentlemen's Magazine*, loc. cit.; *Antiquities of Tewkesbury Church* (1787), 30.
12. W.S. Symonds, 'Historical Notes on some of the Tombs in Tewkesbury Abbey', *Transactions of the Bristol and Gloucestershire Archaeological Society* ii (1878), 208; *New Handbook and Guide to Tewkesbury Abbey Church* (5th edn. 1895), 30.

Notes to Appendix II

1. Clarence held the whole of Richmond honour in Lincolnshire in 1473 and 1478, only two-thirds in 1467.
2. Gloucester's tenure of Speenhamland, Ashley, Mapledurwell and Rotherfield is in doubt, see Hicks, *BIHR* 125n.
3. Chesterfield, Scarsdale and Bushey were exchanged for Cottingham, Falsgrave and Scarborough, see *RP* vi. 101, 125-6.
4. Elfael was exchanged for Ogmore in 1477-8, see above p. 151.

Notes to Appendix III

1. Unless otherwise stated, these three tables are based on *HP* i, ii, *passim*.
2. See also *CLB* 420; Myers, *BJRL* 1.222; *Paston L&P* i.498; *LS* 22; A. Conway, 'The Maidstone Sector of Buckingham's Rebellion', *Archaeologia Cantiana* xxxvii (1925), 108, 114; SC 8/344/1281; SC 6/822/3 mm.12, 13d; DL 29/59/1119 m.3, /1120 m.2, /1121 mm.2, 3, /1123 m.5; DL 29/454/7311 m.2; DL 29/735/12056 m.5, /12059 m.16.
3. See also DL 29/454/7312.
4. See also Rawcliffe, *Staffords*, *passim*. Cokesey was son and heir of Sir John Greville, steward of the Warwickshire estates, Staffs. RO D641/1/2/276 m.5d.
5. See also Hicks, *NH* 85, 85n, 86, 87nn.
6. See also ibid. 85n, 87n; Hicks, 'Northumberland', 86; Petworth House MS. MAC 20 mm.2, 4; Alnwick Castle MS. CVI/2c p. 168.
7. See also Dunham, *Hastings*, *passim*.
8. See also Hicks, 'Clarence', 355-7, 361-2; DL 29/403/6467; *CPR 1467-77*, 218; see above p. 184sqq.
9. *CPR 1461-7*, 537.
10. HMC 12 *Rutland*, i. 2.
11. A tenant of Clarence.
12. J.J. Alexander, 'Sixth Report on the Parliamentary Representation of Devon', *Transactions of the Devonshire Association* lxix (1937), 171.
13. E.L. Guilford, 'Extracts from the Records of the Borough of Nottingham', *Thoroton Society* xxv (1922), 20.
14. Son of Sir Nicholas Latimer.
15. DL 29/639/10374.
16. DL 29/639/10379.
17. SC 6/1089/4 m.3. He contested the 1467 election result, E 13/153 mm.32-33.
18. DL 30/111/1678 m.4d.
19. Nottingham UL MiC5b.
20. *CPR 1476-85*, 137.
21. E 159/255, brevia Hill. 18 Edw. IV m.8d.
22. See also *CPR 1461-7*, 323.
23. *CLB* 381.
24. PROB 11/5 (Godyn) ff.209-11.
25. *CPR 1467-77*, 517-18.
26. SC 6/Hen. VII/1364 m.6.
27. KB 9/347/28.
28. *LS* 158.

Bibliography

Printed Sources

Readers are referred to the excellent bibliography in C.D. Ross, *Edward IV* (1974), 443-56. Printed works most frequently used in this book may be found in the list of abbreviations.

Manuscript Sources

London, Public Record Office.

C 1	Chancery, Early Chancery Proceedings
C 47	Chancery, Miscellanea
C 53	Chancery, Charter Rolls
C 66	Chancery, Patent Rolls
C 67	Chancery, Patent Rolls Supplementary, Pardon Rolls
C 76	Chancery, Patent Rolls Supplementary, Treaty Rolls
C 81	Chancery, Warrants for the Great Seal, Series 1
C 85	Chancery, Significavits of excommunication
C 137	Chancery, Inquisitions post Mortem, Henry IV
C 139	Chancery, Inquisitions post Mortem, Henry VI
C 140	Chancery, Inquisitions post Mortem, Edward IV
C 146	Chancery, Ancient Deeds, Series C
C 237	Chancery, Bails for pardons
DL 26	Duchy of Lancaster, Ancient Deeds, Series LL
DL 27	Duchy of Lancaster, Ancient Deeds, Series LS
DL 29	Duchy of Lancaster, Ministers' Accounts
DL 30	Duchy of Lancaster, Court Rolls
DL 37	Duchy of Lancaster, Chancery Rolls
DL 42	Duchy of Lancaster, Cowcher Books
DL 43	Duchy of Lancaster, Rentals and Surveys

E 28	Exchequer, Treasury of Receipt, Council and Privy Seal
E 36	Exchequer, Treasury of Receipt, Miscellaneous Books
E 101	Exchequer, King's Remembrancer, Various Accounts
E 136	Exchequer, King's Remembrancer, Escheators' Accounts
E 149	Exchequer, King's Remembrancer, Inquisitions post Mortem, Series 1
E 152	Exchequer, King's Remembrancer, Enrolled Inquisitions
E 154	Exchequer, King's Remembrancer, Inventories of Goods and Chattels
E 159	Exchequer, King's Remembrancer, Memoranda Rolls
E 163	Exchequer, King's Remembrancer, Miscellanea
E 164	Exchequer, King's Remembrancer, Miscellaneous Books
E 199	Exchequer, King's Remembrancer, Sheriffs' Seizures
E 202	Exchequer, King's Remembrancer, Ligula Brevium
E 208	Exchequer, King's Remembrancer, Brevia directa baronibus
E 315	Exchequer, Augmentations Office, Miscellaneous Books
E 326	Exchequer, Augmentations Office, Ancient Deeds, Series B
E 357	Exchequer, Lord Treasurer's Remembrancer, Enrolled Escheators' Accounts
E 361	Exchequer, Lord Treasurer's Remembrancer, Enrolled Household Accounts
E 364	Exchequer, Lord Treasurer's Remembrancer, Foreign Rolls
E 368	Exchequer, Lord Treasurer's Remembrancer, Memoranda Rolls
E 379	Exchequer, Lord Treasurer's Remembrancer, Sheriffs' Administrative Accounts
E 401	Exchequer, Treasury of Receipt, Receipt Rolls
E 402	Exchequer, Treasury of Receipt, Issue Rolls
E 403	Exchequer, Treasury of Receipt, Tellers' Bills
E 404	Exchequer, Treasury of Receipt, Warrants for Issue
E 405	Exchequer, Treasury of Receipt, Tellers' Rolls
KB 8	King's Bench, Crown Side, Baga de Secretis
KB 9	King's Bench, Crown Side, Ancient Indictments
KB 27	King's Bench, Coram Rege Rolls
KB 29	King's Bench, Crown Side, Controlment Rolls
LR 12	Exchequer, Auditors of the Land Revenue, Rentals etc.
PROB 11	Prerogative Court of Canterbury, Registers of Wills

PSO 1	Privy Seal Office, Warrants for the Privy Seal, Series 1
PRO 31	Public Record Office, Vatican Transcripts
SC 1	Special Collections, Ancient Correspondence
SC 2	Special Collections, Court Rolls, General Series
SC 6	Special Collections, Ministers' Accounts, General Series
SC 8	Special Collections, Ancient Petitions
SC 11	Special Collections, General Series, Rolls
SC 12	Special Collections, General Series, Portfolios

London, British Library.

Additional MS.6003	Fifteenth-century miscellany of heraldic documents.
Additional MS.48031	Book of transcripts.
Additional Roll 22644	Stafford receiver's declaration of account for Caurs, 1472-73.
Additional Rolls 64808, 64811	Ministers' accounts of Tiverton, 1460-89.
Additional Rolls 64667-68	Court rolls of Okehampton, 1476-78.
Additional Roll 64325	Courtenay of Powderham receiver's accounts, 1476-78.
Cotton Julius BXII	Commonplace book of Richard, Duke of Gloucester.
Egerton MS.2822	Stafford household account book, 1462-63.
Egerton Rolls 8541-42	Ministers' accounts of Walsall borough and foreign, 1460-61.
Harley MS.433	? Signet docket book of Richard III.
Harley MS.543	John Stow's book of transcripts.
Harley MS.3881	Dugdale's transcripts of Hastings records.

London, Guildhall Library.

9531/7	Register of Thomas Kemp

London, Westminster Abbey Muniments.

3526	Account of the receiver-general of Henry Courtenay, 1464-65.

3527, 9215 Accounts of the steward of the household of Henry Courtenay, 1463, 1464-65.

5472, 31795 Private account books of Reginald Bray, 1467-69, 1474.

12181-90 Household account books of Margaret Beaufort, 1466-71.

14717 Wardship transaction, 1470.

Alnwick Castle Muniments.

C III Receivers' accounts

C VI Ministers' accounts

Barnstaple, North Devon Athenaeum.

2003-17 Borough Records, Receivers' Accounts, 1461-78.

Birmingham Reference Library.

168023 Minister's account of Brailes, 1460-61.

331914 Court roll of Perry Bar, 1465.

347863 Court roll of Erdington, 1471.

347914 Rental of Erdington.

347858-934 Ministers' accounts for Pipehall in Erdington, 1445-61.

434600 Minister's account for Yardley, 1460-61.

437204 Arbitration award of Sir Richard Verney v. College of St. Mary, Warwick, 1475.

437205 Execution of the award.

Cambridge University Library.

G/I/5 Ely Diocesan Records, Register of William Grey.

Canterbury Cathedral Library.

F/A 2,5 City of Canterbury, Corporation Archives, Financial Accounts.

Cockermouth Castle MSS. [consulted at Cumberland and Westmoreland R.O.].

D. Lec. 29 Cumberland estate accounts of the Percy family.

299 Courtrolls.

Coughton Court. [consulted at Warwickshire C.R.O.].

Throckmorton MSS. box 59, loose	Appointment of steward 1451.

Exeter Cathedral Library.

2838	Account of steward of cathedral exchequer, 1469-70.

Exeter City Archives Office.

Borough Records, Receivers' Accounts 1-18 Edward IV.

Grigson MSS. CR	183	Court roll of Okehampton 1477-78
	179	Court roll of West Budleigh hundred, 1476-77.
	211	Court roll of Wonford hundred, 1474-78.
	232, 233	Court rolls of Tiverton borough, 1468-69, 1474-76.
	291	Court roll of Tiverton manor, 1466.
	292	Minister's account of Tiverton manor, 1469-70.
	345-48	Court rolls of Tiverton hundred 1465-79.
	405	Court roll of Wonford hundred, 1471-72.
	492-96	Ministers' accounts for Tiverton borough, 1454-90.
	519	Minister's account of West Budleigh hundred, 1454-55.
	538	Receiver's account of Courtenay estates in Cornwall, 1458-59.

Exeter, Devon Record Office.

Exeter Diocesan Records, Register of John Bothe.
Exeter Diocesan Records, Miscellaneous Book 722.

Gloucester, Gloucestershire Records Office.

D 184/M 15/8	Ministers' accounts of Tewkesbury, 1460-61.

Lewes, East Sussex Record Office.

Abergavenny MSS. Aber 68	Rental of Rotherfield, 1466.
Rye Borough Records 33/1-2	Court Books 1475-76, 1478-79.
60/2,3	Account Books 1448-64, 1479-93.

Lichfield Joint Record Office.

B/A/1/12	Register of John Hales

Lincoln, Lincolnshire Archives Office.

Registers 20, 21	Registers of John Chedworth and Thomas Rotherham

London, Corporation of London Record Office.

Journals 6, 7.

Maidstone, Kent Archives Office.

U 1475/M 226-30	De Lisle MSS. Ministers' accounts of Easton by Stamford, 1443-69.
NR/FAc 3,4	New Romney Borough Records, Financial Accounts.
Sa/FAt.4-6	Sandwich Borough Records, Financial Accounts.
Sa/Ac 1	Sandwich Borough Records, Old Black Book.

Nottingham University Library.

Mi C 5b	Middleton Collection. Letter of Duke of Clarence, 1468.

Oxford, Bodleian Library.

Top. Glouc. d 2, Chronica de fundatoribus et de fundatione ecclesia de Theokesburie.

Dugdale MSS. 8,13,15,18,21,39.

Oxford, Magdalen College.

Fastolf Papers 40.

MS. Multon 48.

Oxford, Oxfordshire County Record Office.

Dillon Collection,Dil.II/b/1-16	Ministers' accounts of Spelsbury, 1435-64.
Dillon Collection,Dil.II/b/17	Rental of Spelsbury, 1446.
Dillon Collection,Dil.X/a/II	Court roll of Quarrendon, 1471-72.

Petworth House [consulted at West Sussex C.R.O.].

MD 9/7-9	Manorial documents.
MAC 13,20	Ministers' accounts.

Salisbury Diocesan Record Office.

Register of Richard Beauchamp, I,II.
Chapter Act Books 12, 13.

Shrewsbury, Salop Record Office.

Bridgewater collection, boxes 72,73,76,82,84,86,87 Ministers' and receivers' accounts.

Stafford, Staffordshire Record Office.

D1641/1/2/25, /26, /69, /70	Stafford family's receiver-general accounts.

Stratford-on-Avon, Shakespeare Birthplace Trust.

DR 5/2741-4, /2746-71.	Court rolls of Chaddesley Corbett 1439-82.
DR 5/2845, /2876	Ministers' accounts of Chaddesley Corbett 1468-9, 1484-5.
DR 37/49	Volume containing two versions of the Rows Roll.

Trowbridge, Wiltshire Record Office.

88/1/12	Feoffment
214/8	Arbitration award in John Halle v. Prioress of Amesbury, 1468.

Warwick Castle Muniments [consulted at Warwickshire C.R.O.].

491 Ministers' account of Warwick, 1451-2.

Warwick, Warwickshire County Record Office.

CR 26/4 Extracts from records of Warwick college.

Mi 264 Microfilm of Coughton Court catalogue of additional MSS.

Winchester, Hampshire Record Office.

B/IVa/1/1/2 Register of William Waynflete, I, II.

Worcester, Worcestershire Record Office.

989/30-5 Court rolls of Elmley Castle, 1452-61

989/26, /111-13 Ministers' accounts of Elmley Castle, 1452-61

BA 2648/6(ii, iii) Register of John Carpenter, I, II.

York, Borthwick Institute of Historical Research.

Registers of William Bothe, George Neville and Lawrence Bothe.

Index